BLUEPRINTS

History
Key Stage 2
Teacher's Resource
Book

Second Edition

Joy Palmer

Stanley Thornes (Publishers) Ltd

Do you receive BLUEPRINTS NEWS?

Blueprints is an expanding series of practical teacher's ideas books and photocopiable resources for use in primary schools. Books are available for separate infant and junior age ranges for every core and foundation subject, as well as for an ever widening range of other primary teaching needs. These include **Blueprints Primary English** books and **Blueprints Resource Banks**. **Blueprints** are carefully structured around the demands of the National Curriculum in England and Wales, but are used successfully by schools and teachers in Scotland, Northern Ireland and elsewhere.

Blueprints provide:
- *Total curriculum coverage*
- *Hundreds of practical ideas*
- *Books specifically for the age range you teach*
- *Flexible resources for the whole school or for individual teachers*
- *Excellent photocopiable sheets – ideal for assessment and children's work profiles*
- *Supreme value.*

Books may be bought by credit card over the telephone and information obtained on **(01242) 577944**. Alternatively, photocopy and return this **FREEPOST** form to receive **Blueprints News**, our regular update on all new and existing titles. You may also like to add the name of a friend who would be interested in being on the mailing list.

Please add my name to the **BLUEPRINTS NEWS** mailing list.

Mr/Mrs/Miss/Ms _____

Home address _____

_____ Postcode _____

School address _____

_____ Postcode _____

Please also send **BLUEPRINTS NEWS** to:

Mr/Mrs/Miss/Ms _____

Address _____

_____ Postcode _____

To: Marketing Services Dept., Stanley Thornes Ltd, FREEPOST (GR 782), Cheltenham, GL50 1BR

First published in 1992
Second edition published in 1995 by
Stanley Thornes (Publishers) Ltd
Ellenborough House
Wellington Street
CHELTENHAM GL50 1YW

A catalogue record for this book is available from the British Library.

ISBN 0 7487 2207 6

Typeset by Tech-Set, Gateshead, Tyne & Wear
Printed and bound at The Bath Press, Avon

96 97 98 99 00 / 10 9 8 7 6 5 4 3 2

CONTENTS

Introduction   iv

Study Units

1   Romans, Anglo-Saxons and Vikings in Britain   1

2   Life in Tudor times   41

3a   Victorian Britain   56

3b   Britain since 1930   73

4   Ancient Greece   87

5   Local History   100

6   A past, non-European society   111

Supplementary material

Appendix 1   The history of food and farming   121

Appendix 2   Exploration and encounters, 1450–1550, including material on Aztec civilisation   132

Summary Sheet   144

INTRODUCTION

ABOUT THE MATERIALS

What is *Blueprints: History?*

Blueprints: History is a practical teacher's resource written to fulfil all the requirements of the National Curriculum in history (1995). It is intended to be used flexibly, either as an ideas bank for individual teachers or as a workable core resource for a whole school's scheme of work in history.

Blueprints: History consists of materials for Key Stages 1 and 2. For each Key Stage there is a Teacher's Resource Book and a book of Pupils' Copymasters. This Teacher's Resource Book provides hundreds of practical ideas and activities for Key Stage 2 and may be used on its own, as a freestanding resource, without the accompanying copymaster book. The Pupil's Copymasters consist of 106 photocopiable worksheets linked to the many activities in this book. The worksheets reinforce and extend activities already done and provide opportunities to build up a record of children's work in history. They may also be seen as a tool for teacher assessment. The materials for the two Key Stages can be used together as a continuous and coherent resource for delivering the National Curriculum in history.

Blueprints: History Key Stage 2

Approach

The structure and approach of this Resource Book are designed to help you with the task of meeting the demands made by the National Curriculum in history for Key Stage 2. It is now generally accepted that teaching history through all-embracing cross-curricular topics may not be entirely appropriate. This view has certainly been reflected in the structure of the National Curriculum Programme of Study with its precise Study Units. Such units or topics clearly have history as a discernible and worthwhile core. Their aim is to develop historic knowledge, understanding and skills in an intellectually rigorous way, which is not totally removed from an integrated curriculum structure.

Blueprints: History Key Stage 2 is specifically written to fulfil all the requirements of the National Curriculum in history at this stage, taking account of the need for a balance between a clear historic focus and suggestions for meaningful integrated work. It is intended for all teachers, including non-specialists in this area, and provides a completely comprehensive coverage of the subject. There are practical ideas to use alongside other books and materials, countless suggestions for meaningful and relevant activities for

the children, and a wealth of background information. You can use *Blueprints: History Key Stage 2* either as a complete 'off-the-peg' curriculum resource or flexibly to meet the needs of your own situation.

Structure

The Teacher's Resource Book is arranged in sections which match the National Curriculum History Study Units, as detailed in the next section of this Introduction. Because the coverage of material is so comprehensive, you can develop your own integrated schemes of work using the book as a basis for the essential core of history.

The various activities suggested pay due attention to the importance of historical enquiry and communication, with the aim of providing you with ways of helping pupils to investigate historical topics on their own. A wide variety of opportunities are provided for asking questions; choosing sources for investigation; collecting and recording information; selecting and organising historical information; and presenting results orally, visually and in writing. There is adequate scope for flexibility, and individual use and interpretation.

Record keeping

Straightforward record-keeping materials are provided. At the back of this book there is a child summary sheet which you may photocopy for use in school. The same sheet appears on Copymaster 106 in the photocopiable resource book. Use this to log the contribution made to work at Levels 2, 3, 4 and 5 of the Level Descriptions as children work on the Study Units.

More about the Pupils' Copymasters

The Pupils' Copymasters provide photocopiable worksheets that are linked to and fully integrated with the text of the Teacher's Resource Book. These sheets give the pupils opportunities to record activities and the results of investigations in a structured and organised way, and, in many cases, to consolidate the learning that has taken place.

Copymasters 1 to 90 are clearly linked to particular activities. Roughly speaking, there are nine copymasters per area of study within the Study Units. Each area of study is sub-divided into sections, and the section headings incorporate this device, C1–3 which indicates the numbers of the copymasters that relate to that section. Also, in the notes for the relevant activity, the copymaster that could be used is referred to in bold type.

Copymasters 91 to 105 are general and so are not linked to any particular Study Unit. Their purpose is two-fold: first, to provide information and background facts which can be referred to throughout the teaching and learning of Key Stage 2; and second, to provide recording sheets/pupil activities which are transferable to a variety of Study Units. Notes about the use of these general copymasters are to be found in a separate section at the end of this Introduction.

As mentioned above, Copymaster 106 is a record summary sheet.

Resources

The *Blueprints: History* materials contain a tremendous wealth of background information. It is fully appreciated that you may not have sufficient time to research in libraries and consult reference materials, and so every effort has been made to provide sufficient information to introduce each of the Study Units.

In the Teacher's Resource Book, at the end of each topic section, you will find lists of other publications that you may wish to consult. Compiling these lists was a difficult task, and inevitably there was need for selection. In the main, the non-fiction sections highlight more recently published works, and these are supplemented with annotated fiction lists.

Below is a list of a few general reference books, followed by some addresses that you may find useful.

Blyth, J. *History in Primary Schools*, Open
    University Press, 1989.
Cameron, K. *English Place Names*, Batsford, 1982.
Clark, D. (Ed.) *The Encyclopaedia of Inventions*,
    Marshall Cavendish, 1977.
Cook, J. *Archaeology*, Wayland, 1983.
Ekwall, E. *Concise Oxford Dictionary of English
    Place Names*, OUP, 1960.
Harrison, M. *Homes in History*, Wayland, 1983.
Iredale, D. *Enjoying Archives*, Phillimore, 1985.
Little, V. and John, T. *Historical Fiction in the
    Classroom* (T.H. 59), Historical Association, 1986.
Purkis, S. *Thanks for the Memory* from the 'How
    Do We Know?' series, Collins, 1987.
Steel, D. *Discovering Your Family History*, BBC
    Publications, 1980.
Tatton, E. *My Family Tree Book*, Unwin Hyman, 1983.

The Civic Trust Education Department
17 Carlton House Terrace
LONDON SW1Y 5AW

English Heritage
Education Service
15–17 Great Marlborough Street
LONDON W1V 1AF

National Farmers Union
Information Division
Agriculture House
Knightsbridge
LONDON SW1

The National Trust Education Office
8 Church Street
Lacock
Chippenham
Wiltshire SN15 2LG

Young Archaeologists Club
United House
Piccadilly
YORK YO1 1PQ

Archaeology In Education
Department of Archaeology and Prehistory
University of Sheffield
SHEFFIELD S10 2TN

Museum Education In London
Centre for Learning Resources
275 Kennington Lane
LONDON SE11 5QZ

The Waterways Museum
Stoke Bruerne
Nr Towcester
Northants NN12 7SE

The Black Country Museum
Tipton Road
Dudley
West Midlands DY1 4SQ

The National Maritime Museum
Greenwich
LONDON SE10 9NF

National Portrait Gallery
Publications Department
2 St Martin's Place
LONDON WC2H 0HE

National Army Museum
Royal Hospital Road
London SW3 4HT

Sudbury Hall & Museum
Sudbury
Derbyshire DE6 5HT

Age specificity

In the limited space available, activities can only be suggestions for individual development and interpretation. Individual needs, enthusiasms and detailed organisation, will inevitably shape the way any Study Unit proceeds in practice.

The ideas for work in each Study Unit are not age-specific, but are designed to fit in with and span the general range of expectations for the level descriptions of Key Stage 2.

Whilst clear indications have been provided in the text as to how the various suggested activities may best fit the level descriptions, it is emphasised that the materials are designed to be used flexibly. No doubt you will wish to draw upon and modify ideas and suggestions to suit the needs of individual situations and learners. In so doing, it is hoped that the integrity and intellectual rigour of the history component is maintained within a meaningful and relevant cross-curricular framework. Fitting of activities to level descriptions is indicated within the text of the Teacher's Resource Book in the charts at the end of each unit. Levels 2–5 are indicated, which are those considered appropriate for Key Stage 2 learning.

Coverage of the National Curriculum

Blueprints: History Key Stage 2 provides an extensive range of suggestions for interpreting the precisely defined core content of history, while retaining appropriate elements of integration and cross-curricular development. This is totally in line with the Statutory Orders, which take account of cross-curricular development in stating that:

> The pupils should be taught about important episodes and developments in Britain's past, from Roman to modern times, about ancient civilisations and the history of other parts of the world.

In Key Stage 2 the Programme of Study consists of six Study Units with prescribed content. Each Study Unit should provide opportunities for the development of the knowledge, understanding and skills necessary for the levels of learning appropriate for Key Stage 2 (Levels 2–5). Activities within the Study Units also provide opportunities to:

— explore links between history and other subjects;
— develop information technology capability;
— develop knowledge, understanding and skills relating to cross-curricular themes, in particular citizenship, environmental, health and careers education, and education for economic and industrial understanding.

The Programme of Study for Key Stage 2 (Levels 2–5) requires that:

> Pupils should be helped to develop a chronological framework by making links across the different study units. They should have opportunities to investigate local history and to learn about the past from a range of sources of information.

This is to be achieved by teaching the following six study units:

1 Romans, Anglo-Saxons and Vikings in Britain
2 Life in Tudor Times
EITHER   3a Victorian Britain
OR   3b Britain since 1930
4 Ancient Greece
5 Local history
6 A past non-European society

The *Blueprints* materials have been organised so that they relate directly to these requirements, making their contents readily transferable to any school programme of work for history. In addition, supplementary material is provided in two Appendices, covering Food and Farming, and Exploration and Encounters 1450–1550. The information contained in the Appendices can either be used as alternative material for Study Units 5 and 6, or for background work in history and cross-curricular topics.

Choice of study units

The main section of *Blueprints: History Key Stage 2* is divided into nine units which correspond to the nine possible areas of study outlined in the National Curriculum. (Study Unit 1 covers three areas of study – the Romans, the Anglo-Saxons and the Vikings; Study Unit 3 covers two – Victorian Britain and Britain since 1930). All six of the study units are covered.

Relationship to general requirements and key elements of the Programme of Study

The general requirements of the National Curriculum permeate the materials. For example, the suggested activities enable pupils to be introduced to each Study Unit from a variety of perspectives:

— political;
— economic, technological and scientific;
— social;
— religious;
— cultural and aesthetic.

Suggestions also provide opportunities for pupils to learn about the past from a range of historical sources, as required, including:

— documents and printed sources;
— artefacts;
— pictures and photographs;
— music;
— buildings and sites;
— computer-based materials.

Furthermore, the activities place due emphasis on the development of a range of appropriate skills, e.g. the ability to use dates and terms relating to the passing of time, to make links and connections between the main events studied, both within and across periods, to describe and identify reasons for the results of historical events, developments and changes, and to consider the accuracy and appropriateness of evidence. There is ample opportunity for pupils to ask and answer questions, choose sources for finding out, and collect and record information.

Content of the level descriptions permeates the materials as a whole. Below you will find a ready reference guide to the descriptions of Levels 2–5 and details of the Programme of Study.

Finally, it should be noted that each study unit allows plenty of scope for interlinks with other areas of study in the primary curriculum. No doubt you will wish to plan an overall breadth and balance of topic work across subjects through a period of time.

KEY STAGE 2 PROGRAMME OF STUDY

Pupils should be taught about important episodes and developments in Britain's past, from Roman to modern times, about ancient civilisations and the history of other parts of the world. They should be helped to develop a chronological framework by making links across the different study units. They should have opportunities to investigate local history and to learn about the past from a range of sources of information.

The Study Units and the Key Elements, outlined below, should be taught together.

STUDY OF UNITS

Pupils should be taught SIX Study Units.

■ 1. **Romans, Anglo-Saxons and Vikings in Britain**

The history of the British Isles from 55 B.C. to the early eleventh century, and the ways in which British society was shaped by different peoples. Pupils should be given opportunities to study, in greater depth, ONE of the Romans, Anglo-Saxons, or the Vikings.

■ 2. **Life in Tudor times**

Some of the major events and personalities, including monarchs, and the way of life of people at different levels of society in Tudor times.

■ 3a. **Victorian Britain**

The lives of men, women and children at different levels of society, in Britain, and the ways in which they were affected by changes in industry and transport.

———————————————————— OR ————————————————————

■ 3b. **Britain since 1930**

The lives of men, women and children at different levels of society, in Britain, and the ways in which they were affected by the Second World War and changes in technology and transport.

■ 4. **Ancient Greece**

The way of life, beliefs and achievements of the ancient Greeks, and the legacy of ancient Greek civilisation to the modern world.

■ 5. **Local history**

An aspect of local history.

■ 6. **A past non-European society**

The key features of a past non-European society.

■ 7. **Across the key stage, pupils should be given opportunities to study:**

    a aspects of the past in outline and in depth;

    b aspects of the histories of England, Ireland, Scotland and Wales; where appropriate, the history of Britain should be set in its European and world context;

    c history from a variety of perspectives –political; economic, technological and scientific; social; religious; cultural and aesthetic.

KEY ELEMENTS

The Key Elements are closely related and should be developed through the Study Units, as appropriate. Not all the Key Elements need to be developed in each Study Unit.

Pupils should be taught:

■ 1. **Chronology**

    a to place the events, people and changes in the periods studied within a chronological framework;

    b to use dates and terms relating to the passing of time, including ancient, modern, B.C., A.D., century and decade, and terms that define different periods , *e.g. Tudor, Victorian.*

■ 2. **Range and depth of historical knowledge and understanding**

    a about characteristic features of particular periods and societies, including the ideas, beliefs and attitudes of people in the past, and the experiences of men and women; and about the social, cultural, religious and ethnic diversity of the societies studied;

    b to describe and identify reasons for and results of historical events, situations, and changes in the periods studied;

    c to describe and make links between the main events, situations and changes both within and across periods.

■ 3. **Interpretations of history**

    a to identify and give reasons for different ways in which the past is represented and interpreted.

■ 4. **Historical enquiry**

    a how to find out about aspects of the periods studied, from a range of sources of information, including documents and printed sources, artefacts, pictures and photographs, music, and buildings and sites;

    b to ask and answer questions, and to select and record information relevant to a topic.

■ 5. **Organisation and communication**

    a to recall, select and organise historical information, including dates and terms;

    b the terms necessary to describe the periods and topics studied, including court, monarch, parliament, nation, civilisations, invasion, conquest, settlement, conversation, slavery, trade, industry, law;

    c to communicate their knowledge and understanding of history in a variety of ways, including structured narratives and descriptions.

Attainment Target

LEVEL DESCRIPTIONS

The following level descriptions describe the types and range of performance that pupils working at a particular level should characteristically demonstrate. In deciding on a pupil's level of attainment at the end of the key stage, teachers should judge which description best fits the pupil's performance. Each description should be considered in conjunction with the descriptions for adjacent levels.

By the end of Key Stage 2 the performance of the great majority of pupils should be within the range of Levels 2 to 5.

■ Level 2

Pupils show their developing sense of chronology by using terms concerned with the passing of time, by ordering events and objects, and by making distinctions between aspects of their own lives and past times. They demonstrate factual knowledge and understanding of aspects of the past beyond living memory, and of some of the main events and people they have studied. They are beginning to recognise that there are reasons why people in the past acted as they did. They are beginning to identify some of the different ways in which the past is represented. They answer questions about the past, from sources of information, on the basis of simple observations.

■ Level 3

Pupils show their understanding of chronology by their increasing awareness that the past can be divided into different periods of time, their recognition of some of the similarities and differences between these periods, and their use of dates and terms. They demonstrate factual knowledge and understanding of some of the main events, people and changes drawn from the appropriate programme of study. They are beginning to give a few reasons for, and results of, the main events and changes. They identify some of the different ways in which the past is represented. They find answers to questions about the past by using sources of information in ways that go beyond simple observations.

■ Level 4

Pupils demonstrate factual knowledge and understanding of aspects of the history of Britain and other countries, drawn from the Key Stage 2 or Key Stage 3 Programme of Study. They use this to describe the characteristic features of past societies and periods, and to identify changes within and across periods. They describe some of the main events, people and changes. They give some reasons for, and results of, the main events and changes. They show how some aspects of the past have been represented and interpreted in different ways. They are beginning to select and combine information from sources. They are beginning to produce structured work, making appropriate use of dates and terms.

■ Level 5

Pupils demonstrate an increasing depth of factual knowledge and understanding of aspects of the history of Britain and other countries drawn from the Key Stage 2 or Key Stage 3 Programme of Study. They use this to describe and to begin to make links between features of past societies and periods. They describe events, people and changes. They describe and make links between relevant reasons for, and results of, events and changes. They know that some events, people and changes have been interpreted in different ways and suggest possible reasons for this. Using their knowledge and understanding, pupils are beginning to evaluate sources of information and identify those that are useful for particular tasks. They select and organise information to produce structured work, making appropriate use of dates and terms.

NOTES ON THE GENERAL COPYMASTERS

Copymaster 91 I-Spy archaeology

This shows outline drawings of a range of artefacts derived from archaeological investigations, and from different historical periods. The sheet could be used to introduce a general discussion on the role of archaeology, the work of archaeologists and the nature of evidence obtained through their skills. The children could be asked, 'Which people in history would have used what – and when?' The objects can be coloured accurately and the pupils could write a story about each one.

An alternative way of using this sheet would be to incorporate it within one of the Study Unit projects –asking the question, 'Which of the objects depicted would have been in existence at this time?'

Finally, the children could redraw the articles, putting them in a time sequence, and labelling an adjacent timeline with appropriate dates against each drawing. Starting with the top row and reading left to right, the artefacts are as follows:

Typical pottery of ancient Greek manufacture. The smaller jug is from the early Helladic period (roughly 2500 to 2000 B.C.) and the large round vase from the late Helladic period (1600 to 1200 B.C.). Pottery was an important product of ancient Greece and is very distinctive.

A Viking iron axe-head and sword. The Vikings were skilled metalworkers and produced items of great beauty.

A flint tool from the Neolithic period (3000 to 1800 B.C. in Britain). The New Stone Age was the age of the first farmers, before metal was in use.

Carved reindeer antlers from the Paleolithic period (the earliest age of man, until about 12 000 B.C. in Britain). These particular antlers were found in France.

This life-size bronze head of Claudius I may well have been torn from the bronze body by followers of Boudicca, in the middle of the first century A.D. It vanished until 1907, when it was found in a river in Suffolk.

A bronze sword and spear-head from the late Bronze Age (about 1000 to 600 B.C. in Britain).

This statuette shows King Tutankhamun as Horus harpooning Seth, the enemy of his father. It is one of the grave-treasures of the young king, who reigned, it is thought, for nine years in Egypt in the fourteenth century B.C.

Anglo-Saxon jewellery.

Tableware of the seventeenth century. The plate and mug are made of pewter – a mixture of tin and lead. Until late in the century people used only knives and spoons, but then forks came into general use. For many years people carried their own forks with them, in a leather case.

Copymaster 92: Key dates in world exploration

This copymaster may be helpful when studying Study Unit 6 on study of a past, non-European society, but is useful background chronology to set against knowledge and understanding of events in other periods too. It highlights some of the important journeys made in our world, from the days of the earliest ships in 3500 B.C. to the twentieth century.

Copymaster 93: Key events in Ancient Britain

This is a general information sheet, setting out key events in the history of Britain in the years before the birth of Christ, and it will be particularly useful when studying early invasions and settlements. Some background information on what Britain was like before such invasions is essential.

The sheet also provides a basis for discussion on what we mean by B.C. and A.D., which will be important at many stages when working through the Study Units. Help the children to set the date of the birth of Christ in a chronological framework, and to appreciate that this key event did not take place in England. This discussion could stimulate investigations into what was going on in other parts of the world at this time.

Copymaster 94: Earliest times – how do we know?

This sheet will form the basis for general discussion on how historians find out about places, objects and events that date from thousands of years ago. The work of archaeologists will no doubt be considered in many Study Units. With this sheet you can introduce and discuss other useful methods: counting annual rings on tree trunks (some of the world's trees date from five thousand years ago); using aerial photographs to see things which cannot be spotted from the ground; and the more recent and accurate radiocarbon dating procedures.

Copymaster 95: More about dates

In order to study any unit in this book, children will need a clear understanding about dates and centuries. Explain the meaning of the word 'century', and then ask the children to practise using and interpreting dates by filling in the questions on the sheet. Link this with a general discussion about the use of the terms B.C. and A.D. (see also Copymaster 93).

Copymaster 96: Focus on invention

This is a sheet on which the pupils can record basic facts about inventions or discoveries. It can be used for any period of time, and is therefore relevant to all the Study Units. Ask pupils to draw the chosen invention in the 'thought cloud', draw a portrait of the inventor in the oval frame provided, and then answer the basic questions below. Discussion of the advantages and disadvantages will help the children to appreciate that new discoveries and inventions do not necessarily mean a change for the better for all concerned.

Copymaster 97: Time sequence

Ask the children to colour the outline drawings of people from differing historical periods, and then to arrange them in chronological sequence. This could be simply done by writing the letters of the pictures in correct date order. Alternatively, cut out the portraits, mount them on card and arrange them in sequence as part of a border for a wall-display timeline. Each character could be discussed, and there is infinite scope for both discussion and writing about costume changes, hairstyles, etc. through the years. One key question to consider could be: 'What happened in between?' There are huge gaps of history between the characters depicted, and activities could be devised to fill these in with suitable portraits.

To save you time, here are the identities of the 'portraits':

A A Roman, at the time of the Roman occupation of Britain.
B A modern teenager.
C Elizabeth I.
D A Viking warrior.
E A Victorian lady and gentleman.
F An Ancient Egyptian noblewoman.
G A 'hippie' of the 1960s.
H A Stone Age family.
I Henry VIII.

Copymaster 98: Looking at objects
Copymaster 107 provides a focus for observing and thinking about historical objects/artefacts. The space in the centre allows for the children to draw whatever object is under scrutiny. Encourage them to consider the questions around the outside of the sheet, which promote understanding of the value and importance of the object itself. This copymaster can, of course, be used for objects from any period of historic time, and leads to the all-important consideration of their location and context in the lives of people of the period.

Copymaster 99: What they wore in Tudor times
This copymaster is period-specific, and can clearly be used within the topic on Life in Tudor times. Yet it is also designed to help children appreciate that clothing (as can be observed in historic photographs and paintings) is an extremely important source of evidence about a period. Let the children research the details of what people wore in Tudor times and write the key words at the top of the page by the side of the correct aspect of clothing. Design similar worksheets for other historic periods.

Copymaster 100: The houses of history
This copymaster contains the names of the family or 'house' of the monarchs of Britain from Norman times to the present day. Use it whilst studying a specific period or as a more general theme to help children develop a grasp of the timeline or chronology of British history. Children can either insert the names of the monarchs (and their dates) of each house in the box provided, or design a representative sketch for each house.

Copymaster 100 can also be used in conjunction with Copymaster 101, which provides details of the British monarchs from Norman times to the present day.

Copymaster 101: British monarchs 1066–1952
This has useful value as a reference sheet for both teachers and pupils. Also, the information on it can be used as a basis for practising the skills involved in constructing and drawing family trees of British monarchs.

Copymaster 102: Legacies
This provides a recording sheet which can be used in any of the topics studied. It summarises a framework for discussion and research concerning the legacies that various historic periods have left for present day inheritance. In the context of whatever period you are studying, suggest that the children make notes or sketches of the particular aspects of the legacy of the period in the relevant boxes.

Copymaster 103: A famous life
This Copymaster is designed for use in all topics of the National Curriculum. It provides a useful summary sheet for recording the results of children's research about a famous person such as a monarch, inventor or explorer. The copymaster provides space in the centre for a sketch of the person, plus helpful headings to guide pupils in their task of focusing on the important aspects of the life being analysed.

Copymasters 104–105: Historical vocabulary
These copymasters provide a start to children's research and understanding of historical words. It can be used for discussion, practice in the use of dictionaries and research skills, and recording definitions of the key words and concepts listed. These copymasters can of course be used selectively for research related to specific topics. It could also be used as a basis for the design and compilation of a far more extensive class Dictionary of Historic Vocabulary.

STUDY UNIT 1
THE ROMANS

Pupils should be taught about the history of the British Isles from 55 B.C. to the early eleventh century, and the ways in which British society was shaped by different peoples. They should be given opportunities to study, in greater depth, ONE of the Romans, the Anglo-Saxons, or the Vikings.

1 Pupils should be taught **in outline** about the following:
  a the Roman conquest and occupation of Britain
  b the arrival and settlement of the Anglo-Saxons
  c Viking raids and settlements.

2 They should be taught **in greater depth** about ONE of the above.

a. Romans ● the Roman conquest and its impact on Britain, *e.g. Boudicca and resistance to Roman rule, the extent to which life in Celtic Britain was influenced by Roman rule and settlement, the end of imperial rule*;
  ● everyday life, *e.g. houses and home life, work, religion*;
  ● the legacy of Roman rule, *e.g. place names and settlement patterns, Roman remains, including artefacts, roads and buildings.*

TOPIC WEB

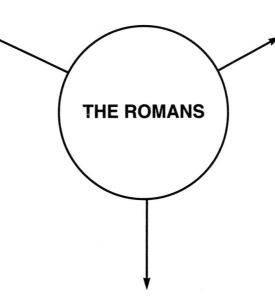

The Roman conquest

● The origins and rise of Rome
● Considering the evidence
● Timeline – the early history of Rome
● The first emperors
● The growth of the Roman Empire
● Reasons for invasion
● Claudius invades Britain
● Soldiers and legions
● Battles and conquest
● Roman roads

The legacy of Roman rule

● Field visits; field evidence
● Towns and cities
● Language
● Architecture
● Writing and literature
● Buildings and technology
● Painting and sculpture
● Place names and travel routes
● Famous Romans

THE ROMANS

Everyday life

● Town life; town plans
● Art in Roman times
● Roman villas
● Occupations
● Modes of transport
● Food and cooking
● Roman numerals
● Religion: gods and goddesses

1

THE ROMAN CONQUEST

> *Pupils should be taught about the following:*
>
> • the Roman conquest and its impact on Britain, *e.g. Boudicca and resistance to Roman rule, the extent to which life in Celtic Britain was influenced by Roman rule and settlement, the end of imperial rule.*

Activity 1: Where was Rome?
Locate the city of Rome on a world map or globe. Discuss its location in Italy and as part of the continent of Europe. Discussion of the background to the invasion is an essential starting point, so find out more about the beginnings of Rome as a small village on one of seven hills, and the rise of the Republic (state without a king).

Activity 2: How do we know?
Consider the key introductory question: *How do we know?* and then find out more about the Romans, their invasions, settlements, and ways of life. (See the illustration on the right.)

Activity 3: A Roman timeline
Draw a timeline like the one shown below, to establish key dates.

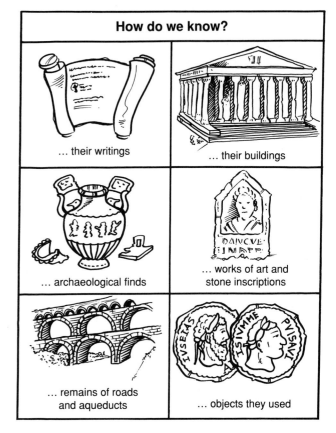

How do we know?

... their writings

... their buildings

... archaeological finds

... works of art and stone inscriptions

... remains of roads and aqueducts

... objects they used

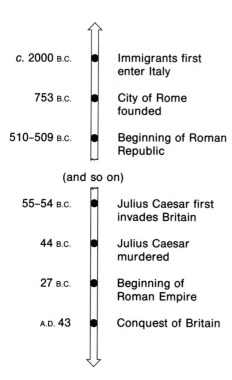

c. 2000 B.C.	Immigrants first enter Italy
753 B.C.	City of Rome founded
510–509 B.C.	Beginning of Roman Republic
(and so on)	
55–54 B.C.	Julius Caesar first invades Britain
44 B.C.	Julius Caesar murdered
27 B.C.	Beginning of Roman Empire
A.D. 43	Conquest of Britain

This timeline can be the basis of a wall-frieze or collage, with illustrations depicting key events or periods in the early history of the Romans. You could divide the class into groups and let each group investigate a different period or issue, using reference books and pictures. Some possible subjects are:

• Migration into Italy, the first settlements (the Etruscans).
• The founding of Rome (the story of Romulus and Remus).
• The early days and expansion of the Republic.
• The rule of Julius Ceasar.
• The republican army.
• From republic to empire – Octavian (Augustus) comes to power.

Activity 4: The early Roman emperors
Divide the children into groups, each to research and write an illustrated account of the significance of the rule of one of the early Roman emperors. Present results as dramatic roleplay – 'My life as Emperor'. The children in each group take turns to become the emperor talking about himself, his life, events of his rule, his ambitions or achievements, and eventual death.

This could be further developed into a tape-recorded radio news programme or a sound version of TV's *This Is Your Life*, with children writing scripts and playing appropriate roles, paying 'tribute' to the wisdom and justice (or otherwise!) of the emperor being featured. Schools with access to video cameras could record visually as well. The same biographical approach can be applied to other characters of the period, e.g. Boudicca, Caractacus.

Background information: *A Roman timeline*
Here is a list of the first Roman emperors.

27 B.C.–A.D. 14 Augustus
A.D. 14–37 Tiberius
A.D. 37–41 Gaius (Caligula)
A.D. 41–54 Claudius
A.D. 54–68 Nero
A.D. 69 Year of 4 Emperors
A.D. 69–79 Vespasian
A.D. 79–81 Titus
A.D. 81–96 Domitian
A.D. 96–98 Nerva
A.D. 98–117 Trajan
A.D. 117–138 Hadrian

Activity 5: Roman invasions
Discuss possible reasons for the early Roman attacks on nearby villages – the earliest Romans were farmers and shepherds who took up arms against neighbouring towns and villages. From the policy of fighting only when danger threatened, a full-time army of trained soldiers eventually developed. More and more land was conquered; soon the whole of Italy was ruled by Rome … and then beyond. (Reasons for the Roman invasions are examined in more detail in Activity 7.

Background information: *Roman invasions*
Julius Caesar was the first Roman emperor to invade Britain from Gaul (France) in 55 B.C., and again in 54 B.C., having already conquered half of Spain and most of France, as well as large areas of Africa, the Middle East and most of Greece. Caesar's visits to Britain were punitive expeditions rather than attempts at colonisation. Some Romans settled and traded in Britain at this time, and almost a century passed before the Romans invaded Britain again.

The real conquest of Britain began in A.D. 43, during the reign of Emperor Claudius, when a Roman general named Aulus Plautius landed with a large army. The emperor himself visited Britain for a short time during the invasion. Tell the story of Caractacus, a British chief who fought against the Romans before being captured and taken to Rome in chains. Aulus Plautius conquered Britain as far north as the River Humber and as far west as the Welsh border.

In A.D. 61 a Roman governor called Suetonius Paulinus led an expedition into North Wales to attack and crush the power of the Druids, priests who incited the native tribes to resist the Romans. He also put down a revolt of the Iceni, another British tribe led by the fierce warrior queen, Boudicca (sometimes known as Boadicea).

Julius Agricola became governor of Britain in A.D. 78. He defeated the savage northern tribes, building a chain of forts across Scotland which pushed the boundary of the Roman colony further north than ever before.

Activity 6: The growth of the Roman Empire
Use **Copymaster 1** as the basis for discussing the pattern of invasion and conquest as the Roman Empire expanded. The map shows phases of gradual expansion until A.D. 138 (the death of Hadrian, during whose time the Empire reached its greatest extent). Ask the children to colour-code the phases of expansion, as indicated in the key.

Activity 7: Why invade?
To focus the children's attention you could display these jumbled-up words, which are some of the main reasons for invasion of Britain:

OOWL   ORNC   ASLEVS   PPCERO
EHELRTA   NIT   LDOG   IESRVL   ALDE

(wool, corn, slaves, copper, leather, tin, gold, silver, lead)

Discuss them as motives for wanting to invade and fight. Ask the children to consider these and any other reasons for invasion that they can think of, and then write about them, commenting on their significance.

Background information: *Why invade?*
Reasons for the Roman invasions may have included:

Produce wool, leather, timber, corn, fruits, oil, glass, wine
Metals lead, copper, silver, gold, tin, iron
Slaves
Conquest for the sake of conquest – 'Rome to rule the world'.

Activity 8: Why invade Britain?
Look back to the jumbled words and list reasons for invasion that are relevant to the United Kingdom. Investigate which regions in Britain would have supplied each commodity. Talk about why Britain resisted the invasion.

Activity 9: Goods from the Roman Empire
Expand on Activity 2 in order to put the United Kingdom in a European context. Make up symbols for the most important products of the Roman Empire. Using these as a key, locate them on a large outline map of Europe, showing where the various products could be found. This will delineate the great range of goods derived from lands within the Empire, highlighting practical reasons for invasion and conquest. Key products include: wool, leather, pottery, corn, timber, fruit, olive oil, wine, glass, metals (lead, copper, iron, silver, gold, tin).

Activity 10: Claudius invades Britain
Copymaster 2, which shows a Roman legionary, can be coloured and used as a cover for topic folders or as an introductory sheet for the project as a whole.

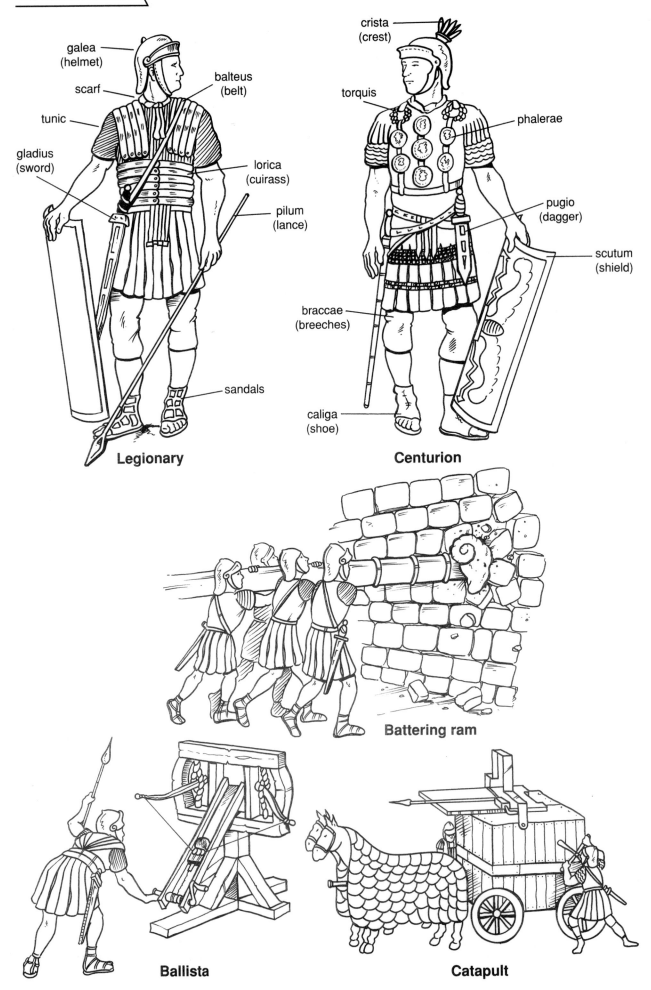

Legionary

galea (helmet)

scarf

tunic

gladius (sword)

balteus (belt)

lorica (cuirass)

pilum (lance)

sandals

Centurion

crista (crest)

torquis

phalerae

pugio (dagger)

scutum (shield)

braccae (breeches)

caliga (shoe)

Battering ram

Ballista

Catapult

Activity 11: The uniform of a soldier

If possible, visit a museum to study and sketch the uniform and weapons of a Roman soldier. Introduce basic vocabulary of uniform, which varied according to the soldier's rank (see page 4).

The children could label the parts of the uniform shown on **Copymaster 2**, including cuirass (the metal 'vest'), scarf, helmet, tunic, sandals, shield, sword, belt, breeches and javelin (or lance).

Activity 12: A legion encampment

Make a model or draw plans of a legion encampment. A camp was always laid out in the same way, marked out as a square. Discuss why the camp had a trench dug around the outside, why the tents were placed a distance from the perimeter, and why the general's headquarters were in the centre.

Activity 13: The life of a soldier

Write imaginative stories (though based on fact) about 'a legion on the march', 'a day in the life of a soldier', 'rules of the army', 'the eagle was captured', and so on.

Activity 14: Siege warfare

The children could research and write about items of Roman siege warfare, particularly the catapult, ballista and battering ram (see page 4). These make challenging subjects for model-making and other craft work. There is scope too for mathematical work on angles and trajectory, and perhaps a computer game or simulation based on hitting targets with a ballista.

Activity 15: 'Soldier mathematics'

Do 'soldier mathematics', appropriate for the age and ability of the children, based on the figures given in the following information.

Background information: 'Soldier mathematics'
Each soldier belonged to a contubernium, made up of 8 soldiers who shared a tent.
10 contubernia made 1 century, with a centurion in command.
Centuries formed cohorts of varying sizes.
10 cohorts made up 1 legion.
An average legion would contain around 5000 soldiers.

Activity 16: The structure of a legion

Using the given information, make a large illustrated frieze depicting the elements of a legion.

Activity 17: A skirmish during invasion

Act out a battle to gain territory. Include discussion on tactics; where and when to attack. Make suitable props, for example, the standard crowned by the legion's eagle. Discuss how native tribes would defend their territory – what weapons would have been used? What were the advantages held by the highly organised and trained Roman army?

Activity 18: A fortified town

Make a case-study of a fortified town captured by the legions, e.g. Maiden Castle in Dorset. Find out how a town such as this would have prepared for the invasion. Draw plans showing ditches, guard chambers and ramparts. Read stories about the attack and its consequences.

Activity 19: A Roman fort

Make a model or plan of a Roman fort. Forts protected the frontiers of the Roman provinces. The Emperor Hadrian linked forts with a huge wall across the north of England.

Activity 20: Britain, as seen by an invader

Write imaginative stories about what it would have been like to enter Britain as a foreign soldier. How would you have felt in this new land – brave, scared, curious? Then imagine how the British would have felt. What differences would there have been in the feelings and attitudes of the two opposing sides? Large drawings of a soldier from each army, accompanied by a series of thought or speech bubbles above their heads, would be a striking way of recording these differences.

Activity 21: Evidence of the Roman invasion

Investigate evidence that exists today of the invasion and conquest battles. Write about the role of archaeologists, who have discovered such gruesome objects as skulls pierced by swords: indeed, a number of shallow graves were found outside the east gate of Maiden Castle, containing skeletons showing sword cuts and one with a Roman arrowhead in its backbone.

Activity 22: An historical newspaper

Using **Copymaster 3** as a template for the front page, the children could write a whole issue of a Roman newspaper, reporting the fall of Maiden Castle, as though they were journalists at that time. Divide them into groups to carry out the research, write accounts of the battle, report interviews with participants, compose headlines and advertisements etc., and create illustrations such as maps and diagrams. Help them to edit and produce the finished paper. If the children have access to word-processing or desktop-publishing facilities, some striking and original work can be produced with help from computer-literate colleagues. In fact, a whole series of such newspapers, covering prominent events or characters during the Roman conquest, would give numerous opportunities for creative work, bringing history back to life. These could be 'published' and displayed in school.

Activity 23: Roman roads

Copymaster 4 can be used to identify and label some Roman place-names on a map. Jumbled answers have been included at the foot of the sheet but you can blank these out if you wish. How many towns or cities of today may have Roman-related names?

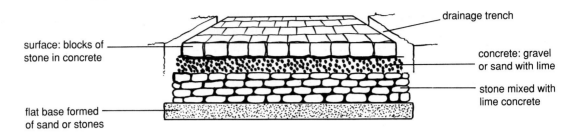

surface: blocks of stone in concrete

drainage trench

concrete: gravel or sand with lime

stone mixed with lime concrete

flat base formed of sand or stones

Cross-section of a Roman road

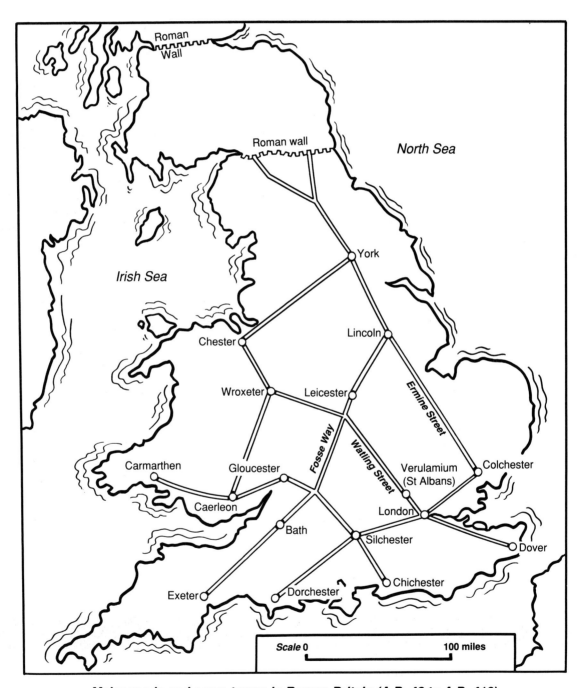

Major roads and some towns in Roman Britain (A.D. 43 to A.D. 410)

Find out about the task of Roman road-making. Roads were constructed to join the forts; discuss why they were always built along the shortest, flattest and straightest route. Ask children to suggest how this was ascertained by surveyors. Write about and illustrate the materials and technology involved in road-building (perhaps a similar study could be made of a Roman aqueduct). Do mathematical calculations on the difference between a Roman mile (1460 metres) and a modern mile (1602 metres). Draw/design and construct cross-section models or diagrams of a Roman road, to include the curved surface or camber (see opposite). Finally, explain the well-known saying 'All roads lead to Rome'.

Background information: *Roman roads*
There were four major military highways, running the length and breadth of the country, connecting the main forts and the main towns of Roman Britain. The road system was reinforced by sea-lanes up the east coast of Britain, and was linked to these by rivers such as the Trent, the Humber and the Ouse, and by canals such as the Foss Dyke.

These roads were equipped with post and relay-stations from 8 to 15 miles apart, providing fresh mounts and overnight accommodation for travellers. In time, many of these stations and some of the towns along the route became market centres, where produce could be gathered, bought and sold.

Towns whose names end in 'chester', 'cester' or 'caster' derive them from the Latin word *castra*, meaning a camp. Nowadays, we take the word 'street' to mean a road with houses alongside it: in Roman times the word meant a paved highway, and came from the Latin *strata*.

Activity 24: The story of Boudicca
Tell the story of Boudicca and the Ninth Legion. The children could produce creative writing and/or illustrations.

Background information: *Boudicca*
Prasutagus was the king of the Iceni tribe in Norfolk. When he died, the Roman government sent officials to take over and rule his kingdom. These officials were corrupt, and treated the native Iceni so unjustly that eventually they rose in rebellion. Led by Boudicca, the widow of Prasutagus, they sacked Colchester, London and St Albans, killing many thousands of Roman settlers. At last the disciplined Roman army under Suetonius Paulinus defeated the rebels. Paulinus was in favour of taking savage reprisals, but Julius Classicianus, the new head of the Roman administration, warned that this would make matters even worse. The government heeded this warning, and Paulinus was succeeded by a more tolerant and enlightened governor.

Study Unit 1a: the Romans in Britain – the conquest and occupation
Suggested levels of work involved in activities

Activity number	Level	Activity number	Level	Activity number	Level
1	2/3	9	2/3	17	2/3/4/5
2	2/3	10	2	18	2/3/4/5
3	2/3/4/5	11	2	19	2/3
4	2/3/4/5	12	2/3	20	2/3/4
5	2/3	13	2/3/4	21	2/3/4
6	2/3	14	2/3/4	22	2/3/4/5
7	2/3/4	15	2	23	2/3
8	2/3	16	2	24	2/3/4

EVERYDAY LIFE

 C5–8

Pupils should be taught about:

everyday life • *houses and home life; work, religion.*

Activity 1: A typical Roman town

Find out from original sites, museums and other secondary resources how the Romans lived in towns. Draw a plan or make a model of a 'typical' town, to include walls and gates, public baths, a theatre, amphitheatre, temples and forum. Pay particular attention to how the streets were laid out. Write about what a typical house was like, and find out about the hypocaust central-heating system (see below).

Activity 2: Roman town life

Make a list of all the ways you can think of in which Roman town life differed from town life today. Do the same for ways in which the adults and children spent their time – both working and at play.

Activity 3: Art in Roman times

Study the work of great painters and artists of the time, and consider the influence of Greek styles and techniques. Design a Roman wall-painting for the classroom, perhaps of portraits, a rural scene, or figures from Greek or Roman mythology.

Make mosaic pictures from small squares of black and white (or coloured) paper or card. Roman mosaics made from small pieces of stone or tile often depicted agricultural scenes, portraits or regular patterns. Black and white mosaic patterns were probably the most common early designs

Activity 4: Roman country life

Compare town life with country life. Wealthy Romans lived for part of the year in large country villas that were surrounded by farmland. A large villa was as grandly decorated as elaborate town houses.

Activity 5: Roman houses

Use **Copymasters 5** and **6** to investigate how Roman houses were furnished and decorated. Many rooms were too small to hold much furniture; the furniture that was used was probably made of wood, marble or metal. Look for museum evidence of interior decoration.

Copymaster 5 can also be used to familiarise the children with the design of a typical Roman villa. In the classroom, draw a large villa outline on a wall-frieze, with 'windows' revealing what the occupants of certain rooms might have been doing, and what furniture or other domestic objects might have been found there.

Background information: Roman houses

A Roman villa might have included:

Bedrooms: usually small and with little in the way of furniture.

Dining-room (Triclinium): this room contained tables for the food and couches for those eating (see **Copymaster 6**).

Kitchen: wood or charcoal-burning ovens were used for cooking.

Shop: a spare room was sometimes let by the owner to local shopkeepers.

Shrine (Lararium): for worship of the household gods.

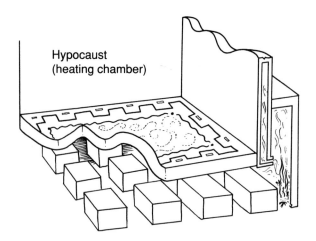

Hypocaust (heating chamber)

Baths: these may have been used by both the house owners and workers.

Living room (Atrium): this would have contained little furniture but perhaps had a pool in the floor.

Activity 6: Different ways of life

Research and write illustrated accounts of the very different ways of life experienced by people from a variety of backgrounds in Roman Britain. These could include 'My life as a …':

trader in the streets	wheelwright
slave in the mines	carpenter
farmworker	tanner
musician at a banquet	cobbler
teacher	potter
bath-house attendant	gladiator
doctor	weaver
blacksmith	charioteer

What qualifications and backgrounds did such people usually have? What might a typical day have been like? What were their 'tools of trade' (see illustrations opposite)?

Activity 7: Tools the Romans used

Using clay or other modelling materials, reproduce tools used by the Romans, based on designs/drawings from museum evidence or secondary resources.

Activity 8: A classroom museum

Establish your own 'museum of the Roman age' in a corner of the classroom. Artefacts might include tools (as above) and weapons, models of houses and forts, plans of towns, clay coins, pottery, plaques and mosaics, even articles of clothing.

Activity 9: A Roman toga

Why not try to make and wear a Roman toga (see diagram opposite)? An old sheet cut to shape might suffice.

Activity 10: Roman transport

Design and construct models of Roman methods of transport, for example, a litter, a farm cart, a galley and a chariot (see illustration on page 10).

Blacksmith

Shoemaker

Carpenter

Weaver

Potter

Farmworkers

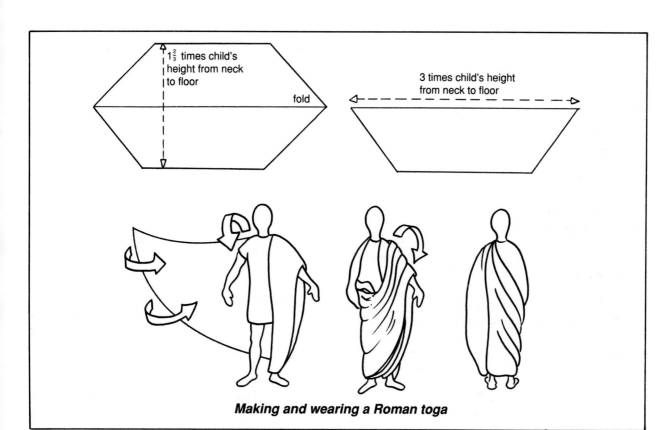

Making and wearing a Roman toga

9

Wealthy Roman citizens were carried around in litters by slaves.

Farm carts had wooden wheels and were drawn by oxen.

A Roman galley

Chariots like this were horse-drawn. The frame, platform and wheels were wooden; the lining would have been leather.

Activity 11: The story of Ben Hur

Read or tell the story of Ben Hur. If possible, enable the children to view the exciting chariot-race sequence from the 1959 film, perhaps on video-tape. This outstanding piece of film-making never fails to generate valuable discussion, as well as vivid creative writing and colourful art/craft work. Another equally effective sequence in the film depicts Ben Hur as a slave on board a Roman galley.

Activity 12: Roman sports and pastimes

The children could investigate, write about and draw pictures of Roman sports and pastimes such as knucklebones, dice, chariot-racing, wrestling, throwing the javelin, visits to the theatre etc.

Activity 13: The story of Spartacus

The story of Spartacus, and his leadership of the slaves in revolt against Rome, also offers scope for creative activities similar to those suggested above. Once again, it may be possible for the children to see extracts from the film, chosen carefully to emphasise aspects of life in Roman times, in this case perhaps the hardships of training in the gladiatorial school. Despite the danger of Hollywood over-indulgence in fiction rather than fact,

films such as these are often exhaustively researched to ensure historical accuracy – at least of set designs and costumes – and may help children to develop a greater sense of the period.

Activity 14: Vocabulary work

Do 'matching words with meanings' exercises associated with the Roman way of life. For example, elaborate on the following:

mosaic	curved surface of a Roman road
villa	Emperor who built a huge wall
camber	writing implement
Hadrian	Roman country house
stylus	picture made with tiny pieces of stone

Activity 15: Roman food

Working with **Copymaster 6**, find out what foods were commonly eaten, both from day to day and at elaborate dinner parties. Colour in the top half of the copymaster, showing the arrangement for a formal banquet.

Activity 16: A Roman banquet

Make plans for an imaginary luxury banquet. Design a menu for the dinner party and write this on the lower half of **Copymaster 6**, with illustrated margins. Ask the children to accompany the work with a written account of the proceedings, perhaps from the point of view of a dinner guest, a serving slave or one of the musicians. Discuss whether they would all have given a similar account of the banquet.

Background information: *Roman meals*

Most Romans ate a breakfast of bread and honey, olives and dates, followed by a simple lunch (prandium) and then dinner (cena), the main meal of the day.

No knives and forks can be seen in the picture on **Copymaster 6**. People used their fingers or spoons. A central table held the food. Slaves served both food and wine. Each of the couches seated three people, and guests were placed according to status.

A Roman dinner usually had three courses:

– *appetizers* such as salads, eggs, fish, mushrooms;
– *a main course* of around seven different dishes of fish, game, poultry and other meat;
– *secundae mensae (the second tables)* of fruits, honey, sweet cakes and nuts.

Activity 17: Roman cooking in the classroom

Cook Roman recipes, and set out your own classroom 'banquet'. A substantial sub-topic could be undertaken on Roman food sources, recipes and techniques of cooking and serving food.

Background information: *Roman cooking*

A most useful book to consult is *Food and Cooking in Roman Britain. History and Recipes (see Resources)*. Bear in mind the impact of the Roman invasion on cookery ingredients. The Romans were responsible for importing and introducing a variety of food sources, including:

game, such as guinea fowl, pheasants, peacocks;
fruits and nuts such as the fig, medlar, walnut and mulberry , and vines;
herbs, including parsley, fennel, mint, chervil, sage, garlic, rosemary and thyme;
vegetables such as cabbage, turnip, lettuce, endive, and others.

Activity 18: Roman numbers

Using **Copymaster 7** to help you, write and count like the Romans. The top half of the sheet gives the basic Roman numerals. Ask the children to work out the missing numerals between 15 and 20. Complete the 'Roman' sums on the bottom half of the copymaster. This activity can clearly be extended by devising sums and numerical games appropriate to the ability of the children.

Activity 19: Writing in Roman times

Explain to the children what it would have been like to be educated in Roman Britain. Writing would have been on wooden tables coated with wax. Take a large piece of thick card and cover it with a thick layer of wax crayon. Let the children experiment with a variety of implements to see which is most effective for writing on this 'tablet'.

Activity 20: Religion in Roman times

Investigate the complex yet fascinating religious beliefs of Roman times. **Copymaster 8** depicts five of the well-known gods and goddesses of the state religion. Ask the children to colour in the pictures, complete the sentences, and then choose one of the figures to research and write about in more detail.

Read or tell the children myths and legends involving the gods and goddesses of ancient Rome.

Activity 21: Christianity in ancient Rome

Tell the children stories of St Alban, the first martyr in Britain, and of others such as St Peter, St Paul, St Prisca, St Valentine and St Patrick. Draw pictures or paint secret Christian symbols, such as the fish. Ask the children to imagine that they are early Christians and to write a story about a secret Christian gathering. Did the Romans capture them?

Background information: *Religion*

The Romans had a variety of gods and goddesses (derived from Greek mythology) that formed the basis of the state religion. People prayed regularly and made sacrifices to their gods. Consider alternatives to the state religion, notably the impact of Christianity. Christians believed that there was only one god, and would not worship the gods of the Roman state. Official toleration of Christianity began in A.D. 313, and it became the official state religion in A.D. 394. For fear of persecution, the early Christians met in secret.

Study Unit 1a: the Romans in Britain – everyday life
Suggested levels of work involved in activities

Activity number	Level	Activity number	Level	Activity number	Level
1	2/3/4	8	2/3	15	2/3
2	2/3	9	2	16	2/3/4
3	2/3	10	2	17	2/3/4
4	2/3/4/5	11	2/3	18	2
5	2/3	12	2/3	19	2
6	2/3/4/5	13	2/3	20	2/3/4/5
7	2/3	14	2/3	21	2/3/4

THE LEGACY OF ROMAN RULE

C9

Pupils should be taught about:

the legacy of Roman rule

- place-names and settlement patterns, Roman remains, including artefacts, roads and buildings

Activity 1: A field visit

The legacy of the Roman Empire in our country is vast, and will probably be best appreciated and understood by a field visit to a Roman site or a specialist section of an art gallery or museum. Consult Ordnance Survey maps and the gallery or museum to ascertain the position of any Roman sites near your school. Where possible, undertake a case-study of one place, and consider its influence on the local area and beyond.

From field visits, archaeological evidence, reading and the study of other secondary resource material, ask the children to think of those aspects of Roman life that still affect our lives today.

Activity 2: A wall-display

Design a 'legacy of a settlement' wall-display wheel as shown here, with specific examples illustrated in each section. Individual ideas and data for this can be collected on **Copymaster 9**. The mosaic pattern can be coloured in, and the children can write or illustrate in mosaic design their own legacy ideas and discoveries in the space below. The copymaster as a whole could form part of the 'legacy of a settlement' wall-display, or an introductory sheet for the topic as a whole.

Activity 3: Considering the evidence

Consider to what extent art, architecture and writing are reliable forms of evidence about Roman times. Talk about ways in which they may be unreliable.

Activity 4: Learning the language

Learn some words of Latin. Expand the chart shown below.

Background information: *The language*

The native languages of new kingdoms after the decline and fall of the Empire adopted many of the words of the old Roman world. The Latin language forms the basis of a number of modern languages including Italian, French, Portuguese and Spanish. There are also many Latin words in the English language.

Latin	Meaning	English	French	Italian
populus	people	populace	peuple	popolo
aqua	water	aquatic	eau	acqua
nox	night	nocturnal	nuit	notte

Activity 5: Write a biography

Write and illustrate biographies of famous Romans, for example:

Julius Ceasar (100–44 B.C.)
Augustus (63 B.C.–A.D. 14)
Vergil (70–19 B.C.)
Hadrian (A.D. 76–138)

Describe their lives, influence and legacy. Display key facts about who did what, on pieces of card set beneath paintings of influential Romans. Lined up on the classroom wall, these will make an impressive 'who's who' display.

You may be able to look through translations of Roman writings such as those of Suetonius (*The Twelve Caesars*) and unearth short quotations which may be of interest to the children:

> 'Julius Ceasar was a bid of a dandy, always keeping his head carefully trimmed and shaved. . . He was a most skilful swordsman and horseman, and showed surprising powers of endurance. He always led his army, more often on foot than in the saddle, went bare-headed in all weather, and could travel for long distances at incredible speed in a little cart, with very little luggage.'
>
> (Suetonius)

> 'The Britons use the word 'strongholds' to describe densely wooded spots defended with a mound of earth and a trench, to which they retreat in order to escape the attacks of invaders.'
>
> (From *The Conquest of Gaul* by Julius Caesar)

Explain what a translation is, and that the invading Romans like Suetonius and Caesar did not write or speak English as we know it today. Where did these Roman translations come from? Do they provide reliable evidence about the Roman settlement?

Activity 6: Roman clues in the locality
Visit a local church. Study prayer books, service books and perhaps talk to clergy. What evidence can you find of the legacy of Rome, its religion and language?

Activity 7: A Roman timeline
Complete an illustrated timeline of the key events in the history of Rome and its Empire. This can be done in individual topic books or as a major class wall-display. Fill in boxes for Rome, than add other columns to show

Rome	Europe	Britain
800 B.C.		
Rome founded on seven hills by the River Tiber (735 B.C.)		

the development of events in Britain, Europe or other continents of the world. After 800 B.C. you could organise the boxes around, say, 500 B.C., 100 B.C., A.D. 50, etc.

Background information: *A Roman timeline*
A sample timeline showing some significant dates is shown below. Modified or extended versions of this can be produced, with illustrations, depending upon the ability of the children.

Activity 8: The end of imperial rule
Research reasons for the withdrawal of Roman troops from Britain in A.D. 410. Discuss the impact of Barbarian tribes in Europe and the effect this had on decision-making by the Roman emperor. Find out the meaning of the word 'barbarian' as it was used in this context.

Background information
Romans withdrew troops from Britain because of barbarian invasions in Europe. The army was therefore focused on the European mainland. Romans attributed the name 'barbarian' to anyone living outside the Empire who did not follow the Roman way of life. The final major invasion was by the Vandals in A.D. 455, who sailed into Italy and destroyed Rome. The last Emperor of the West was Romulus Augustus, deposed in A.D. 476 by Odoacer from Germany, who pronounced himself king of Italy. Barbarian kingdoms were set up in Britain, France and Germany.

Britain	Date	Europe
	B.C.	
New Stone Age	*c.* 2000	Beginnings of Greek Civilisation
Bronze Age invasions	*c.* 1600	
First Iron Age invasions		
	c. 400	
Later Iron Age invasions		
Caesar raids Britain	55–54	
	44–31	Augustus and Antony
	31 B.C.–A.D. 14	Augustus
	A.D.	
	14–37	Tiberius
	37–41	Gaius (Caligula)
Roman conquest of Britain	41–54	Claudius ⎱ period of luxury
Revolt of Boudicca	54–68	Nero ⎰ and debauch
Advance to Wales and North	69–79	Vespasian
Agricola's governorship	79–81	Titus
Town centres built in stone	81–96	Domitian
	96–98	Nerva
	98–117	Trajan
The Wall built	117–138	Hadrian, peace, and favour to the Greeks
Town houses of brick and stone Modest villas	138–161	Antoninus Pius. Peace and encouragement of the west
Carausius Emperor in Britain Coastal forts built	284–306	
Prosperity especially in the south-west	306–363	*House of Constantine* Christian Emperors
367 Great barbarian raid in Britain	378	Army of the East destroyed by the Goths
383–388 Magnus Maximus, Emperor in Britain, Gaul, Spain, Italy	383–395	
407 Constantine III Emperor in Britain, Gaul, and Spain	395–450	
410 Goths sack Rome		
Honorius instructs cities of Britain to look to their own defence		

Study Unit 1a: the Romans in Britain – legacy of Roman rule
Suggested levels of work involved in activities

Activity number	Level	Activity number	Level	Activity number	Level
1	2/3/4/5	4	2	7	2/3/4/5
2	2/3/4/5	5	2/3/4/5	8	2/3/4/5
3	2/3/4/5	6	2/3/4		

RESOURCES

Non-fiction

Burrell, R. *The Romans*, Oxford University Press, *Oxford Children's Ancient History, 1991.*

Corbishley, M. *What do We Know About the Romans?* Simon & Schuster, 1991.

James, S. *Ancient Rome*, See Through History Series, Heinemann.

Wood, T. *Roman Palace*, What Happened Here Series, A & C Black.

Roman Britain, History in Evidence Series, Wayland.

The Romans, Look into the Past Series, Wayland.

Family Life in Roman Britain, Family Life Series, Wayland.

Food and Feasts in Ancient Rome, Food and Feast Series, Wayland.

The Romans, Illustrated World History Series, Usborne.

Ancient Rome, Everyday Life Series, Usborne.

Living in Roman Times, First History Series, Usborne.

The Romans, Jump History Series, Two-Can.

Rome and The Ancient World, Illustrated History of the World Series, Simon & Schuster, 1991.

A Roman Villa, Inside Story Series, Simon & Schuster.

The British Museum has published an activity book on The Romans (British Museum General Enquiries – Tel: 0171-636-1555)

Fiction

Dupasquier, P. *The Sandal*, Andersen Press, 1989. A picture story about a sandal lost by a little Roman girl, which eventually finds its way into a museum of today.

Garland, S. *Shadows on the barn*, A & C Black, 1990. Children discover a Roman mosaic in a hen house. An easy-reading story.

Horace, *Two Roman mice*, Kaye & Ward, 1975. Retold by M.K. Roach, with illustrations based on Roman buildings, customs and decoration.*

Maris, R. *Cornerstone*, Heinemann, 1977. Set in Britain soon after the conquest, the story includes information about Roman stone-working techniques.*

Snelling, J. *Roman myths and legends*, Wayland, 1988.

Sutcliff, R. *Circlet of oak leaves*, Hamish Hamilton, 1968. Two Romans change identities in a battle against the Picts.*

The following stories will be enjoyed by more fluent readers, and extracts would be useful for reading aloud:

Clarke, J. *Take your time*, Jonathan Cape, 1990. Time travel to Roman Britain (also includes Plague 1666, Victorian London, and World War II).*

Ray, M. *Eastern Beacon*, Jonathan Cape, 1965. Illustrates the remoteness of parts of Britain under the Roman occupation.*

Ray, M. *Rain from the west*, Faber, 1980. Early Christianity in frontier Britain in the first century of the Roman Empire.*

Rees, D. *Beacon for the Romans*, Pergamon, 1981. A story about the end of Roman rule in Britain.*

Sutcliff, R. *Capricorn bracelet*, Red Fox, 1990. Six stories, set near Hadrian's wall, A.D. 61 – A.D. 383.

Sutcliff, R. *Eagle of the Ninth*, Puffin, 1977. Based on the unexplained disappearance of the Roman Ninth Legion in A.D. 117, and tells about the British having to adapt to Roman ways.

Sutcliff, R. *Frontier Wolf*, Puffin, 1984. Set on the northern border of Roman Britain.

Sutcliff, R. *Outcast*, OUP, 1980. Contrasts between Roman and Celtic ways of life. Part of the story is set in the Romney Marsh.

Sutcliff, R. *The Silver Branch*, Puffin, 1980. Plots, intrigue and adventure in Britain as Roman power begins to wane.

Treece, H. *Legions of the Eagle*, Penguin, 1970. A first-century A.D. story about Roman and Celtic conflict and friendship.

Treece, H. *The Queen's Brooch*, Hamish Hamilton, 1966. A tale of Boudicca's time, about a young tribune who becomes friendly with a youthful Celtic chieftain.*

*These books are out of print but are still available from libraries and second-hand bookshops.

Blueprints links

You will find related technology activities on the Romans in *Blueprints: Technology Key Stage 2*. The following other Stanley Thornes books will also prove useful: *Investigating History: Invaders and Settlers*.

STUDY UNIT 1 ANGLO-SAXONS IN BRITAIN

Pupils should be taught about the history of the British Isles from 55 B.C. to the early eleventh century, and the ways in which British society was shaped by different peoples. They should be given opportunities to study, in greater depth, ONE of the Romans, the Anglo-Saxons, or the Vikings.

1 Pupils should be taught in outline about the following:
   a the Roman conquest and occupation of Britain
   b the arrival and settlement of the Anglo-Saxons
   c Viking raids and settlements.

2 They should be taught in greater depth about ONE of the above.

b. Anglo-Saxons ● the arrival and settlement of the Anglo-Saxons and their impact on England, *e.g. early settlement, the conversion of the Anglo-Saxons to Christianity, King Alfred and Anglo-Saxon resistance to the Vikings*;
● everyday life, *e.g. houses and home life, work, religion*;
● the legacy of settlement, *e.g. place names and settlement patterns, myths and legends, Anglo-Saxon remains, including artefacts and buildings.*

TOPIC WEB

The arrival of the Anglo-Saxons

- Reasons for invasion
- Map of invasion routes
- The seven Kingdoms
- A timeline
- From warriors to kingdoms
- Sea transport
- The legend of Arthur
- Saxon kings
- Alfred the Great
- The family tree of Alfred
- The decline of the Saxon age

Everyday life

- Anglo-Saxons as people and personalities
- Homes and settlements
- Agriculture
- A thane and his wife
- Feasting, sport and entertainment
- Religious beliefs; missions for Christianity
- The Venerable Bede
- Writing and scholarship
- 'Then and now'

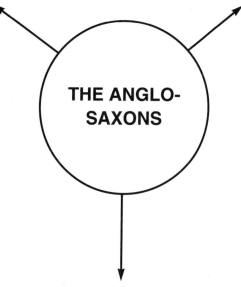

THE ANGLO-SAXONS

The legacy of settlement

- Sutton Hoo
- The nature of evidence
- Language and place names

THE ARRIVAL AND SETTLEMENT OF THE ANGLO-SAXONS

C10–12

Pupils should be taught about:

- the arrival and settlement of the Anglo-Saxons and their impact on England, *e.g. early settlement, the conversion of the Anglo-Saxons to Christianity, King Alfred and Anglo-Saxon resistance to the Vikings.*

Activity 1: Setting the scene

Set the scene for understanding the raids of the Anglo-Saxons by discussing the end of the Roman invasion. As the Romans departed, the Britons remained … until new invaders arrived. Angles, Saxons and Jutes soon set sail across the North Sea to Britain: these peoples had raided during Roman times and been repulsed but, in the absence of Roman defenders, the island was now virtually powerless to resist.

Activity 2: Why invade?

Reasons for invasion must be considered against a background of understanding of the existing situation in Britain, and the nature of the lands from which the invaders came. In this context, ask pupils to imagine they are Angles and Saxons, and to write a list of ideas which might explain their actions. Such a list might include:

'We are being attacked in our own lands.'
'Britain has better farming land.'
'The Romans have left and the Britons are weak.'
'We are tough and brave. We like to fight.'
'Britain has plenty of grain and livestock.'

Debate these and any other suggestions, asking whether it is possible to rank them in order of importance.

Describe the scene that would have faced the Angles and Saxons as they entered Britain for the first time – a mixture of farmland, rural life and grand Roman towns.

Activity 3: Weapons and warfare

Ask the children to research into what the Anglo-Saxon warriors might have looked like, and produce some writing and artwork on the subject. What sort of weapons did they use? And, most importantly, how do we know? Where does our evidence come from?

Activity 4: Anglo-Saxon invasion

The outline map on **Copymaster 10** can be used as an ongoing recording sheet as the topic progresses. Arrows from Europe show the directions of invasion of the Angles, Saxons and Jutes. Ask the children to add labels showing where each of these peoples came from. As the invasion is studied in detail, use the map on **Copymaster 11**. Depending on the age and abilities of the children, the Seven Kingdoms of the Saxon age can be simply labelled, or colour-coded in a key to show their importance at different times.

Background information: *Anglo-Saxon invasion*

The Seven Kingdoms were (as numbered on **Copymaster 11**):

1 Northumbria	5 Kent
2 Mercia	6 Sussex
3 East Anglia	7 Wessex
4 Essex	

In the sixth century Kent was the leading kingdom but it was overtaken by Northumbria in the seventh century. Mercia became the dominant kingdom in the eighth century, followed by Wessex, which maintained its supremacy until the end of the Saxon age.

Activity 5: Adding to the map

At an appropriate time, ask the children to label the remaining areas on the map on **Copymaster 11**:

A Strathclyde and Cumbria
B North Wales
C West Wales

These were inhabited throughout the Saxon period by Britons and Celtic tribespeople, many of whom had fled to the hills during times of invasion.

Activity 6: An Anglo-Saxon timeline

Begin a timeline of the Anglo-Saxon age. Again, this can be an ongoing recording chart which can be regularly added to as events and issues unfold throughout the topic. Children can construct their own individual timelines or make this a class activity. Below is a section of such a timeline to convey the general idea. Any classroom display or timeline should be illustrated with paintings and/or collage work based on key events of the period. The rise of the kingdoms, mentioned above, can be one key general issue to record, with details of particular kings as appropriate to your work. Other ideas are offered on page 20.

It is, of course, inappropriate to make a complete separation of the Anglo-Saxons from their contemporaries, the Vikings. Some of the ideas and activities suggested in the section on Vikings may well be relevant for incorporation into a topic on the eighth, ninth and tenth centuries in Britain. Certainly there is a good deal of overlap in the reasons for invasion, the distinction between raids and settlement, and many facets of everyday life and beliefs.

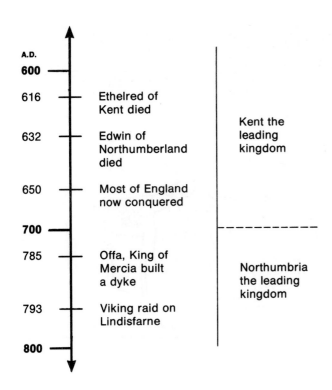

600

616 — Ethelred of
Kent died

632 — Edwin of
Northumberland
died

Kent the
leading
kingdom

650 — Most of England
now conquered

700

785 — Offa, King of
Mercia built
a dyke

Northumbria
the leading
kingdom

793 — Viking raid on
Lindisfarne

800

Activity 7: From warriors to kingdoms

Write about the transition 'from warriors to kingdoms'. and about the gradual establishment of a differentiated society as the kingdoms became established. In the earliest days, the Anglo-Saxons were 'as one', fighting together and establishing their settlements. Ask the children to suggest reasons why certain individuals emerged as leaders and as nobles, while others remained as fighters or serfs.

Design a series of posters (like those on page 18) to illustrate the rise of the kingdoms. Introduce the word 'bretwalda', the overlord, who became the eventual king.

Background information: From warriors to kingdoms
The title 'bretwalda' is said to mean 'Britain-ruler', though no Saxon chief ever ruled the whole of Britain. It may best be considered as describing a powerful local ruler.

Activity 8: Arrival of the early warriors

Find out about the arrival of the early warriors. All were young men – no women or children sailed with them.

Dates	Rulers	Events/people	Background
400–600	Angles and Saxons settle in Britain.	Hengist & Horsa.	British tribes put up a long and stubborn resistance for 200 years.
About 461 About 560 597 About 603 to 680	Pope Gregory. Kings Edwin, Oswald, Oswy of Northumbria.	Death of St. Patrick. St. Columba in Scotland. St. Augustine in Kent. St. Aidan. Abbess Hilda and Caedmon. Bede (672–735).	Spread of Christianity. Perpetual warfare, esp. against Penda of Mercia.
757–96	King Offa of Mercia.	Offa's Dyke.	Period of the Heptarchy (or Seven Kingdoms).
825	Egbert ('the Great') of Wessex, first King of all England (802–836).	Defeated Mercia at Battle of Ellanddune.	Saxon open-field system of Agriculture.
About 835	The Danes.	Viking raids.	E. Anglia, North and Midlands overrun. Christianity destroyed temporarily.
871–99 (or 900)	Alfred the Great, King of Wessex.	Inevitable clash with invaders.	
878		Guthrum defeated at Ethandune. Peace of Wedmore. *Anglo-Saxon Chronicle.*	Division of England into Danelaw and Wessex.
900–24	Edward the Elder.	Reconquered Danelaw.	Gt. period of Wessex Kings.
925–50	Athelstan.	Conquered S. Scotland.	Spread of building and learning.
959–75	Edgar.	St. Dunstan.	Incr. power of the Church.
978	Ethelred the Unready.	New Danish raids.	Danegeld.
1013	Sweyn of Denmark.	Invaded Britain.	
1016–35	Canute.	Edmund Ironside fought him.	Canute ruled an Anglo-Danish Empire.
1042–66	Edward the Confessor.	Introduced Normans. Built Westminster Abbey.	Danes built towns and fostered trade. Use of stone for building.
1066	Harold. (son of Earl Godwin of Wessex).	Defeated Tostig and Harald Hardrada at Stamford Bridge (nr. York)	Wm. of Normandy prepared to invade.

Stage 1

Warriors build simple homes on patches of land they have seized.

Stage 2

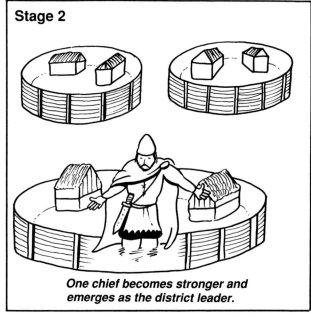

One chief becomes stronger and emerges as the district leader.

Stage 3

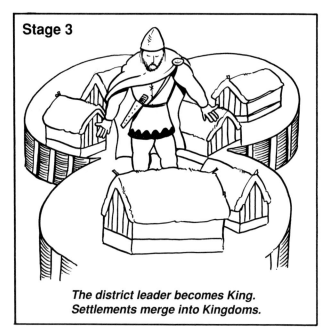

The district leader becomes King. Settlements merge into Kingdoms.

Stage 4

The King gathers his followers. Different levels of society are formed.

Draw or paint pictures of the longboats used for transport. Discuss what they might have brought with them – food, clothing, weapons. Their boats were actually quite small, around 20 metres in length and 3 metres wide. Each carried 40–50 people. Consider how the warriors moved about once they landed on the shores of Britain.

Think about the invasion from the point of view of the Britons. How would they have reacted? How did these newcomers differ from the Romans? Then consider the invasion from the point of view of the invaders. Would the established Roman towns have appealed to them as dwelling places? Finally, consider what the Romans might have thought of the Anglo-Saxons. The children could draw pictures of the Britons and the Anglo-Saxons, writing some of their responses to the above questions in thought or speech bubbles.

Background information: *The early warriors*
The Anglo-Saxons, whilst lacking the military organisation and discipline of the Romans, were fierce warriors. They won most battles easily, with the result that the Britons retreated into the north and west, allowing scope for the establishment of the Saxon settlements and eventual kingdoms in the east and south. Writing in about A.D. 730, Bede recorded that

'… these heathen conquerors (the Anglo-Saxons) devastated the surrounding cities and countryside … priests were slain at the alter; bishops and people alike, regardless of rank, were destroyed with fire and sword, and none remained to bury those who had suffered a cruel death.'

Use an atlas to study the shape and physical geography of the British Isles. Consider the places to which the Britons might have retreated in order to escape the invasion from the south-east (link this to the information shown on **Copymasters 10** and **11**).

Find out more and write about some of the battles against the Anglo-Saxons. Mark Offa's Dyke on **Copymaster 11**.

18

Activity 9: The spread of Christianity

First let the children locate on the map on **Copymaster 11** likely areas of settlement for the Celtic Christians.

Find out about the lives of those who set out on missions to teach about the Christian way of life. It is appropriate to include the stories of St Patrick (who went to Ireland in A.D. 432), St Columba (who visited Iona in A.D. 563) and St Aidan, who built the monastery at Lindisfarne and ruled there as bishop for 16 years until his death in A.D. 651. Consider also the significance of Roman church missionaries, including St Augustine who had a major influence in the conversion of Saxons to Christianity.

Add to your timeline, with appropriate illustrations, the names of these and other missionaries, such as St Swithin (Bishop of Winchester between A.D. 852 and 862), St Kentigern or Mungo (Bishop of Glasgow, who died in A.D. 651), and St Wulfstan (1009–1095) Bishop of Worcester, the last of the Anglo-Saxon saints. Sites such as Iona and Lindisfarne could be added to the map on **Copymaster 11**.

The children could also investigate the life of a monk in Anglo-Saxon times, reporting in writing and/or by drawings, paintings or collage work. A scene in the monastery chapel or perhaps in the cell of a monk would make a good subject for a diorama or model.

Activity 10: King Arthur – truth or legend?

Tell the story of King Arthur, the legendary hero who is believed to have battled against the Saxon invasion. This story provides much scope for the vital historical skill of considering the reliability of evidence. Find as many pictures as possible of the legendary Arthur and discuss how these differ – some place great emphasis on him as a warrior in armour, others show him as King with Queen Guinevere. Paint your own picture gallery explaining some of the legends, stories and events in the life of Arthur. **Copymaster 12** provides a basic set of typical pictures.

Ask pupils to write down what we actually know about Arthur, e.g. that legends were written about him. Many historians believe that King Arthur did exist. It is documented that he was born at Tintagel Castle in Cornwall, to a father who was King of the Britons, and that at the age of fifteen he became king upon the death of his father. Consider how we know these things, and also what we do not know for certain – nothing was actually written about him during his lifetime although legends tell of the great hero who battled against the Saxons.

Investigate and write about Arthur's involvement with the invaders, bearing in mind its legendary qualities. It is suggested that he won countless battles, aided by Caliburn (or Excalibur), his special sword, a gift from the Lady of the Lake. A sub-topic on Arthur's life could involve the children in reading stories and poems, and developing these in art and craft lessons.

Activity 11: How do we know about Arthur?

Find out the names of people who documented Arthur's deeds. Gildas, a Welsh monk, wrote about a victory for the Britons at the battle of Mount Badon, in which Arthur is alleged to have played a key role (though Gildas does not mention Arthur by name). Nennius, another Welsh monk, writing a *History of the Britons* in A.D. 830, names Arthur as leader in battles against the Anglo-Saxons. Nennius wrote

> '… on that one day (the battle of Mount Badon) there fell in one onslaught of Arthur's, nine hundred and sixty men; and none slew them but he alone, and in all his battles he remained victor.'

Badon is thought to be somewhere in the south – perhaps a village called Bradbury, alongside an ancient British hill-fort near Swindon, or another hill-fort called Bradbury Rings in Dorset, or perhaps even the city of Bath. But … did Arthur really kill 960 men single-handed, in one battle?

Organise a class debate on 'The man called Arthur'. As well as having fun in this debate, tease out the real nature of the historical evidence on which we can depend. You can glean much useful information from books (see *Resources*).

Paint a large wall-frieze showing Arthur and his company of knights (including Lancelot, Gawain, Bedivere, Bors, Ector, Pellinore, Mordred and Kay) sitting at the round table. As a background, show Sir Galahad riding out to battle on his charger.

Read T.H. White's story *The Sword In The Stone* for a lively though fictionalised account of Arthur's early life. Let the children hear some of the music from Rick Wakeman's 1975 LP 'The Myths And Legends of King Arthur And The Knights Of The Round Table' (A&M Records Ltd, number AMLH 64515). The record contains a rousing overture, beginning with the words:

> *Whoso pulleth out this sword from this stone and anvil, is the true-born king of all Britain.*

Other suitable tracks might include 'Sir Lancelot and the Black Knight' and 'Merlin the Magician'. Ask children what pictures the music conjures up in their minds: hopefully, some vivid artwork and creative writing will follow.

Note: This was one of the first and most successful of the numerous concept albums, issued in the mid-seventies, blending some of the Arthurian characters and stories with contemporary rock music. The children would probably benefit by having a copy of the lyrics in front of them when listening: these are provided, along with numerous illustrations, in a booklet contained in the sleeve of the record. The record cover includes two pictures of the sword Excalibur, buried to the hilt in an anvil on the front of the sleeve and being held aloft by the Lady of the Lake on the back, which might well inspire further art and craft work.

Activity 12: Arthur on film and television

It may be possible for the children to watch extracts from films, television series or documentaries about King Arthur, thereby increasing awareness of the period.

A number of productions have been made about the

Arthurian legend, though few are historically accurate. *The Knights Of The Round Table* (1953) had a medieval setting but in essence is little more than a colourful adventure story: it may entertain, but it is doubtful whether it will really inform. The film *Excalibur*, made in 1981, is more realistic (and inevitably more violent): teachers intending to show extracts in order to stimulate creative work should choose them with care.

Activity 13: More about the Saxon kings

Investigate the lives and activities of the well-known Saxon kings. The first of these was Ethelred of Kent, followed by Edwin of Northumberland. King Offa of Mercia is well remembered for the building of a dyke as a defence against the attacks of the Britons from North Wales, but probably the greatest king of all was Alfred of Wessex.

Activity 14: Alfred the Great

Undertake a sub-topic on the story of the best-known figure of Saxon times – Alfred the Great. From the outset, ask the children to bear in mind that he is the only king of England to have been labelled 'the Great', and to find out why. Afterwards, ask them if it is their considered opinion that he really was 'a leader above all leaders'? What were his greatest achievements?

Start by compiling biographies of Alfred, King of Wessex from 871 to 899. Write about and illustrate key events of his life, and document what evidence we have to substantiate the truth of his reign. Note the relevance of the work of writers such as Bishop Asser, who wrote a *Life of Alfred*. Ask the children if they can find out what the name 'Alfred' meant. Why might he have been given this name?

Make a large illustrated wall-chart to summarise some of Alfred's achievements. Set out key headings, and add writing and pictures to explain their significance. Alfred is said to have invented a candle-clock which was marked into eight equal sections, each of which burned for one hour. Perhaps the children could try to design and/or construct a candle-clock of their own (be aware of safety considerations at all times).

Write about another well-known, but less glorious achievement of Alfred's life – the burning of the cakes. Read the story of this and other legends.

Find out the details of Alfred's long battle with the Viking invaders, and how he defended the Kingdom of Wessex to the end. On a map of Britain, locate Edington where Alfred defeated the Vikings – leaving much of the south and west of England under the rule of Alfred in Wessex. Ask children whether they think that Alfred was justified in adopting the title 'King of all Anglo-Saxons'. Paint or make collage pictures of Saxon people hard at work constructing a burh, a fortified hilltop stronghold, with enemy ships approaching on the horizon.

Background information: *Alfred the Great*

Alfred was born in A.D. 849 at Wantage. He was the youngest son of King Aethelwulf of Wessex, and could trace his ancestry back to the leader of a sixth-century band of Saxon raiders, called Cerdic. Cerdic, it was said, could trace his ancestry back to Odin, the 'All-Father'! (see page 37 for more about Odin.)

At the time of Alfred's birth, Wessex was the most powerful of the Saxon kingdoms. His name, which may originally have been spelt 'Aelfraed', is said to mean 'elf-counsel' –perhaps a reference to his intelligence and wisdom? As he grew older, Alfred grew fond of hunting, an excellent way of learning about his kingdom when few maps existed. According to Bishop Asser, Alfred 'remained ignorant of letters until his twelfth year, or even longer,' though he had an excellent memory and could learn poetry off by heart from a very early age.

Alfred's first success against the Danes came at the battle of Ashdown in A.D. 871, when he was second in command. He was unable to defeat the Danes completely, but his resistance was stiff enough to persuade them to leave Wessex in peace for the next few years and seek plunder elsewhere. As time went by, some of the Danes and the native Saxons began to intermarry. Others, led by a notable warrior, Guthrum, still had designs on Wessex.

In January of 878 the Danes took the Saxons by surprise, driving Alfred and a small band of soldiers into hiding in the Somerset marshes. Alfred set up his headquarters on the isle of Athelney, determined to continue the fight. By May he had gathered a strong enough force to attack Guthrum at Edington (or Ethandun). Eventually the Danes were forced to surrender, swearing on oath that they would leave the kingdom – and that Guthrum would become a Christian. Guthrum and the Danes were as good as their word: it appears that Guthrum and Alfred had developed a mutual respect which enabled such an agreement to be reached without loss of face on either side.

A penny coin of Alfred was struck in 880 or thereabouts, bearing the inscription Aelfred Rex Anglor(um) meaning 'Alfred, King of the English'. According to the *Anglo-Saxon Chronicle*, 'All the English people that were not under subjection to the Danes submitted to him.'

Activity 15: Alfred's descendants

Design and build up a large family tree, like the one on page 21, to show the kings of Saxon England who descended from Alfred. Illustrate this with paintings of each ruler, and add sentences summarising their significance. (For preliminary work on family trees, see activities suggested in the section Life in Tudor Times in this book, pages 41 to 55.) Divide the children into working groups to research more about the personalities and lives of these men. Explain why some of the kings have nicknames – why was Ethelred known as 'Unready', Edgar as 'the Peaceable' and Edward as 'the Confessor'? If the children were to give themselves a nickname, what would it be? Find out what is meant by 'The Golden Age of the Saxons'. Write about the eventual decline of the Golden Age, and the closing years of Saxon England. Tell the stories of King Canute who spoke to the waves of the sea, Harold Godwinsson's visit to Normandy, and William of Normandy's claim to the English throne.

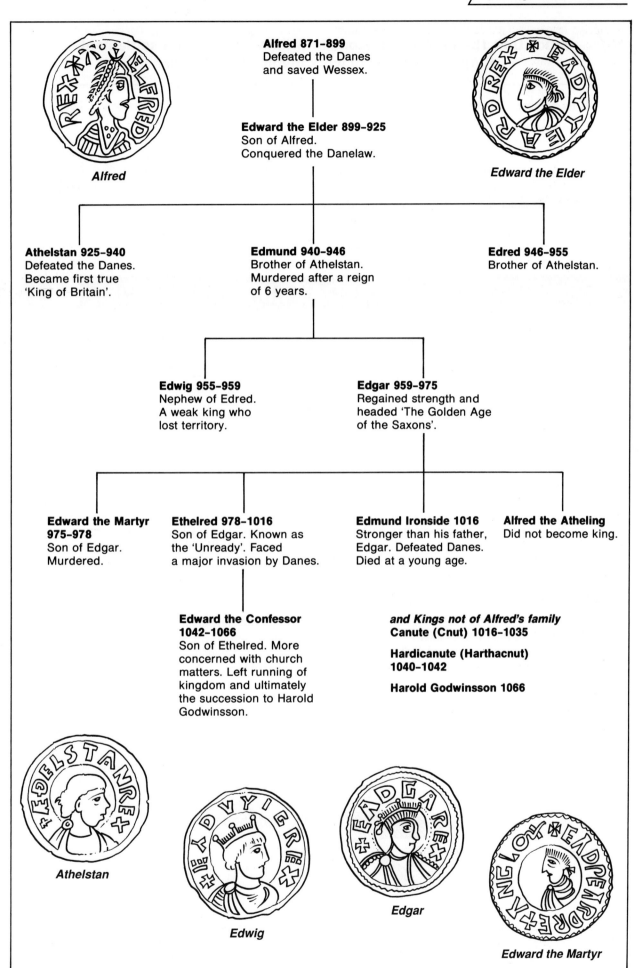

Alfred 871–899
Defeated the Danes
and saved Wessex.

Alfred

Edward the Elder 899–925
Son of Alfred.
Conquered the Danelaw.

Edward the Elder

Athelstan 925–940
Defeated the Danes.
Became first true
'King of Britain'.

Edmund 940–946
Brother of Athelstan.
Murdered after a reign
of 6 years.

Edred 946–955
Brother of Athelstan.

Edwig 955–959
Nephew of Edred.
A weak king who
lost territory.

Edgar 959–975
Regained strength and
headed 'The Golden Age
of the Saxons'.

**Edward the Martyr
975–978**
Son of Edgar.
Murdered.

Ethelred 978–1016
Son of Edgar. Known as
the 'Unready'. Faced
a major invasion by Danes.

Edmund Ironside 1016
Stronger than his father,
Edgar. Defeated Danes.
Died at a young age.

Alfred the Atheling
Did not become king.

**Edward the Confessor
1042–1066**
Son of Ethelred. More
concerned with church
matters. Left running of
kingdom and ultimately
the succession to Harold
Godwinsson.

and Kings not of Alfred's family
Canute (Cnut) 1016–1035

**Hardicanute (Harthacnut)
1040–1042**

Harold Godwinsson 1066

Athelstan

Edwig

Edgar

Edward the Martyr

Study Unit 1b: the Anglo-Saxons in Britain – arrival and settlement.
Suggested levels of work involved in activities

Activity number	Level	Activity number	Level	Activity number	Level
1	2/3/4	6	2/3/4	11	2/3/4/5
2	2/3/4/5	7	2/3/4/5	12	2/3
3	2/3/4	8	2/3/4/5	13	2/3/4/5
4	2/3/4	9	2/3/4/5	14	2/3/4/5
5	2	10	2/3/4/5	15	2/3/4/5

EVERYDAY LIFE

C13–16

Pupils should be taught about:

everyday life ● houses and home life; work; religion.

Activity 1: Who were the Angles and Saxons?

Consider the Angles and Saxons as personalities, and as people. Draw accurate pictures to represent them as they were – most were very tall and exceptionally strong, with fair hair and blue eyes. Write a list of suitable words describing their personalities and skills to aid written accounts, for example:

tough	adventurous	warriors
strong	farmers	oarsmen
brave	fighters	hunters

Activity 2: What were their homes like?

Draw pictures of the types of homes that the Anglo-Saxons lived in, with notes about how they were constructed. This activity would lead quite naturally to the construction of diorama scenes of Anglo-Saxon homes and lifestyles, The simplest homes were huts, perhaps made out of tree-trunks, constructed over a pit in the earth. Reeds or turf were used to thatch the roof. Other houses had wattle-and-daub walls.

Discuss how the differentiated society resulted in buildings of various sizes and degrees of elaboration. The lord or chief of a village owned a 'hall', the largest building in the settlement. Lowly serfs lived in simple huts.

Construct a model hut, or a more elaborate model of an entire settlement surrounded by fence and ditch, using card, scrap materials and papier mâché on a hardboard base.

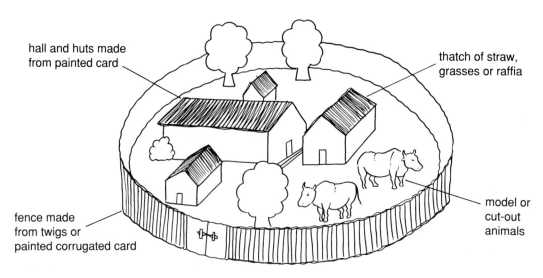

hall and huts made from painted card

thatch of straw, grasses or raffia

fence made from twigs or painted corrugated card

model or cut-out animals

To construct a simple rectangular hut, take a piece of thin card and rule it into 16 squares. Make cuts and then fold and secure the end flaps with glue, as shown in the following diagram.

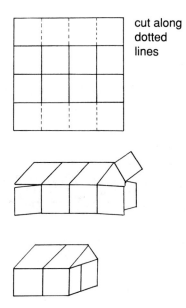

cut along
dotted
lines

On a much grander scale, and if space in the school grounds allows, construct a 'life size' hut – a splendid project for design and technology. Aim to build a hut measuring 4 metres by 3 metres (see below).

Activity 3: Village life
Prepare other pictures and writing about village life to augment your model hut or settlement. The Anglo-Saxons were very good at farming. Find out about the tools and implements they developed, for example, an ox-drawn plough, and about their system of organising fields and crops. Use **Copymaster 13** to introduce the children to the Anglo-Saxon system of cultivation. Discuss why the early settlers operated this 'three-field system'. Why did they need to have a fallow year? What advantages of modern farming did they lack?

Background information: Village life
Anglo-Saxon farmers cultivated three different fields, which were divided into a number of narrow strips. Each family had strips scattered about the three fields in order to share out the good and bad soil fairly, and thus they had a farm in various places around the village. One field was allowed to rest (i.e. remain fallow) each year, so that the soil would have the chance to regain its nutrients. During this fallow year, animals grazed in the field and on common land on the outskirts of the village. The chief crops grown in the other two fields were wheat and barley. The pictures on page 24 illustrate an Anglo-Saxon farming year.

Activity 4: Anglo-Saxon society
Use **Copymaster 14** to introduce the word 'thane', meaning the chief of the settlement. He would have lived in the 'hall' with his wife, family and servants. Children can colour the outline drawings, paying attention to authenticity with the splendid, brightly coloured clothes and Anglo-Saxon liking for jewellery. Using a second copy of **Copymaster 14**, the children could colour and cut out the figures, mount them on

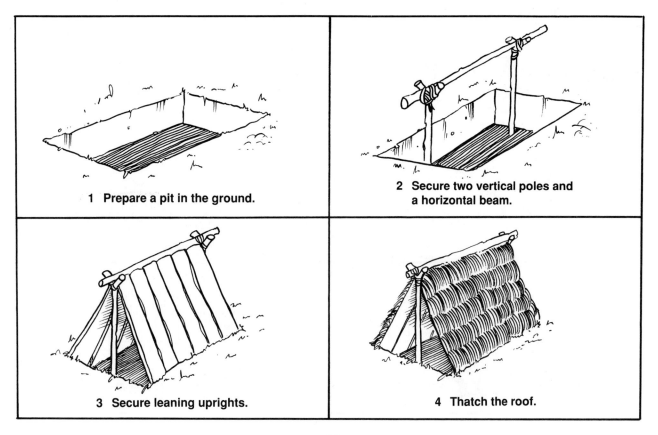

1 Prepare a pit in the ground.

2 Secure two vertical poles and a horizontal beam.

3 Secure leaning uprights.

4 Thatch the roof.

An Anglo-Saxon farming year

January – ploughing

February – pruning

March – preparing the soil and sowing

April – a time for feasting

May – looking after the flocks

June – cutting wood

July – haymaking

August – harvesting

September – hunting

October – hawking

November – preparing for winter

December – threshing and winnowing

24

card and stand them alongside dioramas or models of the hall or village, or include them on a 3-D display of Anglo-Saxon life. Ask the children to research and write about a day in the life of the thane.

Make other freestanding Anglo-Saxon figures using papier mâché and wire on a wooden frame. They can be dressed with scraps of leather, wool and other material. Copy items of Anglo-Saxon jewellery, using scrap materials, card and spray paints. Use them to make a display, or to adorn any model figures you may make.

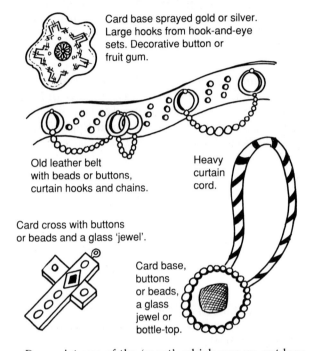

Card base sprayed gold or silver. Large hooks from hook-and-eye sets. Decorative button or fruit gum.

Old leather belt with beads or buttons, curtain hooks and chains.

Heavy curtain cord.

Card cross with buttons or beads and a glass 'jewel'.

Card base, buttons or beads, a glass jewel or bottle-top.

Draw pictures of the 'moot', which was an outdoor meeting place in the settlement where people came to discuss affairs, as well as to trade food, tools and weapons. Investigate aspects of family and village life such as feasts, sports, entertainments, crime and punishment. Sundays and 'feast days' were holidays. Sports and dances took place in the moot, and from time to time the thane would host a splendid banquet. Write stories about some of these episodes in village life.

Two of the greatest pleasures of the Anglo-Saxons were eating and drinking. Paint or make collage pictures of a feast, showing the men enjoying their ale and mead, animals roasting on spits, and musicians entertaining the company. The scene might also include acrobats and jugglers. Don't forget to show tapestries hanging from the walls of the hall, and weapons at the ready in case of a surprise attack during the festivities. Write about the feast as well, from the different points of view of these people – the women preparing the food, the thane or his steward organising the proceedings, the servants rushing to prepare the hall, the guests enjoying the hospitality, and those left to clear up afterwards. Would everyone have enjoyed the proceedings to the same extent? The children may need to research each of these activities before writing, but their findings will add colour to the subject.

Perhaps small groups of children could investigate in more detail one aspect of the sport and/or other entertainment of the times – for example, Saxon musical instruments (harp, flute, trumpet, horn, etc.); favourite foods (fish, pork, hare, rabbit, poultry, etc.); and popular games (hunting, horse-riding, ballgames, wrestling). The groups could share their discoveries by making oral presentations to the rest of the class, with the aid of paintings, drawings and reference books.

Activity 5: Then and now
Compare the lifestyle of Anglo-Saxons with that of modern Britain. Design quiz sheets for pupils, as suggested below, or ask them to devise their own drawings of 'gadgets of the day' and 'gadgets they did without'.

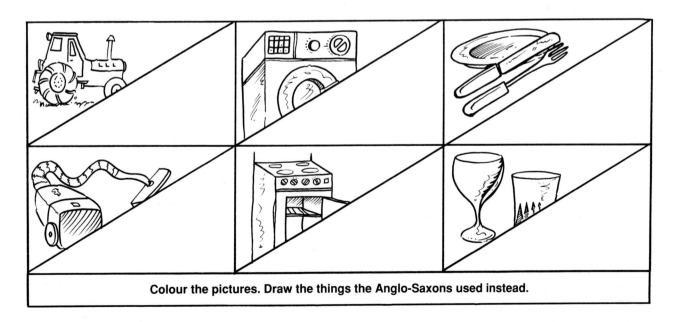

Colour the pictures. Draw the things the Anglo-Saxons used instead.

Activity 6: The Anglo-Saxon alphabet

The Anglo-Saxons had a runic alphabet similar to that of the Vikings (see page 38). Perhaps the children could compare these symbols and write messages using them.

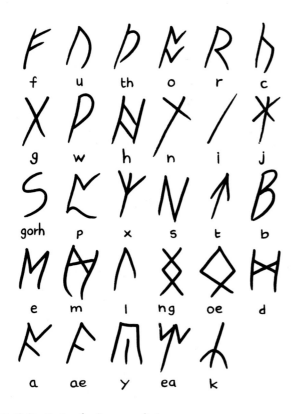

Activity 7: Anglo-Saxon religion

Find out about religious customs and beliefs, and in particular about the relationships between Saxons and the Christian religion.

Background information: *Anglo-Saxon religion*

The Anglo-Saxons were pagans who worshipped many different gods. The chief of these was Woden, from whom comes our Woden's day or Wednesday (see also the unit on the Vikings, page 37). Most Christians were terrified by the pagans and fled to safety in the west, where they were known as Celtic Christians.

Activity 8: The Venerable Bede

Copymaster 15 could form an introduction to a more detailed study of one very influential monk – the Venerable Bede. The drawing can be coloured in 'Saxon style' and used as a cover for a 'Biography of Bede'. Find out why he is referred to as the 'Venerable' Bede (the word 'venerable' meant 'worthy of love').

A study of the life and work of Bede will raise awareness of this period of history as being very significant in the development of literacy. Monasteries became well known for their libraries and schools. Famous scholars and literary works such as the poem *Beowulf* began to emerge during Anglo-Saxon times.

Background information: *The Venerable Bede*

Bede was influential for many reasons, not least among them being his ability as a writer. His famous work on the history of the Church and Saxon England, called *Ecclesiastical History of Britain*, is a major source of evidence about the period which historians have consulted throughout the centuries.

Activity 9: Illuminated manuscripts

Copymaster 16 can be used to introduce the subject of illuminated manuscripts. Look at museum evidence or pictures of some illuminated texts of the time. Discuss the technology available for writing books and manuscripts, and the sheer beauty of some of the works produced. Children can use the copymaster to do their own illuminated lettering – ask them to colour in the given outlines and then design their own letters in the space provided. Discuss what a time-consuming activity this must have been!

Use the 'Old English' style of lettering to make labels for your pictures and other work on the Anglo-Saxons. It is possible to purchase dry-transfer lettering in this style from Letraset® and other sources. The Helix® company produces a set of two plastic templates in upper and lower-case Old English lettering, should a larger size be required for frieze-boards and other display work.

Study Unit 1b: the Anglo-Saxons in Britain – everyday life.
Suggested levels of work involved in activities

Activity number	Level	Activity number	Level	Activity number	Level
1	2/3	4	2/3	7	2/3/4/5
2	2/3	5	2/3/4	8	2/3/4/5
3	2/3/4	6	2	9	2/3

THE LEGACY OF SETTLEMENT

C17– 18

Pupils should be taught about:

the legacy of settlement

● place names and settlement patterns; myths and legends; Anglo-Saxon remains, including artefacts and buildings

Activity 1: What the archaeologists found

If a visit to a museum or an Anglo-Saxon site is not possible, tell a story of well-known discoveries of Anglo-Saxon remains, such as those found at Sutton Hoo in Suffolk. Locate Sutton Hoo on a map, and use reference books to find out about and make drawings of what archaeologists discovered, including the outline of an entire burial ship, weapons, jewellery, pottery and household utensils. Find out how the archaeologists worked to draw conclusions from their amazing finds. What have we learned about Anglo-Saxon life from the Sutton Hoo treasures? What do such things *not* tell us?

Ask the children to find out about the Alfred Jewel, discovered in 1693 near Athelney, in Somerset. What did it look like? How did it get its name? What might it have been used for?

Background information: *The Alfred Jewel*

The Alfred Jewel was so called because of an inscription around the edge, reading *AELFRED MEC HET GEWYRCAN* ('Alfred ordered me to be made'). The Jewel was made of gold, with an enamel portrait of a figure carrying what appear to be two sceptres – could this be Alfred himself?

Activity 2: At home with the Anglo-Saxons

Look further into the legacy of Anglo-Saxon place-names remaining today. Are the children 'at home with the Anglo-Saxons'?

Using **Copymaster 17**, ask the children to study the signposts and then match the Anglo-Saxon words on them with the modern equivalents given at the foot of the page. The children can then complete the sign-posts by putting in real place-names, from the school's local area if possible. The modern equivalents of the Anglo-Saxon words are as follows:

hurst: wood
tun: an early settlement, hence 'home'
ham: a number of huts, hence a 'village' or 'town'
mere: pool
field: field
minster: religious building
ing: the people of
worth: protected place
ford: river-crossing
ley: a clearing in the forest

This activity can be extended to an investigation into well-known place-names elsewhere in England, which are derived from the Anglo-Saxon. Consider, for example, the meaning of names such as 'Birmingham' and 'Stratford'. Remember also to discuss the derivation of the word 'England' ('Angle-land').

Activity 3: Anglo-Saxon Chronicle

Investigate the origins and content of the 'Anglo-Saxon Chronicle', a key source of information about the period. Discuss the reliability of evidence such as this. This activity could also be related to a more general study of the legacy of King Alfred (see Activity 14).

Background information

Alfred was very keen on learning and intellectual matters. He made the clergy learn Latin as this was the language of their church. Noblemen were encouraged to write and to read English. It is believed that the Anglo-Saxon Chronicle (a yearly account of events) was begun during Alfred's reign. This is a most useful source of facts of the period.

Activity 4: Investigate the locality

Find out from your local library or books on the locality, where the nearest buildings are which date from Anglo-Saxon times – perhaps a castle or church. If possible, visit and make a detailed study of this aspect of Anglo-Saxon legacy, still available for us to see today.

Activity 5: Off to England

Play the ship's voyage game on **Copymaster 18** towards the end of your project: it will reinforce many facts learned and hopefully teach others. The games should be mounted on stiff card and covered in clear plastic film for greater durability. You might like to let the children colour their copies first. Play in pairs, throwing a standard dice and following the simple instructions on the track. A correct answer to a question wins another 'go'; a wrong answer means that the player misses a turn. Who will be the first to be at home in England?

Decide how to provide answers, perhaps on cards for consultation? The answers (in order of questions) are as follows:

Northumberland	Oxen	Sutton Hoo
20 metres	Beowulf	a fine
Arthur	Yule	Eostre

Activity 6: Give us a game!
Perhaps the children could adapt or design other games for their classmates to enjoy. Insist upon an educational element. If you have access to a computer, you could create a variety of quiz and database programs on the Anglo-Saxon period. Perhaps the children could contribute material too.

Study Unit 1b: the Anglo-Saxons in Britain – legacy of settlement.
Suggested levels of work involved in activities

Activity number	Level	Activity number	Level	Activity number	Level
1	2/3/4/5	3	2/3/4/5	5	2/3
2	2/3/4	4	2/3/4/5	6	2/3/4/5

RESOURCES

Non-Fiction

Honnywill, J. *The Anglo-Saxons and Vikings*, Collins Primary History Series, 1991.

Stoppleman, M. *Anglo-Saxon village,* What Happened Here Series, A & C Black.

Saxon Life, Family Life Series, Wayland.

Saxon Villages, Beginning History Series, Wayland, 1991.

Saxon Britain, History in Evidence Series, Wayland.

Saxon Invaders and Settlers, Invaders and Settlers Series, Wayland.

The British Museum has published an activity book on The Anglo-Saxons (British Museum General Enquiries – Tel: 0171-636-1555)

Fiction

Crossley-Holland, K. *The Sea Stranger/The Fire Brother/ The Earth Father*, Heinemann, 1969–1976. A trilogy about the coming of Christianity to the East Saxons, and the villagers' uneasy relations with the newly-founded monastery.*

The following stories are more demanding in terms of reading stamina. They provide useful background, and selected passages could be read aloud.

Crossley-Holland, K. *The Faber Book of Northern Legends*, Faber, 1977. Includes Germanic heroic legends such as *Beowulf*.

Cumberlege, V. *Carry a long knife*, Andre Deutsch, 1970. Set in Sussex and Hampshire when Britain is attacked on all sides by invaders, including the Saxons.*

Hodges, W. *The Namesake*, Puffin, 1964. The emergence of King Alfred, successful against the Danes.*

Hodges, W. *The Marsh King*, Puffin, 1967. The Danes return, are overcome, and the enemy is baptised into the Christian faith.*

Stanley-Wrench, M. *The Silver King*, World's Work. 1968. The story of Edward the Confessor, and the founding of Westminster Abbey.*

Sutcliff, R. *Dawn Wind*, OUP, 1961. A description of the years following the final defeat of the Britons by the Saxons at Aquae Sulis. The aftermath of conquest and the arrival of St Augustine.

Sutcliff, R. *Dragon-slayer: the story of Beowulf*, Puffin, 1970. This dramatic retelling of the Anglo-Saxon poem recounts Beowulf's three great battles.

Sutcliff, R. *The Lantern Bearers*, OUP, 1959. Roman withdrawal, and the beginning of the Saxon invasions.

Sutcliff, R. *Shining Company*, The Bodley Head, 1990. Based on *The Gododdin*, an early North-British poem, about a foray against the invading Saxons in about A.D. 600.

Treece, H. *The Eagles Have Flown*, The Bodley Head, 1954. Arthur against the Saxons, between about A.D. 490 and A.D. 520.*

Walsh, G.P. *Hengist's Tale*, Chivers, 1988. *The story of Hengist, one of the first successful Saxon invaders.*

Walsh, J.P. *Wordhoard*, Macmillan, 1969. Classic collection of Anglo-Saxon stories for young people.*

*These books are out of print but are still available from libraries and second-hand bookshops.

Blueprints links

You will find related technology activities on the Anglo-Saxons in *Blueprints: Technology Key Stage 2*. The following other Stanley Thornes books will also prove useful: *Investigating History: Invaders and Settlers*.

STUDY UNIT 1 VIKINGS IN BRITAIN

Pupils should be taught about the history of the British Isles from 55 B.C. to the early eleventh century, and the ways in which British society was shaped by different peoples. They should be given opportunities to study, in greater depth, ONE of the Romans, the Anglo-Saxons, or the Vikings.

1 Pupils should be taught **in outline** about the following:

        a the Roman conquest and occupation of Britain

        b the arrival and settlement of the Anglo-Saxons

        c Viking raids and settlements.

2 They should be taught in greater depth about ONE of the above.

  c. Vikings ● Viking raids and settlement and their impact on the British Isles, *e.g. their settlement in different parts of the British Isles, King Alfred and Anglo-Saxon resistance to the Vikings*;

        ● everyday life, *e.g. houses and home life, work, religion*;

        ● the legacy of settlement, *e.g. place names and settlement patterns, myths and legends, Viking remains, including artefacts, and buildings.*

TOPIC WEB

Raids and settlements

- Anglo-Saxon kingdoms
- Viking homelands and voyages
- Timeline
- Viking raiders
- Longships
- Raids (including Lindisfarne)
- Raids or settlement?
- Comparing reasons
- Places settled
- Great Viking figures
- Trade and skills

Everyday life

- Vikings as people – names and appearance
- Homes
- Everyday tasks
- Food and cooking
- Feast days
- Gods and beliefs
- Runes
- Law, order and punishment

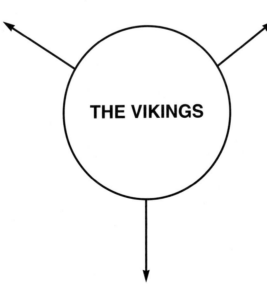

THE VIKINGS

The legacy of settlement
- Place-names
- Language
- Artefacts
- Key towns
- Dates to remember

VIKING RAIDS AND SETTLEMENT

C19–20

Pupils should be taught about:

- Viking raids and settlement and their impact on the British Isles, *eg their settlement in different parts of the British Isles, King Alfred and Anglo-Saxon resistance to the Vikings.*

Activity 1: The Seven Kingdoms of Britain

In order to appreciate the nature of and reasons for the Viking raids and settlement, children will need to have some appreciation of other events and periods in the early history of the British Isles. In particular, this topic is in many ways inextricably linked with an understanding of Anglo-Saxon Britain (see pages 15 to 28 of this book).

At the outset, use **Copymaster 19** to help children to understand that at the time of the Viking raids and invasion (about the middle of the eighth century), Britain was divided into Saxon kingdoms, each with its own king. Ask the children which of the Seven Kingdoms they would be living in if they still existed today. Ask them to colour this kingdom so that it stands out on the map. If you wish the children to discover the names of the kingdoms for themselves, blank out the labels on the map before photocopying.

Activity 2: Who were the Vikings?

An interesting way into this topic would be to pose five key questions to investigate the theme of 'the Vikings – who, what, why?' This would be a good project title because it places due emphasis at the outset on enquiry and investigatory modes of learning. The children could work in groups to investigate the following questions:

Who were the Vikings?
Where did they come from?
Why did they come?
How did they live?
What did they leave behind?

Copymaster 20 will help in answering the first two key questions. Ask the children to complete the simple sentences beneath the map (answers are 'Vikings' and 'Normans'). They can then colour the countries of Norway, Sweden and Denmark, familiarising themselves with the lands from which the Norsemen came – an important first stage. Use this map as an ongoing recording sheet and, as the topic progresses, let the children plot (by drawing arrows) the directions of Viking voyages for raid or invasion. This will help to give them an understanding of the spatial relationships of the Viking settlements, and teach the idea of Britain as part of a wider Viking world. Perhaps you could make up other sentences that will enable them to differentiate between raids and settlement.

Activity 3: A Viking timeline

Begin a timeline of Viking voyages. The Viking age in Britain began in A.D. 789 when ships first appeared off the coast, and ended after 1066 when the Normans won the battle at Hastings, a period of almost three hundred years. If this timeline is constructed as a large wall-display all the children will have access to it, and it can be added to with notes and illustrations as the topic progresses.

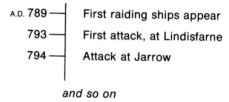

Viking voyages

A.D. 789	First raiding ships appear
793	First attack, at Lindisfarne
794	Attack at Jarrow

and so on

Activity 4: Viking raiders

The children can colour, cut out and piece together the Viking figure on **Copymaster 21**. Mount it on stiff card and use paper-fasteners to secure it. Why not try to design other figures to represent a Viking woman and/or children?

Paint or make collage pictures of the Viking raiders, with appropriate weapons. Remember that Viking warriors wore a simple helmet made of leather or metal: it is extremely unlikely that they wore the elaborate horned or winged helmets seen in so many illustrations. The children should label their pictures with all the appropriate names which may be applied – Vikings, Norsemen, Danes, Northmen …

Why not try making a freestanding Viking figure using papier mâché, and wire on a wooden frame? Dress it with scraps of leather, wool and other material, and make suitable weapons.

Accompany these different figures with detailed and accurate descriptive writing to explain the appearance of such fierce and terrifying attackers. Discuss the origin of the term 'Viking'.

Background information: *Viking raiders*

The word Viking probably derives from the Scandinavian word 'vik' or 'vig', meaning 'an inlet from the sea, a creek or fiord', and 'ing' meaning 'people'. Hence, 'Viking' – 'a person from the fiord'. Other scholars refer to the Old English word 'wic' (a camp or a trading place). Vikings might be traders, warriors, or both – as many were (see top of next page).

Warrior   **Trader and settler**

Activity 5: A Viking longship

The Vikings depended on sea transport for their voyages. Make a detailed study of their longships.

Copymaster 22 introduces basic facts about Viking ships and provides an outline drawing which can be coloured before more elaborate art and craft work is developed. It is also an aid to familiarisation with the basic language used to describe their sea vessels. Ask children to label the drawing to show appropriate parts of the ship, and complete the sentences. Younger children can be helped by providing the answers in a different order, for example:

SAILS   FIGUREHEADS   OAK   OARS   SQUARE

Other versions of **Copymaster 22** could be produced with the letters of each answer jumbled, or with just the first letter of each answer given as a 'clue'.

Ask pupils to complete the copymaster by writing a sentence to explain why the title is 'Serpent of the Sea'. Viking longships were also known as 'dragon ships'.

Activity 6: How the longships were built

Follow on from Activity 5 by writing about the construction of longships. They were built outdoors and usually close to the shore. Consider and write about why the Vikings were so good at shipbuilding. Investigate their technology, for example how were the planks of oak joined together? How were the ships made watertight? And, most importantly, how do we know the answers to these questions?

Activity 7: How do we know about the longships?

Use reference books or, if possible, visit a museum to learn about Viking ships that have been found intact. Try to find out where such critical evidence has been located, and where it is possible to see in Britain today artefacts from the Viking era.

Background information: *Longships – the evidence*

Perhaps the most famous of Viking longships is the Gokstad ship, excavated in Norway as long ago as 1880. It was made of oak, with a pine mast and a large steering paddle on the right or starboard ('steer-board') side of the stern. The ship had been buried in a mound of blue clay, which helped to preserve it. It contained the body of a dead Viking king, surrounded by his weapons and other possessions. Unfortunately, any treasures buried with him had been stolen by thieves.

In 1904 a local farmer found some wooden remains in a large mound on his land at Oseberg. When the mound was excavated it was found to contain a Viking longship, dating from the ninth century and decorated with magnificent wood carvings. In the ship were found skeletons of two women, together with a wonderful range of wooden artefacts including sledges, chairs, beds, spades, forks and hoes, boxes and chests, casks, buckets, cooking utensils, an iron cauldron and an intricately carved four-wheeled cart. These artefacts give a fascinating picture, not only of the everyday life of the Vikings, but also of the fine quality of their workmanship.

The design of the Oseberg ship reveals that it was built earlier than the Gokstad ship since the latter had improved on some of the weaknesses of the former. The Gokstad and Oseberg ships are both on display in the Viking Ship Hall in Oslo.

Activity 8: Build you own longship

Construct a longship in craft and technology lessons, using either wood or stiff card. Paint the figurehead in gold and silver and attach a cloth sail, using string for ropes. Think of a colourful name for your ship – one Icelandic sailor called his 'Reindeer of the Ice Road'; others were called 'Dark Horse of the Sea' and 'Hawk of the Waves' Track'.

Compile a construction guide or detailed factual inventory about a real Viking longship. Here are some useful facts to include.

An early longship had:
16 planks of oak on each side, overlapping and fastened with bolts and iron nails.
A square sail that could be lowered.
32 oars.
An oar-shaped rudder.
A mast up to 12 metres high.
A speed of up to 12 knots.

The Gokstad ship measured 23.33 metres in length, 5.25 metres in width and 1.95 metres deep from gunwhale to keel. Measure and draw the length and width of the ship in the playground so that the children can try to imagine it more clearly. Read extracts from some of the Norse sagas to add colour to the subject. For example, this extract from *King Harald's Saga* (translated by M. Magnusson and H. Palsson, Penguin Classics, 1966) was written by Snorri Sturluson, a famous writer of Norse sagas who lived in the thirteenth century:

Men will quake with terror
Ere the seventy sea-oars
Gain their well-earned respite
From the labours of the ocean.
Norwegian arms are driving
This iron-studded dragon
Down the storm-tossed river,
Like an eagle with wings beating.

Write imaginative stories about 'setting sail' in a Viking ship. Include details of what the ship was likely to be carrying, including a crew of around 50 men with their sea-chests, weapons and food rations. How did the Vikings navigate? Ask children to imagine that they are a longship captain and to write about the qualities they would look for in a crew – an appropriate description of 'an ideal Viking'. Being tough, brave, fierce, adventurous, skilled with weapons and powerful oarsmen are presumably some of the attributes which might be suggested.

Paint a magnificent wall-frieze, showing the coast of England – perhaps Lindisfarne – on one side, and Viking ships with brightly coloured sails ploughing their course through the waves towards it. Write a caption in large letters beneath the frieze, such as: The Vikings – Raiders, Warriors, Adventurers and Sailors.

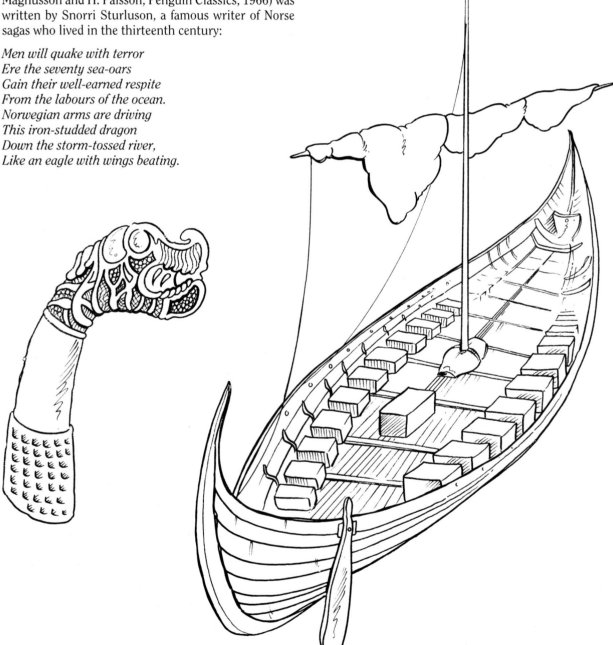

Activity 9: Viking raids

Find out more and write about some of the key raids, for example, Lindisfarne (site of the first Viking attack in A.D. 793) and Jarrow in A.D. 794. For those in the north of England a visit to Lindisfarne may be possible and would be extremely valuable. If a visit is not possible, use reference books to find out about the nature of these raids and about the evidence that remains.

Write an imaginative story or description of a Viking raid, and illustrate it with paintings or collage work. Paint pictures of the ruins of Lindisfarne that remain today and then superimpose collage pictures of Vikings – an excellent way of blending the 'old' with the 'new' in children's minds.

This art activity could be extended into 3-D form in craft lessons. Make a Viking scene, and house it in a diorama. Take a large cardboard box and cut away the front rectangle. Paint the outer faces white or cover them with neutral coloured paper. On the inner faces of the box, paint scenes of Lindisfarne today. Construct cardboard figures of Vikings and stand these on the floor of the box, in front of their scenic 'backcloth'. Add other details if you like, such as rocks, grass and bushes. This idea could be applied to other aspects of the topic – perhaps you could paint a seascape in the background and add models of Viking ships.

Write about the Viking raids from the point of view of the monks in the monasteries under attack. Write about how they might have prepared for the fierce Norse warriors, their inner feelings of terror, and of the losses they suffered.

Ask the children if they can find out what 'Danegeld' was, and what it was used for.

Investigate original source material which helps us to understand the stories of the raids; for example, the *Anglo-Saxon Chronicle*, written by monks in various locations, relates key events of the time and includes such information as:

> 'The heathen men destroyed God's church on Lindisfarne through brutal robbery and slaughter.'

Consider the reliability of such writings. All accounts of the Viking raids were written by English monks. Discuss whether their ideas and descriptions are likely to be reliable evidence. Is there a possibility of bias in their accounts? If so why?

Activity 10: Raids and settlements

Help the children to appreciate the difference between raids and invasion for settlement. Indicate the timing of these activities on your timeline. Raids began with the attack on Lindisfarne and became regular events in the years that followed, resulting in many deaths and the devastation of monasteries. However, it was not until A.D. 851 that large numbers of ships arrived and Vikings came to settle on a permanent basis. Consider separately the reasons for these two forms of attack, although many will overlap. Record the results in pictorial form as shown overleaf, perhaps as a Viking thinking or speaking his intentions.

Make a list of countries visited or settled by Vikings

(helping to build up the pattern of voyages on **Copymaster 20**). These will include Britain, France, Spain, Russia, Iceland, Greenland and America. Divide the class into groups, each to find out as much as possible about Viking colonies in places outside Britain, thus helping to set events in Britain as part of the wider Viking world. Investigate, for example, the discovery of Iceland in around A.D. 870 by Vikings from Norway; the invasion of Greenland in A.D. 984 by Eirik the Red; and the story of Leif Eiriksson, who sailed to the east coast of America in A.D. 1002.

Compile a book on the 'Great Figures of the Viking Age', to include illustrations, stories associated with these Viking heroes, and details of the evidence that still remains of the colonisation.

Include a sub-topic on Viking merchants and trade in Europe. Record results in tabular form, as indicated below, showing how in the days of permanent settlements they built up significant trade between north and south. Discuss the skills and activities of Viking settlers which resulted directly from their trading habits. Many were accomplished general craftsmen, silversmiths, wood and antler carvers, carpenters, blacksmiths and farmers. Why was there such a strong tradition of Viking craftsmanship, particularly in wood and metal work?

Background information: *Viking craftsmanship*

In common with the Greeks and Romans, the Viking told stories of a blacksmith-god, a skilled craftsman who possessed secret knowledge and supernatural powers.

To the Vikings, iron was more valuable than gold or silver, since it was used to make tools and weapons. Superstitions about the lucky horseshoe may have sprung from this idea, as might the saying 'See a pin and pick it up, all the day you'll have good luck.' The Vikings believed that meteoric iron had been flung from the heavens by angry gods: in their view, a man with the skill to shape mighty weapons from metal was not only likely to be a descendant of the gods, but also to possess magical powers.

Activity 11: The years of battle

Draw or annotate prepared outline maps to show the areas of Viking attack in the British Isles (see maps below and **Copymaster 19**). Through the years of relentless aggression, the Saxon kingdoms fell to Viking rule, though the kingdom of Wessex resisted to the end (see page 16 in the unit on the Anglo-Saxons).

Find out the names of key sites where Viking battles were fought in Britain (link this with activities on page 39 relating to the legacy of settlement), and locate them on a map. Perhaps the final battle for the Vikings in Britain took place at Stamford Bridge, seven miles outside York, in 1066. Harald Hardrada and Tostig, brother of the English King Harold Godwinsson, were defeated – shortly before Harold himself was killed at the Battle of Hastings. If possible, when telling this story refer to the Bayeux Tapestry. Perhaps the children could retell the story of the battle at Stamford Bridge by creating their own sequence of collage pictures in the style of the Bayeux Tapestry.

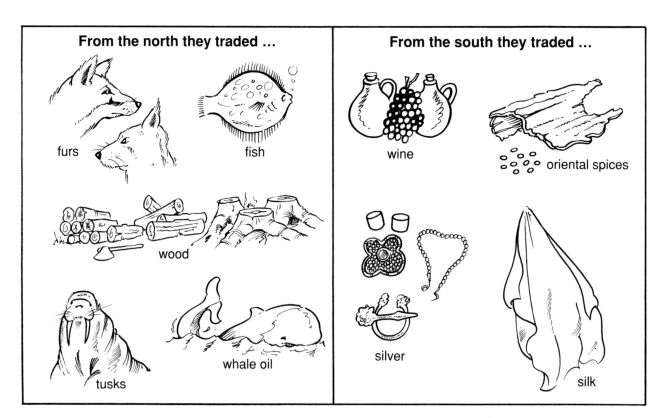

From the north they traded ...

furs
fish
wood
tusks
whale oil

From the south they traded ...

wine
oriental spices
silver
silk

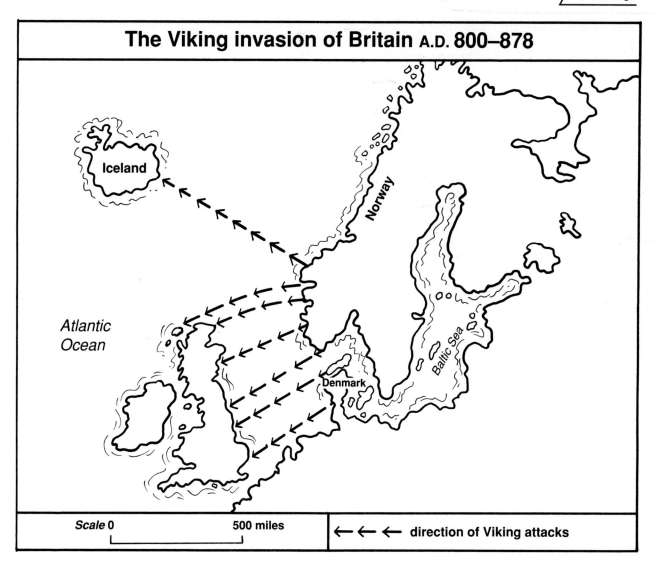

The Viking invasion of Britain A.D. 800–878

Iceland

Norway

Atlantic
Ocean

Baltic Sea

Denmark

Scale 0   500 miles

← ← ←   **direction of Viking attacks**

**Study Unit 1c: the Vikings in Britain – raids and settlement.
Suggested levels of work involved in activities**

Activity number	Level	Activity number	Level	Activity number	Level
1	2/3/4/5	5	2	9	2/3/4
2	2/3/4/5	6	2/3/4	10	2/3/4/5
3	2/3/4/5	7	2/3/4/5	11	2/3
4	2/3	8	2		

EVERYDAY LIFE

C23–26

Pupils should be taught about:

everyday life   ● houses and home life; work; religion.

Activity 1: What were the Vikings like?

Talk about what the Vikings were like as people. Discuss and write about their personalities and appearance, and the nature of the evidence that helps to form our viewpoint. Consider what is fact (some Vikings were unusually tall, others blonde) and what is opinion (they were all savages and cruel murderers who revelled in bloodshed and death). Consider why books about Vikings almost always show pictures and tell stories of men, rather than women and children. Indeed, when reading some history books, it is difficult to imagine that there were any Viking women!

Investigate personal names – Wolf, Leif, Erik or Eirik, Thorfinn, Thorvald – which reflect their Scandinavian origins. Have any of these names survived the ages to become common in Britain today? This study may reveal that many Viking names (or perhaps more accurately, nicknames) were based on the personal characteristics or attributes of the owner. Harald Harefoot may have been a swift runner and Ari the Learned noted as a scholar, while Bjorn Ironside and Eirik Bloodaxe were perhaps known as mighty warriors. It may be easy to explain how Svein Fork-Beard, Sigtrygg One-Eye and Thorkel the Tall got their names; but what of Ragnar Hairy-Breeks, Harald Fine-Hair, Olaf the Peacock, Halfdan of the Wide Embrace, Ivar the Boneless, and Thorolf Butter? Ask the children to speculate and/or write a story in connection with the origin of one or more of these names, and draw colourful illustrations.

Let the children speculate what their names might have been had they been Vikings. Perhaps they could each make up a colourful name for themselves … and the story of how they came by it.

Background information: *Viking names*

Thorolf Butter seems to have gained this name when he returned from Iceland with the (no doubt exaggerated) claim that 'butter dripped from every blade of grass', i.e. that the land was fertile. Halfdan was said to have been a Viking warrior of widespread conquests. The other Vikings mentioned above have equally curious stories connected with the origins of their names! (These stories can be found in *Vikings!* by Magnus Magnusson, published by Book Club Associates, by arrangement with The Bodley Head Ltd and BBC Publications, 1980. The book is packed with fascinating information about the Viking civilisation, and copiously illustrated.)

The names of Viking women included Thyri, once a Queen of Denmark; and Thjodhild, wife of Eirik the Red, who was converted to Christianity and had a small church built at Brattahlid, in Greenland. Many others are mentioned in Magnusson's book.

Activity 2: Daily life

Research details of everyday life in a Viking settlement. What would a typical home have been like?

Use **Copymaster 23** in conjunction with reference books and museum information. Ask the children to colour the drawing and label it appropriately (showing earth floor, fire, wooden frame, shutters, thatched roof and simple furniture). Write a sentence beneath (composed by children or structured by you, depending on abilities) to explain that most families lived in one large room with a raised fireplace in the centre. The Viking house is another good subject for diorama construction.

Houses of this simple rectangular shape are easy to construct out of card and you can thatch their roofs if grasses, straw or reeds are available. Use these models to make a Viking settlement. In the centre of the settlement place a much larger dwelling – the Chief's house. Add outbuildings such as barns, stables and workshops. Arrange the settlement model on a table, and surround the buildings with pieces of writing mounted on freestanding cards which tell of everyday life. Appropriate writing for the scene would include 'Growing up as a Viking child', 'My household life … by a Viking woman', 'Working on the farm', and 'Family feasts'.

To aid an understanding of 'who did what' in the Viking home, devise language games to match tasks with individuals. For example, the children could draw a Viking family and write out a list of tasks they undertook, with lines connecting the task with the person who would perform it.

Activity 3: Viking cookery

Find out more about food ingredients and cooking techniques. Make a list of commonly eaten foods – fish, meat, wheat, barley, oats, rye, peas, beans, milk, cheese and nuts. Draw pictures of food-related practices, such as the hanging up of dried fish and meat on the walls of the house, salting or pickling meat to preserve it, and making breads and scones over the open fire.

Activity 4: Around the house

Investigate, from real artefacts if possible, the useful objects in a Viking home that were made from the bones and antlers of wild animals, for example sewing needles and pins, combs and knife handles. What other household items might the children find?

Activity 5: Feast days

Find out about feast days and how they were celebrated. What was a 'skald'? Paint pictures or make a large collage of a celebration of one of the three major feast days – one at the end of December, one in April and one in October. Include details of people dressed in their best clothes and jewellery, elaborate rectangular-shaped platters of food, and slaves pouring drink. Perhaps a skald is reciting one of his stories.

Background information: *Feast days*

Feast days were family holidays when major celebrations were held, involving a great deal of eating and drinking. Men often got very drunk on mead, beer or wine. Entertainment was provided by musicians, or storytellers called skalds who recited poems or long tales about the brave deeds of Viking heroes, or the adventures of the gods themselves. These long stories were called sagas, a word which is still in use today.

Activity 6: A Viking saga

If possible, tell or read some of the Viking sagas to the children. A well-known poem of the 8th century is

Beowulf, as portrayed on **Copymaster 24**. Several versions for children are available of this work, an old English poem of 3,182 lines. The children should need no encouragement to draw Grendel, the monster, on the copymaster and colour the scene. Other tales are about Sigurd and the Dragon, Sampo Lappelill (published in *The Sea King's Gift and other tales from Finland* by Frederick Muller, 1973), Thor and the Frost Giants, Baldur the Bright, and Authun (or Audun) and the Bear. This latter story is included in a book of five short *Icelandic Stories* as told by Magnus Magnusson on *Jackanory*, and published by the BBC in 1969.

The Viking literary tradition is an extensive and colourful one. Many Norse stories contain strange and magical creatures such as giants, dragons and trolls. These characters offer a wealth of opportunities for creative writing, drama, music and movement (Grieg's *In The Hall Of The Mountain King*), and artwork of all kinds.

Activity 7: The Viking code

Ask the children to explain the meaning of the following quotation from a thirteenth-century Viking poem, translated into a book called *The Poetic Edda*, edited by U. Dronke and published by OUP in 1969:

> *Wealth dies, kinsmen die, a man himself must likewise die; but word-fame never dies, for him who achieves it well.*

This concept of 'word-fame' tells much about the moral values of the Vikings, involving as it does high standards of personal behaviour, honour and integrity. Reputation was everything. Here are some more Viking sayings. What do the children make of them?

> A gift always looks for its return.

> There is no better load a man can carry than much common sense; no worse a load than too much drink.

> Confide in one, never in two; confide in three, and the whole world knows.

In connection with the first of these three sayings, and the Viking belief that gifts or favours must be repaid, tell the story of Egil Skallagrimsson. Egil was captured and sentenced to death by King Eirik Bloodaxe, his great enemy. Egil had friends at court who persuaded King Eirik to delay the execution until morning. That night Egil wrote a long poem praising King Eirik, who was then honour-bound to offer Egil a gift in return. Egil asked for his own 'wolf-grey head', and his life was spared. The full account can be found in *Egil's Saga* (chapters 59, 60 and 61) translated by Hermann Palsson and Paul Edwards, published by Dent 1975, Penguin 1976. It would probably be best read (or retold) by you in selected extracts.

Activity 8: The Viking religion

Write and illustrate accounts about religious beliefs and practices. The Vikings were not Christians, but pagans: they worshipped numerous heathen gods, and had some strange ideas of the world in which they lived. They envisaged their world encircled by a sea and beyond the sea was Jotunheim, where the frost-giants lived. Under the ground dwarves of darkness dwelt in Svartalfheim, where they mined gold and gems. The dwarves were clever craftsmen and worked in under-ground caverns, where they built forges and work-shops. They could only walk above ground at night, because the sun's rays turned then into stone. Above the earth but below the sky lived the elves of light, in Alfheim; and above that was Asgard – the home of the gods. A rainbow bridge joined Asgard to Midgard, the earth.

Copymaster 25 will be useful for introducing ideas and facts about Viking gods, the most important of whom was Odin or Woden, the All-Father – from whose name is derived the Wednesday (Woden's Day) of our week. From his throne in the Norse heaven known as Asgard, Odin could see out over all the world. The drawing on the copymaster shows Odin with his eight-legged horse. Ask the children to research details of Odin and colour his picture. They could then draw similar pictures and write stories of other well-known gods in the Norse Pantheon.

Ask the children to find out who the Valkyries were, and draw pictures of them. Let them hear Richard Wagner's music, *Ride of the Valkyries*, and produce creative writing and/or artwork to portray such creatures.

Discuss the relationship between beliefs of the heaven of Asgard and the palace of Valholl, associated with the pleasures of continual food and drink, and the great courage of the Viking warriors based on their desire to please Odin and arrive there!

Draw pictures of a Viking burial, indicating the great range of goods buried with the dead for use in the next life. Even entire ships were buried! (See the picture on the next page.)

Background information: The Viking religion

Odin was regarded as the wisest of the gods; indeed, according to legend, he had sacrificed one eye in his constant quest for knowledge. At dawn each day his two ravens, Hugin and Munin (Mind and Memory) were let out to fly around the world and report back to Odin on what they had found. The children can design a background for the picture on Copymaster 25 – perhaps the palace of Valholl (incorrectly known in English by its plural name of 'Valhalla'), the Hall of the Slain, where the spirits of the bravest warriors spent the afterlife feasting and fighting. Are words like 'valiant' and 'valour' connected with Valholl in some way?

Apart from Odin, perhaps the most widely recognised of the Norse gods was Thor the Thunderer, from whom the name Thursday derives. Other prominent deities included Frey the god of nature and fertility; Loki, the mischievous god of fire; and Frigga, from whom we get the name Friday. Thor was a giant red-haired figure, god of the sky and hurler of thunderbolts, who rode in a chariot drawn by two sacred goats. He protected the world against the threat of evil giants, aided by his mighty hammer Mjollnir, which returned to his hand each time he flung it at an enemy. The gods were worshipped in the open air, and received regular sacrifices from the people.

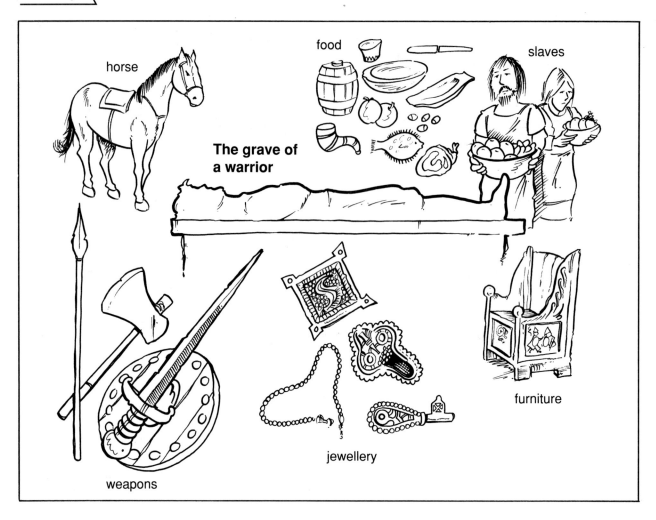

horse

food

slaves

The grave of a warrior

furniture

jewellery

weapons

Activity 9: Viking runes

The children could learn to write as the Vikings did.

Copymaster 26 introduces them to the nature of a Viking runic alphabet. The runes, said to have been discovered by Odin, were used for carved inscriptions, magic charms and curses. First, ask pupils to fill in the gaps at the top of the sheet (the answers are 16, straight and carved). Below that is the runic alphabet, which can be used to decode the message around the edge of the sheet and then as the basis for a wide range of activities. Discuss why not every letter in our modern alphabet is represented. Children can write their names in runes (if letters permit), write and translate messages to each other, and study genuine runic inscriptions found documented in reference books or on artefacts. In the case of incomplete names or messages, the class could avoid frustration by agreeing on new runic letters for those in our present alphabet which are not already represented.

Design Viking memorial stones or wood carvings and decorate them with runes. If possible, make these out of slate, stone or wood, and of course, the runes should be carved or scratched rather than written, if materials permit. Be aware of safety at all times, particularly if children are working with sharp objects. Alternatively, draw a sword or some other object with runic signs on it – make the runes spell out a word which will give the object special powers.

Activity 10: Law and order

Consider law and order in Viking days. Disputes were often resolved in open-air meetings attended by freemen of the area. Punishments for those found guilty were severe. Criminals may have been stoned to death, drowned or had their heads chopped off. In Iceland the was a custom of making an accused woman pick stones from a cauldron of boiling water. If her wounds healed, she was declared innocent; if they did not, she was found guilty. Find out more about 'blood feuds' and 'duels to the death'.

Activity 11: Viking vocabulary

Ask the children to think about the following list of words and decide which seem appropriate to describe Vikings, and to give evidence and reasons for their answers:

brave   fearless   timid   weak   gentle

cowardly   determined   strong   adventurous

Perhaps the children could add words of their own to this list.

Discuss the origin of the word 'berserk' which is still in use today. What does it mean to us?

**Study Unit 1c: the Vikings in Britain – everyday life.
Suggested levels of work involved in activities**

Activity number	Level	Activity number	Level	Activity number	Level
1	2/3/4/5	5	2/3	9	2/3
2	2/3/4	6	2/3	10	2/3/4
3	2/3	7	2/3/4	11	2/3
4	2/3	8	2/3/4/5		

THE LEGACY OF SETTLEMENT

Pupils should be taught about:

the legacy of settlement

- place-names and settlement patterns; myths and legends; Viking remains, including artefacts and buildings.

Activity 1: Visit the Vikings
The Vikings are still with us in many ways, and by far the best method of considering their legacy is by field-work. Try to visit a Viking museum or settlement: York and its Jorvik museum is one of the most elaborate and worthwhile of such sites.

Activity 2: Viking place-names
Make a study of place-names that carry the Viking influence. A knowledge of some Viking words and their meanings will be necessary for this, so compile a Viking dictionary to help. Here are some words with their modern equivalents to start you off.

vik/wick (creek or bay)   bie/by (village)
thorpe (hamlet)   beck (stream)
toft (homestead)   thwaite (clearing)
kirk (church)

Ask the children to think first of any local names that may have Viking connections, and then to consult maps and books of place-names of the British Isles to work towards a more comprehensive list. Perhaps these could be marked on a map. From previous activities the children should be aware of which parts of our country are more likely to reflect the Viking influence, i.e. the north and east.

Activity 3: Evidence about the Vikings
Write about the vital role of archaeologists in discovering traces of the Viking era. Evidence exists in the form of original ships, tools, shields, swords, jewellery and household objects. Try to find out where some of these artefacts have been dug out of the ground.

Ask the children to imagine themselves as someone – an archaeologist, a farmer, a worker on a building site, or even a child at play – who uncovers a Viking king's burial mound. Write about what happened.

Find out the names and locations of modern cities such as York and Dublin which owe their importance to Viking settlement and trade. Why were such places selected as trading centres? Perhaps the children could mark them on a large wall-map of the British Isles, together with a suitable picture or emblem.

Copymaster 27 will serve as an end-of-project quiz or reinforcement summary sheet. It can also be used to assist in the compilation of the ongoing timeline. Ask the children to match the dates to the specific illustrated events.

Activity 4: Vikings on film and television
From time to time documentary films of the Viking civilisation may be screened outside school hours. You could video-record such programmes and show selected 'highlights' where these would enhance the work already being done.

Probably the best of the Hollywood films on this subject is *The Vikings*, made in 1958 with Tony Curtis, Janet Leigh and Kirk Douglas. Children will hopefully gain an impression of the atmosphere of the period by watching what is essentially an adventure film, made for reasons of entertainment and not necessarily for historical accuracy. This in itself would be a good teaching point – if the film were viewed some time after the commencement of work on the Vikings, children may be able to spot some of these inaccuracies for themselves!

Study Unit 1c: the Vikings in Britain – legacy of settlement.
Suggested levels of work involved in activities

Activity number	Level	Activity number	Level	Activity number	Level
1	2/3/4/5	3	2/3/4/5	4	2/3/4/5
2	2/3				

RESOURCES ▶

Non-fiction

Honnywill, J. *The Anglo-Saxons and Vikings*, Collins Primary History Series, 1991.
Viking Britain, History in Evidence Series, Wayland.
Viking Invaders and Settlers, Invaders and Settlers Series, Wayland.
The Vikings, Look Into The Past Series, Wayland.
Viking Explorers, Beginning History Series, Wayland, 1991.
Viking Warriors, Beginning History Series, Wayland, 1991.
Vikings And Their Travels, Making History Series, Simon & Schuster.
The Vikings, What Do We Know About Series, Simon & Schuster.
Viking Street, What Happened Here Series, A & C Black.
Vikings, Insight Series, Oxford.
Viking World, Illustrated World History Series, Usborne.
Viking Raiders, Time Traveller Series, Usborne.
The Vikings, Young Researcher Series, Heinemann.
The British Museum has published an activity book on The Vikings (British Museum General Enquiries – Tel: 0171-636-1555)
The Jorvik Viking Centre is in Coppergate, York. (Tel. 01904 643 211)

Fiction for younger readers

Atterton, J. *The shape-changer*, Walker Books, 1989. Kari, son of Viking settlers, helps neighbouring farmers to break a magic spell.
Jones, T. *Saga of Eric the Viking*, Penguin, 1985. Fun story of an imaginary epic voyage.
Knight, F. *Olaf's Sword*, Heinemann, 1969. Voyage of discovery with the Vikings.*

Fiction for more competent readers

These longer stories are for more fluent readers, or for reading aloud.

Crossley-Holland, K. *Axe-age, Wolf-age*, Faber, 1988. A selection from the Norse myths, grippingly told.
Crossley-Holland, K. *Havelock the Dane*, Macmillan

1964. A story of Saxons and Danes. How Havelock wins back the kingdom of Denmark, and his wife's kingdom of Norfolk.*
Green, R.L. *Myths of the Norsemen*, Puffin, 1988. New edition of the *Saga of Asgard*.
Lowe, P. *Gods and Heroes from Viking Mythology*, P. Lowe, 1978. Colourfully and informatively illustrated.
Maddock, R. *Northman's Fury*, Macdonald, 1970. A story about the misery of constant guerrilla warfare, the longing for peace, and the baptism of Guthorm after Alfred's victory.*
Serraillier, I. *Havelock the Warrior*, Hamish Hamilton, 1968. Another retelling of the legend of Havelock, Saxon invader.*
Treece, H. *Horned Helmut*, Macmillan, 1979. Written in the style of an Icelandic saga.*
Treece, H. *Viking Saga: Viking's Dawn/The Road to Miklagard/Viking's Sunset*, The Bodley Head, 1955–1960. Trilogy about the life and voyages of the Viking, Harald Sigurdson, and his friend, Grummoch.
Snelling, J. *Viking Myths and Legends*, Wayland, 1987. Well illustrated and simply told.
Sutcliff, R. *Blood Feud*, Puffin, 1978. Story of Vikings in the 10th and 11th centuries, close to home and as far afield as Constantinople.
Swindells, R. *Voyage to Valhalla*, Heinemann Educational, 1977. A Viking 'ghost' story.

Poetry

Sailing by D. English; *O'er the wild gannet's bath* by G. Darley; and *Thorkild's song* by R. Kipling, which can all be found in *The Book of Salt Sea Verse*, compiled by Charles Causley, Puffin 1978.*

*These books are out of print but are still available from libraries and second-hand bookshops.

Blueprints links

You will find related technology activities on the Vikings in *Blueprints: Technology Key Stage 2*. The following other Stanley Thornes books will also prove useful: *Investigating History: Invaders and Settlers*.

STUDY UNIT 2 LIFE IN TUDOR TIMES

Pupils should be taught about some of the major events and personalities, including monarchs, and the way of life of people at different levels of society in Tudor times:

Major events and personalities

a Henry VIII and the break with Rome, *e.g. the divorce question, the dissolution of the monasteries;*
b exploration overseas, *e.g. the voyages of Sebastian and John Cabot, Francis Drake and Walter Raleigh;*
c Elizabeth I and the Armada (1588);

The ways of life of people at different levels of society

d Court life, *e.g. the progresses of Elizabeth I, the role of a personality such as Thomas More or the Earl of Essex;*
e ways of life in town and country, *e.g. home life, work and leisure, health, trade;*
f arts and architecture, including Shakespeare, *e.g. Elizabethan theatres, music, paintings, town houses, manor houses, and country houses and their estates.*

TOPIC WEB

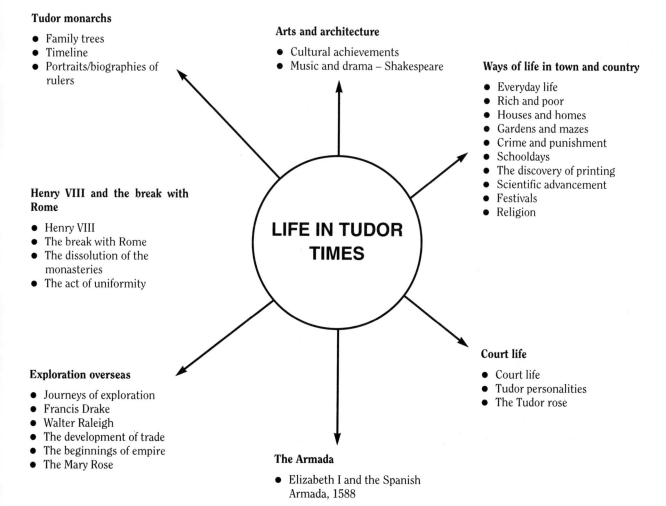

Tudor monarchs

- Family trees
- Timeline
- Portraits/biographies of rulers

Arts and architecture

- Cultural achievements
- Music and drama – Shakespeare

Ways of life in town and country

- Everyday life
- Rich and poor
- Houses and homes
- Gardens and mazes
- Crime and punishment
- Schooldays
- The discovery of printing
- Scientific advancement
- Festivals
- Religion

Henry VIII and the break with Rome

- Henry VIII
- The break with Rome
- The dissolution of the monasteries
- The act of uniformity

LIFE IN TUDOR TIMES

Exploration overseas

- Journeys of exploration
- Francis Drake
- Walter Raleigh
- The development of trade
- The beginnings of empire
- The Mary Rose

The Armada

- Elizabeth I and the Spanish Armada, 1588

Court life

- Court life
- Tudor personalities
- The Tudor rose

MAJOR EVENTS AND PERSONALITIES

Pupils should be taught about:

major events and personalities

a Henry VIII and the break with Rome, *e.g. the divorce question, the dissolution of the monasteries*
b exploration overseas, *e.g. the voyages of Sebastian and John Cabot, Francis Drake and Walter Raleigh*
c Elizabeth I and the Armada (1588)

TUDOR MONARCHS

Activity 1: A family tree
Familiarise pupils with the names of the rulers of the Tudor period, and the dates of their reigns. A good way of approaching this would be through portraits and family trees. Prepare picture cards of the Tudor kings and queens, complete with labels showing names and dates. Discuss the design and construction of family trees – children can draw their own, beginning at the very simple level with their parents, brothers and sisters. Later the line for grand-parents can be added. There may well be a need for you to exercise sensitivity where some family backgrounds are concerned.

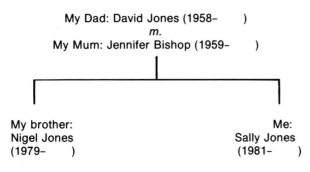

Discuss what information diagrams of this kind can provide (dates of birth; death, marriage(s), number of children, etc), and how they are useful in helping us to record and recall details of our history.

Transfer the skills of drawing and reading personal family trees to those of the Tudor monarchs. Ensure that the children are not confused about whether dates refer to birth and death or to the duration of a monarch's reign. Depending on the age and ability levels of the children, it may be appropriate to construct a simple family tree for the Tudors which can be elaborated upon later so that the pupils are able to place the Tudor era in the context of a broader chronological framework.

The diagram at the top of the next page is helpful background material for the construction of a comprehensive family tree linking the Tudor monarchs with those of the Houses of York and Stuart.

Copymaster 28 provides the basis for the construction of a Tudor family tree. Use picture cards or reference books to 'bring it to life'. Children can underline or otherwise highlight the names of the Tudor rulers, and in the five boxes underneath they can draw and colour their own portraits of the five Tudor kings and queens. Less able children can be helped in this task by prior labelling of the boxes: Henry VII; Henry VIII; Edward VI; Mary I; Elizabeth I.

Activity 2: Jane (July 1553)
Copymaster 28 does not contain the name of Lady Jane Grey, who reigned as queen for nine days. Discuss the background to this short reign, and perhaps pupils could add her name to the tree.

Background information
Henry VIII's only son, Edward, became king when he was ten years old. When he was 15 he became terminally ill. He was persuaded to name a cousin, Jane Grey, a Protestant, who would be his heir. Yet Lady Jane Grey had no serious wish to be queen. Nine days after she technically inherited the throne, Mary Tudor marched on London with the support of the people and was declared queen.

Activity 3: A Tudor timeline
A major decision has to be made at the outset of this topic – whether to progress chronologically through events in the reigns of the different monarchs, or to adopt a thematic approach in order to investigate, for example, major topics such as religion, exploration, or aspects of everyday life throughout the various reigns. Whichever approach is adopted, a timeline of the era will be very valuable. This can obviously be elaborated upon as and when it is appropriate.

Use **Copymaster 29** to record key events of the Tudor period. Some key dates are provided for the children

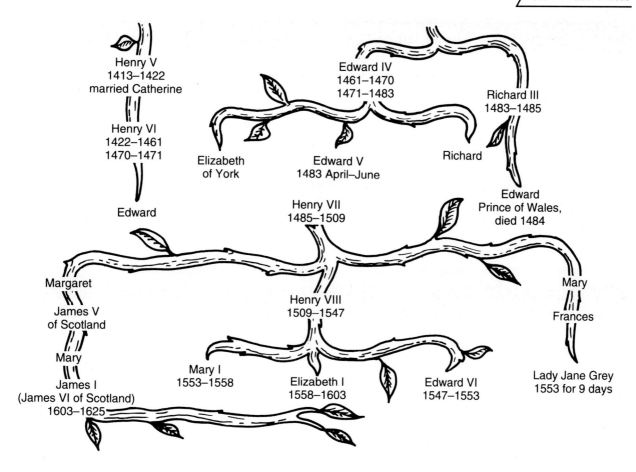

Henry V
1413–1422
married Catherine

Henry VI
1422–1461
1470–1471

Edward

Edward IV
1461–1470
1471–1483

Richard III
1483–1485

Elizabeth
of York

Edward V
1483 April–June

Richard

Edward
Prince of Wales,
died 1484

Henry VII
1485–1509

Margaret

James V
of Scotland

Mary

James I
(James VI of Scotland)
1603–1625

Henry VIII
1509–1547

Mary I
1553–1558

Elizabeth I
1558–1603

Edward VI
1547–1553

Mary

Frances

Lady Jane Grey
1553 for 9 days

down the left-hand margin of the sheet. As the topic progresses, ask them to record the key event(s) that occurred on those dates. The right-hand side of the sheet can be illustrated – perhaps at the end the children could draw what they consider to be the three most influential happenings of the period, or the one single event that they have found most interesting. If necessary, the children can be given help with this sheet by providing a jumbled list of 'answers'. These are (in the correct order):

1485   Henry VII becomes king
1488   Bartholomeu Dias reaches the Cape of Good Hope
1492   Christopher Columbus lands in the Caribbean islands and names them the West Indies
1509   Henry VIII becomes king
1534   Act of Supremacy
1536   Wales united with England
1536–1539   Dissolution of the monasteries
1547   Edward VI becomes king
1549   Act of Uniformity
1553   9-day rule of Lady Jane Grey
1553   Mary Tudor becomes queen
1559   Elizabeth I becomes queen
1562–1598   Civil wars in France
1564   Birth of William Shakespeare
1587   Elizabeth accepts James VI of Scotland as her heir
1588   The Spanish Armada is defeated
1603   Death of Elizabeth I. James becomes James I, of England

Activity 4: Royal biographies
Develop the above activities by researching, writing and illustrating biographies of the Tudor rulers. There is so much material to cover in this study unit that it is clearly impossible to do all of these in depth. Divide the children into groups, each to do an in-depth research study into the reign of one ruler.

Begin by discussing how to go about such a research study – how do we know about the lives of historic kings and queens? What is the nature of reliable evidence? Ask each group to consult books, pictures, and any original source material (documents and artefacts) if a visit to an historical museum is possible.

The end-product from each group could be an illustrated biography which other children in the class can read and refer to, a wall-display, and perhaps an oral presentation to the rest of the class.

Activity 5: Tudor personalities
Use a variety of sources of evidence including portraits, descriptive writing, accounts of actions and factual events, as the basis for discussion about the characters and personalities of the Tudor monarchs. Ask the children to say or write down key words that come to their minds and which they associate with the various monarchs, e.g. brave, selfish, cowardly, lively, adventurous.

Perhaps pupils could write about which Tudor king or queen they admire most, giving reasons why, with substantiated evidence.

Study Unit 2: Life in Tudor Times – major events and personalities: Tudor monarchs.
Suggested levels of work involved in activities

Activity number	Level	Activity number	Level	Activity number	Level
1	2/3/4/5	3	2/3/4/5	5	2/3/4/5
2	2/3	4	2/3/4/5		

HENRY VIII AND THE BREAK WITH ROME

Activity 1: Henry VIII

In compiling accounts of the lives of Tudor rulers, the children will come across a wide range of significant events of the time. Inevitably you will need to select the events you wish to study in detail, perhaps guided by the availability of evidence and resources. Wherever possible debate events, drawing attention to the fact that the course of history is seldom straight-forward – many situations have complex issues and arguments surrounding them. For example, organise a debate about some of the actions of King Henry VIII:

Why did he end his marriage with Catherine of Aragon?
Do you think this was the right thing to do?
Why did he make himself head of the Church of England?
Do you think this was appropriate?

Display the results of such a debate on wall-posters, and discuss how the course of history might have been very different if certain actions had not been taken.

Activity 2: Two faces of Henry VIII

Extend the above activity by discussing the apparent changes that took place in the appearance and personality of Henry VIII during his lifetime. Find appropriate sources of evidence to substantiate beliefs that Henry's appearance changed dramatically between his youth and his later years. (e.g. portraits, descriptive writing of authors of the time). Suggest that the children create their own portraits of the king, either in his youth or mature years.

Background Information

In his youth, Henry VIII was an excellent sportsman. He was a tennis player, horseman, huntsman, dancer, and jouster. He was a handsome prince, with an outgoing, lively personality. He was tall, slim and good looking. In his mature years, however, he became very overweight and ugly. Portraits of the king often portray him as he was during these later years of his life.

The young Henry aged around 20 years

The mature Henry

Activity 3: The break with Rome

Many events of the Tudor period lend themselves to critical debate. A good example is the break with Rome and its associated events. Let the children read about this, or tell them the basic facts. Construct a large wall frieze of people or places associated with the actions of the king. Debate the rights and wrongs of the break with Rome and of execution for treason.

Background Information

Henry VIII decided that it was in his interests to take control of the Church of England. In 1534 Parliament passed the Act of Supremacy which declared the King the Supreme Head of the Church in England. People had to take an oath accepting Henry's heirs and his supremacy in the church. A number of people refused to take this oath, including Sir Thomas More, and John Fisher, Bishop of Rochester. They were executed for the crime of treason. Henry was excommunicated by the Pope for heresy in 1535. Whilst Henry denied the Pope's authority, he did not reject the teachings of the Roman Catholic Church. In 1536, the King issued the 6 Articles, which set out aspects of the Roman Catholic faith still to be followed. Henry believed that the convents and monasteries of England were not economically viable and set about closing them down or destroying them. This was accomplished during the years 1536–1539, in a period known as the time of the dissolution of the monasteries.

Activity 4: Act of Uniformity

Extend debate and discussions concerning the break with Rome by considering events of the reigns of Tudor monarchs who succeeded Henry VIII. Talk and write about the impact of various laws and decisions on society and consider why monarchs may have acted in the way that they did with respect to religious affairs.

Background information

During the reign of King Edward VI, Henry's son by Jane Seymour, the Duke of Somerset acted as regent (someone who rules on behalf of a monarch who is unable to do so. In the case of Edward VI, he was too young.)

During this time, serious changes were made in religion which brought the Church of England much closer to Protestant doctrines. The Act of Uniformity of 1549 made the First English Prayer Book the only permitted prayer book in the land.

During the reign of Mary Tudor (1553–1558), such protestant legislation was repealed, and catholicism was reinstated. Some 300 protestants who refused to accept catholic doctrine were burnt to death for the crime of heresy. Queen Elizabeth I was protestant, though she attempted to establish a church that would be universally acceptable. As in the days of Henry VIII, the monarch became Supreme Head of the Church of England. The Church's doctrines were defined in 1563 in what are known as 'the 39 articles'. Many catholics were displeased with the content of the 39 articles, and in 1570 the Pope excommunicated Elizabeth.

Mary Queen of Scots, a catholic cousin of Queen Elizabeth, was involved in four plots against the English Queen, and was eventually executed in 1587 for the crime of treason.

Activity 5: Dictionary

Compile an illustrated class dictionary containing entries of words associated with activities and events of Tudor monarchs. This need not be very extensive, and may consist of a loose leaf book with a page per word, with suitable definitions and illustrations. Possible words for inclusion are:

heresy

regent

excommunication

depose

treason

succession

independence

Study Unit 2: Life in Tudor Times – major events and personalities: Henry VIII and the break with Rome.
Suggested levels of work involved in activities

Activity number	Level	Activity number	Level	Activity number	Level
1	2/3/4/5	3	2/3/4/5	5	2/3
2	2/3/4/5	4	2/3/4/5		

EXPLORATION OVERSEAS

Activity 1: Seadogs and sailing ships

Plot the journeys of exploration of the well-known Tudor seadogs, including Drake, Raleigh, Hawkins and Frobisher, on a world map. Find out from reference books and an atlas the names of places they visited. Discuss the benefits and discoveries that Britain gained from the voyages of these English sailors. What were the dangers they encountered?

Activity 2: The Golden Hind

Paint pictures of *The Golden Hind*, or perhaps assemble it from a model-making kit. What was/is a hind? Write about the ship's voyages and adventures and, if possible, measure it out in the playground. Make comparisons between ships such as this and ocean-going vessels of today. (Some of the dimensions of the *The Golden Hind* were as follows: length 102 feet; breadth 20 feet; mainmast 59 feet high).

What does the word 'circumnavigate' mean? Ask the children to rewrite the story of Elizabeth I's knighting of Drake, ending the story with the words, 'Arise, Sir Francis Drake'. Find out more about the goods that Drake brought home from his famous voyage on *The Golden Hind* (1577–80), including silver, diamonds, pepper, nutmegs and ginger. Link this to discussion on the development of trade in Tudor times, and the vital role of merchant ships and seamen in the development of trade links and the growth of Britain's Empire.

Draw a cross-section of a merchant ship of the time, showing the various decks and spaces to store cargo. Write about the life of a sailor on board ship – tasks, food, hazards and diseases. Locate on a map the busy seaports from which such ships would have sailed, including London, Hull, Newcastle, Bristol and Plymouth.

Activity 3: Booty and buccaneers

A colourful and lively sub-topic could be undertaken on the activities of pirates in the Spanish Main, particularly the career of Sir Henry Morgan (1635–1688), who seems to have been the most successful buccaneer in history. He is said to have amassed 950,000 pieces-of-eight, not to mention other valuables such as gold and jewels, between 1669 and 1671.

Activity 4: Places to visit

As well as being an interesting place to visit, it is possible to obtain publications and other information on maritime history from the reign of Henry VII to the present day, by contacting the Education Department at the National Maritime Museum, Greenwich.

The Tower of London is also a fascinating place to visit. In fact, a sub-topic on the history of the Tower would include a number of events which occurred in or close to Tudor times – Sir Walter Raleigh's captivity (1603–1616); the escape of John Gerard, a Catholic priest (1597) – which offer much scope for creative writing and artwork.

Further information on the weapons and tactics of the Civil War is obtainable from the National Army Museum's Education Service in London. Illustrated talks are available to school visitors, the children can handle artefacts of the period, and worksheets are available or can be constructed to follow up a particular aspects of the topic. Indeed, teachers are encouraged to liaise with the museum's Education Services in order to construct a suitable programme for a visit.

Activity 5: Period films

Perhaps the best known of all adventure films set in Tudor times is Errol Flynn's *The Sea Hawk*, made in 1940. It may not be historically accurate, but it gives a flavour of court intrigue and swashbuckling on the high seas, both of which relate to Elizabethan times. If possible, let the children hear the opening soundtrack music from the film (without necessarily telling them what it is), and ask them what they think the music is about. (This sumptuous musical score is available on an LP *The Sea Hawk: The Classic Film Scores of Erich Wolfgang Korngold* on RCA Red Seal, SER 5664.)

Activity 6: The Mary Rose

Help children to appreciate that, whilst the defeat of the Spanish Armada is a very well known event in the history of our country, England had been fighting naval battles against various countries for some considerable time.

Tell them the story of the *Mary Rose*, one of Henry VIII's ships which sank when defending our land against the French fleet. The wreck of the *Mary Rose*, recovered over four hundred years later, represents one of the most exciting sources of evidence of the Tudor age. Visit the *Mary Rose* herself, or find out about the ship from the *Mary Rose* exhibition at Portsmouth.

Copymaster 30 enables children to colour an outline drawing of this splendid piece of historic evidence. The space beneath can be used for a variety of purposes, such as writing an account of the sinking of the ship, drawing objects recovered from the wreck, or explaining the significance of the evidence in telling us about life in Tudor times. The children might care to write separately an imaginative story of how the *Mary Rose* came to be discovered – perhaps as extracts from the diary of the diver who discovered the wreck, describing his discoveries and his feelings as he first explored the vessel.

Study Unit 2: Life in Tudor Times – major events and personalities: Exploration overseas.
Suggested levels of work involved in activities

Activity number	Level	Activity number	Level	Activity number	Level
1	2/3	3	2/3	5	2/3/4
2	2/3	4	2/3/4/5	6	2/3/4/5

ELIZABETH I AND THE ARMADA ▶

Activity 1: A portrait of Elizabeth
Copymaster 31 can be coloured and used by the whole class at some stage in the project, and is given as a suitable cover design for the biography, which can be followed for biographies of the other rulers. If similar sheets are designed for the others, they could also form a classroom wall-display and gallery of 'Portraits of Tudor Monarchs', or be used as the illustrations on a large family tree. After being decorated and mounted on card, **Copymaster 31** could also form the centrepiece of large collage pictures of Queen Elizabeth I and her reign.

Activity 2: The Spanish Armada
Why was the Spanish Armada launched against England? Try to explain the background at the conflict. Undertake a sub-topic on the defeat of the Armada, plotting the route of the invasion on an outline map, as shown on page 48. Write dramatic accounts of the appearance of the Armada in the English Channel, and the Queen's inspiring speech to her army. Discuss how and why the Spanish fleet was defeated. What effect did this event have on the respective powers of Spain and England as seafaring nations?

Background information: *The Spanish Armada*
The Spanish monarch, Philip II, was angered by the way Drake and other English seadogs were attacking his New World colonies and capturing his treasure ships. Philip was a devout Catholic. He believed that it was his duty to invade and conquer England in order to force her back to the Church of Rome.

The Spanish fleet was commanded by the Duke of Medina Sidonia, a nobleman who knew little about seamanship – unlike Drake, Hawkins and Lord Howard of Effingham, three of the most experienced and doughty seadogs in the world at that time.

The two fleets met in the English Channel and, though the English ships were outnumbered and outweighed by their opponents, they were more manoeuvrable and the gun crews more skilled. The Spaniards were driven back to the French port of Calais, only for the English to send fire-ships amongst them as they lay at anchor. The Spanish fleet emerged in total confusion: the English ships, aided by a fierce storm, scattered them far and wide. A number of Spanish galleons tried to escape by sailing north, only to be wrecked by storms on the coasts of northern Scotland and Ireland. Of the original 130 ships in the Spanish fleet, less than 80 eventually struggled back to port.

Activity 3
Use **Copymaster 32** as a basis for practice in the use of research skills and writing about historic times. Pupils can be asked to read about the Spanish Armada, look up references to the words printed on the page, then write a dramatic poem or piece of creative writing about the Armada, incorporating all of the words on the Copymaster. The writing can be done in the space below the drawing.

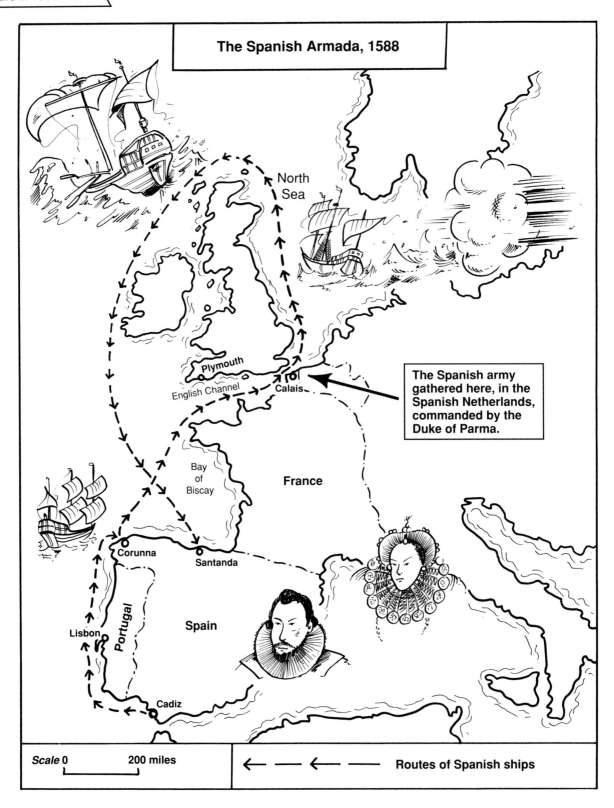

The Spanish Armada, 1588

North Sea

Plymouth

English Channel

Calais

The Spanish army gathered here, in the Spanish Netherlands, commanded by the Duke of Parma.

Bay of Biscay

France

Corunna

Santanda

Portugal

Spain

Lisbon

Cadiz

Scale 0   200 miles

← — ← — Routes of Spanish ships

Study Unit 2: Life in Tudor Times – major events and personalities: Elizabeth I and the Armada.
Suggested levels of work involved in activities

Activity number	Level	Activity number	Level	Activity number	Level
1	2	2	2/3/4/5	3	2/3

THE WAYS OF LIFE OF PEOPLE AT DIFFERENT LEVELS OF SOCIETY

C33–35

Pupils should be taught about:

the ways of life of people at different levels of society

d Court life, *e.g. the progresses of Elizabeth I, the role of a personality such as Thomas More or the Earl of Essex*

e *ways of life in town and country, e.g. home life, work and leisure, health trade*

f *arts and architecture, including Shakespeare, e.g. Elizabethan theatres, music, paintings, town houses, manor houses, and country houses and their estates*

COURT LIFE

Activity 1: Court life in Tudor times

Read stories and study pictures of court life in Tudor times. Find out about Hatfield House and Hampton Court. Ask the children to imagine that they are visitors to the court of Queen Elizabeth I, perhaps as foreign leaders or ambassadors. They should write an account of their visit, describing in detail the appearance and talents of the Queen, the food and entertainment provided, topics of conversation, and the role of servants and advisors to the Queen. Where was the Paradise Chamber? How did it get this name? It might be possible to play some recordings of Tudor music for the children to hear.

Draw, paint or make collage pictures of 'The Court of Good Queen Bess'. Discuss whether this seems an appropriate nickname for this highly gifted monarch who ruled for the 45 years of the great Elizabethan age. Why did she attract so much admiration?

Make an illustrated 'shopping list' of appropriate gifts to deliver to the Queen if you were invited to visit her court –perhaps jewellery, petticoats, gloves or a musical instrument. What strange gift(s) might Sir Walter Raleigh have brought the Queen from the New World?

Ask the children to each imagine that he or she is a courtier in Elizabethan times. The Queen announces that she intends to pay them a visit. What would their feelings be? What would they do to make her stay an enjoyable one? What might happen if she did not enjoy herself? What might they hope for it she did enjoy her stay? They should write about this, and about what happened during the visit.

Background information: *Tudor court life*

Henry VIII is said to have spent £300 000 a year on food and £50 000 a year on drink, vast sums of money at that time. There was a daily allowance of beer or wine for everyone in the royal household – no coffee or tea in those days!

Entertainments at court included jousting (sometimes in 'fancy dress'!), tennis (played with leather balls filled with hair), hunting, hawking, archery, dancing, firework displays and even play-acting.

Elizabeth I once stayed at Gorhambury, home of Lord North, for three days. Her short stay cost Lord North £761.21, a not inconsiderable sum in those days!

Activity 2: Thomas More

Research, debate and write about the life of the well known Tudor personality Sir Thomas More.

Use **Copymaster 33** as the basis for recording results of research. This provides an opportunity for the children to search for pictures of Sir Thomas More (such as the well known portrait by Holbein) and sketch him in the frame provided; also to fill in the blanks correctly in the sentences.

Data recorded on this Copymaster can then be used as a basis for more expansive writing on the subject.

Answers to blanks in Copymaster 33

- Chancellor
- Utopia
- King
- 1535
- Treason

Activity 3: The Tudor rose

Discuss the origins of, and let the children undertake creative art work using, the symbol of the Tudor Rose.

Background information
Until the year 1485, the throne of England had been contested by two family 'Houses', those of Lancaster and York. The wars that took place between them were called the Wars of the Roses, as each House had a rose as an emblem. The Tudor Rose was thus the symbol of Henry Tudor, who belonged to the House of Lancaster. In 1485 he defeated King Richard III from the House of York in the famous Battle of Bosworth. Henry became the first Tudor monarch.

Note: **General Copymaster 90** is also directly relevant to the study unit on life in Tudor times.

The Tudor rose

Study Unit 2: Life in Tudor Times – the ways of life of people at different levels of society: court life.
Suggested levels of work involved in activities

Activity number	Level	Activity number	Level	Activity number	Level
1	2/3/4	2	2/3/4/5	3	2/3

WAYS OF LIFE IN TOWN AND COUNTRY ▶

Activity 1: Everyday life in Tudor times
Through their reading and investigations, children will gain a general overview or 'feel' of everyday life in Tudor times. Write stories and paint pictures of such topics as 'a rural town' (villagers feeding chickens, pigs and sheep in gardens, carts loaded with vegetables trundling through the streets, men going off to work in the fields, beggars wandering past), or 'the market place' (shops with wooden shutters and swinging signs busily selling goods, country people arriving to display and sell their wares, children and animals playing in open spaces, the town crier shouting out his messages).

Background information: *Life in Tudor times*
It is estimated that only about four million people lived in Tudor England – how many are living in England today? London was the largest city, with a population of about 200 000 in 1600. The city streets were narrow and crowded, and there was no street lighting or regular police force.

Activity 2: Rich and poor
Draw attention to the great differences between the lives of the rich and the poor. Write imaginative autobiographical accounts of 'a day in the life of':

a street bellman
a village vagabond
a servant in the Tudor mansion

a town watchman
a milkmaid
a town crier
a rich merchant.

Many poor people earned a precarious living from crime. The children will know what a pickpocket did, but what do they think a 'cutpurse' used to do?

Draw, paint or make collage pictures of these and other characters, together with a suitable background scene for them. More ambitious children might care to make freestanding Tudor figures, using papier mâché and wire on a wooden frame, and dressing them appropriately.

Activity 3: Health of the Tudors
Discuss why many Tudor people did not live above the age of 40. Research medical and sanitary facilities of the times, and compare with the present day. If a visit to a museum is possible, investigate the primitive equipment of the period; if not, consult reference books and other secondary sources.

Background information
Many Tudor children died in early childhood, and the majority of people did not live beyond the age of 40. Diseases were rife; houses were overcrowded and streets littered with animal dung and flies. Sewers were open and carried diseases into water supplies. Many houses

had only holes in the ground as toilets. Medical equipment was extremely primitive and people depended on herbal medicines as remedies. Common diseases of the time were the plague, typhus and malaria.

Activity 4: Lifestyles

In comparison with the opulent lifestyle of the royal court, investigate how ordinary families occupied their time. The sons of the rich went to school, while the girls stayed at home to learn domestic skills. Leisure time was often spent singing or playing musical instruments, or enjoying morris dancing. Games included cards, chess, draughts and dice. Sports included archery, hunting, hawking, fishing, wrestling, bowls, tennis and 'football'. Another popular pastime was a visit to the theatre. Illustrate these and other activities, perhaps as a large montage of 'Life and Leisure in Tudor Times'.

Activity 5: The maze craze

Using **Copymaster 34**, discuss the 'maze craze' of Tudor times. Why was a maze a popular feature of so many elaborate gardens? **Copymaster 34** is a fun puzzle sheet which reinforces historical understanding. Ask children to find their way from the entrance to the fountain in the centre, and out again. They can then attempt to

draw mazes for other children to follow (and no doubt discover that this is not an easy task!). Find out where original garden mazes exist today. What other features were common in mansion gardens of the time? Remember to include sundials, fountains, herb and 'knot' gardens.

Activity 6: Crime and punishment

Find out about crime and punishment in Tudor times. Crime was very common and punishments were severe. Make a chart like the one shown below. Ask the children to find out what a 'scold' was and how she might be punished. How were witches dealt with? What was a pillory?

Discuss the nature and severity of these punishments (a woman was hanged for stealing two bedsheets). How do they compare with what happens to criminals in this country today? Ask the children to debate the death sentence and what they consider to be appropriate penalties for various crimes.

Debate other evils of the time, such as bull or bear-baiting and cock-fighting. Find out when these sports were made illegal, and why views have changed on such practices.

Activity 7: At school

Research and then write an account of a day at a Tudor school. Who attended? For how long? What was taught?

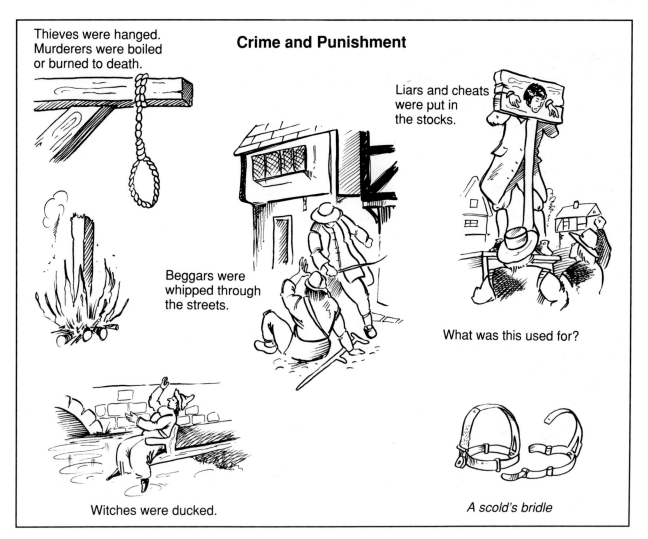

Crime and Punishment

Thieves were hanged. Murderers were boiled or burned to death.

Liars and cheats were put in the stocks.

Beggars were whipped through the streets.

What was this used for?

Witches were ducked.

A scold's bridle

A horn book

A Tudor Classroom

What equipment was used? What happened to pupils who did not pay attention, or learn their lessons? What was often used instead of a real book? (See the illustrations above).

Background information: At school

Only the children of wealthy parents were educated; boys at school, girls usually at home by a tutor. Poor children received no teaching.

Writing was considered less important than reading, which was the first skill taught. Boys learnt Greek, Latin, mathematics and music. Very little science was taught. Girls learnt music, dancing, needlework and perhaps Latin and French. Discipline was harsh – a birch was used in schools to beat children to make them learn.

Books were expensive to produce and pupils often learnt to read using a hornbook. This 'book' consisted of a wooden holder containing a sheet of writing or print, and over this a thin protective sheet of horn was fixed. The pupil read from this, holding it rather like a large hand-mirror.

Activity 8: Trade and industry

A sub-topic on the trade and industry of the period could involve different groups of children in investigating aspects of the woollen industry, coal-mining, iron manufacture, and transport. The development of roads alone would make a worthwhile investigation – include methods used to improve the state of roads, the development of turnpikes and tollgates, stage-coach travel and the activities of highwaymen. There is scope for useful comparisons with present-day travel times and modes of transport. Children can find out if there are any toll-houses or old coaching inns in their local area and, if so, visit them and make them a basis for factual and imaginative writing.

Activity 9: The discovery of printing

Investigate some of the important discoveries of the period, especially those such as printing which had an impact upon cultural matters. Write about the life of William Caxton, the first great printer in England, who set up his first printing press in London in 1477. Find out about the legacy of Caxton's work, including his most famous publication, Chaucer's *Canterbury Tales*. Discuss how the invention of printing dramatically altered the lives of many people, since it meant that it was no longer the privilege of the rich to read books.

Make your own printing blocks from potatoes or other available materials, and experiment with the production of a set of alphabet letters. Discuss the complexity of having to make 'back to front' letters if you want to print words. The children could try to print and illustrate short sentences, paragraphs or perhaps a whole page of their own work, commenting afterwards on any difficulties they may have met. This activity could be carried out using a modern child's printing set, if such a resource is available.

Activity 10: Sir Isaac Newton

Compile a biography of one of the most famous scientists of the age, Isaac Newton. His most important discovery was the Law of Gravity, but he also calculated how comets move. What had many people believed about comets in the past? How did Newton prove them wrong?

With older children, reflect on how thinking about the moon and planets changed dramatically during the Tudor years. Why do you think this was so? In part, this discussion can be related to a study of trade and travel, and the need for improved methods of navigation.

Find out the names and ideas of other famous scientists of the time, such as Robert Boyle, William Harvey and Robert Hooke, and about the establishment (during Charles II's reign) of the 'Royal Society for Improving Natural Knowledge'.

Background information: Scientific advancement
The Royal Society was founded in 1662 to stimulate scientific progress, and soon brought a notable advance in the knowledge of physics, astronomy, medicine and mathematics. Harvey discovered how blood circulated in the body, Boyle learned about the air that we breathe, and Hooke used the microscope to advance our knowledge of how living things are formed.

Activity 11: Maypoles and morris dancing

Learn how to do morris dancing or maypole dancing. Both of these activities would make a splendid centre-piece to a wall-display of pastimes and festivals of the period. Link this to writing about the ways in which May Day, Midsummer's Eve and other festivals were celebrated in great and colourful style. Create a 3-D maypole collage, surrounded with writing about associated customs, music and folklore.

Activity 12: Religion

Help the children to appreciate how very important religion was in the everyday lives of people in Tudor times. Fines were levied if church attendance was missed. Investigate the far more serious punishments associated with religious beliefs, and the lives of some of the martyrs – include the stories of Archbishop Cranmer and Bishops Ridley, Hooper and Latimer at Oxford. Explain terms like 'martyrdom' and 'persecution'.

Consider the main disagreements of Tudor times between Protestants and Catholics. Issues relating to this will no doubt have been raised and discussed when learning about the lives of the monarchs. Find out more about the impact of the 1559 abolition of the Catholic Church by Queen Elizabeth I. For example, services in the new Church of England were no longer conducted in Latin but in English.

Study Unit 2: Life in Tudor Times – the ways of life of people at different levels of society: ways of life in town and country.
Suggested levels of work involved in activities

Activity number	Level	Activity number	Level	Activity number	Level
1	2/3/4/5	5	2/3	9	2/3/4/5
2	2/3/4/5	6	2/3/4	10	2/3/4/5
3	2/3/4	7	2/3/4	11	2/3
4	2/3/4	8	2/3/4/5	12	2/3/4

ARTS AND ARCHITECTURE

Activity 1: Cultural achievements

Research and record notable achievements and styles of art, architecture, literature, music and drama of the period, perhaps by finding out more about the lives and works of such notable individuals as Sir Christopher Wren (1632–1723), the architect of the new St Paul's Cathedral; Sir John Vanbrugh, the architect of a number of grand Stuart mansions; John Milton (1608–1674), the writer of the epic poem *Paradise Lost* and other works; and of course William Shakespeare, poet and playwright.

Activity 2: The Globe and Drury Lane theatres

Using **Copymaster 35** as a starting point, find out as much as possible about the Globe Theatre, including the origin of its name. Paint pictures of its interior, showing male actors with their brightly coloured costumes, The Globe Theatre is a challenging subject for diorama or model-making from scrap materials.

Ask the children to find out how the plays were staged. This will help them to understand why the building was designed in the way it was. How were music and sound-effects introduced? Rumour has it that the first Globe Theatre was burned down when the effects required for a battle scene got out of hand. It is said that the actors and audience escaped safely, though one man's trousers caught fire! This episode would make a lively subject for creative writing, drawing and painting, and is well suited to the production of an historical newspaper.

The Drury Lane Theatre was built in the reign of Charles II, an enthusiastic theatregoer. Compare it with the Globe Theatre, and paint pictures of a play in performance there. What was the major difference in the membership of the theatre company at this time?

Who was Nell Gwyn (or Gwynne)? Her story might enable the children to understand that not every monarch was the paragon of virtue that one might expect the holder of such high office to be!

Ask the children to find out what a visit to the theatre might have been like, and to write an imaginative story about it. If possible, make a visit to Stratford-upon-Avon, or find out about the activities of the Royal Shakespeare Theatre Company today.

Background information: *The theatre*
The answers to the questions on **Copymaster 35** are as follows. William Shakespeare was probably born in Stratford-upon-Avon in Warwickshire. He was baptised there in Holy Trinity church on 26 April 1564. He died on 23 April 1616 and is buried in the same church. His wife's name was Anne Hathaway. His plays are comedies, tragedies and histories.

A useful book to consult in this connection is *The Story of the Theatre* by David Male, published by A & C Black Ltd, London, in 1967. It contains a complete chapter on Shakespeare and the Globe Theatre, as well as information on the Drury Lane Theatre of Charles II's day, together with many fine illustrations.

Activity 3: Tudor music
Search your nearest music library and encyclopaedias of music to find out about musical instruments of the period and well known musicians and their works. Listen to some famous Tudor music and discuss the circumstances under which it would have been played. Consider how it differs from musical compositions of later periods and today.

Background information
Two of the most famous musicians of the Tudor period were Thomas Tallis and William Byrd. They composed a great deal of church music; also music to be played at home in the grand mansions of the period. Thomas Tallis lived 1505–1585, William Byrd lived 1540–1623.

Activity 4: Houses and homes
Make models of Tudor houses. Design and construct frames out of cardboard or suitable boxes, cover them with paper and then paint them to resemble the traditional black and white timber-and-plaster dwellings. Use the models to make a town street, and add other appropriate buildings such as shops and taverns, as well as street furniture. Find out the location of and, if possible, visit Tudor buildings that still exist today.

Discuss why many shops had a painted sign or picture outside, rather than writing, to advertise their wares? Perhaps the children could design some tavern and/or shop signs (butcher, baker, shoemaker, and so on) for a classroom wall-display.

Draw 'cutaway' illustrations of the interiors of various houses during the Tudor period, comparing the houses of different sections of society. Identify the 'special features' of wealthy Tudor houses for which they are now famous, for example four-poster beds, grand oak staircases and long galleries.

Draw the appropriate furniture in each 'cutaway' room, and then compare these dwellings with our own homes today. Perhaps the children could make a list of modern household comforts that were not available to people in Tudor times, thereby increasing their awareness of the fairly primitive nature of domestic arrangements – many families lived in one small room with little or no furniture, and perhaps only straw for bedding.

Activity 5: Tudor mansions
Make a model or do paintings of a Tudor mansion or manor house. Write stories along the lines of 'a day in the life of a rich Tudor family', or 'my friend the Lord of the Manor'. Discuss reasons why some people lived in this grand style. Research evidence of Tudor mansions or manor houses which can still be observed today.

Background information
The richest people in Tudor times lived in country mansions. Many of these were manor houses set in acres of countryside owned by the 'Lord of the Manor'. Often this land would include a village, whose people farmed their own crops on strips of land near to their homes. The villagers would pay the wealthy manor owner money for using his land for growing crops and perhaps also for keeping sheep and cows. The mansions themselves were very large houses, often with many servants. Tudor country houses which are worth visiting include:

Hardwick Hall, Derbyshire
Little Moreton Hall, Cheshire
Longleat, Wiltshire
Cotetele House, Cornwall
Hampton Court, London
Oxburgh Hall, Norfolk
Loseley House, Surrey
Barrington Court, Somerset
Doddington Hall, Lincolnshire

Activity 6: Growth of the wool trade

Investigate and write about the impact of the growth of the wool trade on rural life. Perhaps a classroom debate could be organised with children putting points of view forward from the Lord of the Manor and from village people.

Background information

Many wealthy land owners decided to rear large flocks of sheep around their country mansions. This activity provided much needed wool for England's expanding trade in cloth and was thus financially rewarding. Much common land, previously available to villagers for rearing their animals, was fenced in for the flocks of sheep. The villagers clearly suffered as a result, and many became short of food and clothes. In many instances, they fled as beggars to nearby towns, an act which only pleased the wealthy manor lords as they could demolish the villagers' homes and acquire extra land for grazing sheep.

Study Unit 2: Life in Tudor Times – the ways of life of people at different levels of society: arts and architecture. Suggested levels of work involved in activities

Activity number	Level	Activity number	Level	Activity number	Level
1	2/3/4/5	3	2/3/4/5	5	2/3/4/5
2	2/3	4	2/3	6	2/3/4

RESOURCES ▶

Non-fiction

Unwin, R. *Tudors and Stuarts*, Oxford Primary History.
Tudor Britain, History in Evidence Series, Wayland.
Family Life in Tudor England, Family Life Series, Wayland.
Tudor Sailors, Beginning History Series, Wayland, 1991.
The Tudors and Stuarts, Look into the Past Series, Wayland.
Newbery, E. *Tudor Farmhouse*, What Happened Here Series, A & C Black.
Tudors and Stuarts, Collins Primary History.

Fiction

Stories for young readers

Beresford, E. *Armada Adventure*, Methuen, 1988. A stirring story set at the time of the attempted Spanish invasion.*
Gerrard, R. *Sir Frances Drake: his daring deeds*, Gollancz, 1988. Drake's voyages, told in rhyme. Humorous picture storybook.
Richemont, E. *Time Tree*, Walker Books, 1989. A time-slip story that tells about the trauma of being deaf in Tudor times.
Trease, G. *Masque for a Queen*, Hamish Hamilton, 1970. Elizabeth I plans to visit Fairfield Hall, and a masque is in preparation for her entertainment.*

*These stories are out of print but are still available from libraries and second-hand bookshops.

Stories for more competent readers

The following stories are suitable for more fluent readers, or for reading excerpts aloud.

Harnett, C. *Stars of Fortune*, Methuen, 1956. A story of the Washington family at Sulgrave Manor, during the reign of Mary Tudor.*
Harnett, C. *The Woolpack*, Penguin, 1989. A Cotswold woolmerchant's family in the time of Henry VII.
Melkinoff, P. *Plots and Players*, Blackie, 1988. Struggles and adventures of Jewish children in Elizabethan London.*
Sutcliff, R. *Brother Dusty-feet*, OUP, 1952. Strolling players of Elizabeth I's time.*
Trease, G. *Cue for Treason*, Penguin, 1970. A story that ranges across Tudor England, involving strolling players and a plot against Elizabeth I.
Uttley, A. *Traveller in Time*, Penguin, 1977. Time-slip story about the Babington plot, to put Mary Stuart on the throne.
Willard, B. *The Mantlemass Novels* (various editions are available). Stories that span the years 1485 through to the Civil War.

Poetry

Drake's Drum by Sir Henry Newbolt; and *The Queen's Speech* (anon) can both be found in *The Book of Salt Sea Verse*, compiled by Charles Causley, Puffin, 1978.*
The Revenge: A Ballad of the Fleet by Lord Tennyson is published in *Poems for over 10-year-olds*, compiled by K. Wilson, Viking Kestrel, 1984.

Blueprints links

You will find related technology activities on the Tudors in *Blueprints: Technology Key Stage 2*. The following other Stanley Thornes books will also prove useful: *Investigating History: Life in Tudor and Stuart Times*.

Pupils should be taught about the lives of men, women and children at different levels of society in Britain and the ways in which they were affected by changes in industry and transport:

Changes in industry and transport

    a steam power, factories and mass production, *e.g. economic growth and the provision of jobs for men and women, the impact of mass production on living and working conditions;*

    b the growth of railways, *e.g. the work of Robert Stephenson and Isambard Kingdom Brunel, the impact of railways on everyday life;*

The lives of people at different levels of society in town and country

    c at work, *e.g. factory life, Lord Shaftesbury and factory reform, Florence Nightingale and nursing, domestic service, agriculture, the armed forces, the merchant marine, workhouses;*

    d at home, *e.g. family life at different levels of society, Victoria and the royal family, the role of religion, public health and medicine;*

    e at leisure, *e.g. music, sport, holidays, the Great Exhibition;*

    f at school, *e.g. Sunday schools, voluntary schools, board schools, public schools.*

TOPIC WEB

Everyday life

- At work
- At home
- At leisure
- At school

VICTORIAN BRITAIN

Setting the scene

- Life and legacy of Queen Victoria
- A Victorian timeline

Industry and transport

- Steam power, factories and mass production
- Industrial revolution
- Impact on working and living conditions
- Railways in Britain
- Canals

SETTING THE SCENE

C36

Activity 1: Life and legacy of Queen Victoria

Set the scene for development of this topic by finding out about the life and legacy of Queen Victoria, who ruled for longer than any other English monarch has done. Perhaps the compilation of illustrated biographies of Victoria and her life would make a useful lead into, and unifying activity for, the project as a whole. Because there is so much about the Victorian era that could be considered, it is necessary to provide a focus of this kind, and a clear starting point, otherwise such a wide-ranging topic could merely become a collection of interesting yet unrelated facts. If Victoria herself is taken as the lead into further aspects of the age, perhaps groups of children could then research and investigate specific areas of importance in her reign, such as public health, religion, growth of towns, railways, etc.

Use **Copymaster 36** as an introduction to the topic as a whole. It provides a possible topic-book cover, helps the children to appreciate what Queen Victoria looked like, and reinforces basic facts such as the dates of 'Victorian Britain'. Ask the pupils to look at photographs and artists' impressions of Queen Victoria and colour the drawing appropriately. The sentence can then be completed (answers are 64 years, 81 years and 1901). Ensure that the children understand that the year 1837 is the year she came to the throne, at the age of eighteen. Clearly there is scope for further 'Victorian mathematics', for example, when was she born?

Activity 2: Who was Victoria?

Answer this question by drawing a family tree (for details of preliminary work on family trees, see the topic Life in Tudor Times). This could be extended to include details of her own family, and the line of succession to the English throne.

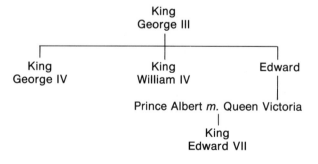

Copymaster 36 can be used as the basis for ongoing recording of legacy, as the biography of Queen Victoria progresses. The frame around the portrait has been left blank so that the children can write in key words that emerge from their investigations, summarising the legacy of Victoria's reign. For example:

BUILDING	TRANSPORT
(Royal Albert Hall)	(Growth of railways)
INVENTIONS	LAWS
(Stainless steel)	(Public Health Act)
COMMUNICATIONS	MACHINES
(Telegraph, telephone Morse Code)	(Sewing machines)

As the topic progresses, the children will build up a picture of the queen as a person. Ask them to gather a list of words to describe her personality – stubborn? ambitious? determined? intolerant? cruel? strong? hot-tempered? loyal? kind? caring? devoted? These are all possible words to consider and discuss. Organise a class debate about the queen, putting forward opposing views of her personality. Ask the children to substantiate their arguments with evidence of her actions. Develop this issue by asking them what personal qualities they think are important in a king or queen. (Gilbert and Sullivan had an amusing comment on royalty in *The Gondoliers*. Provide a copy of the lyrics, and let them hear the song 'A Regular Royal Queen'.)

Activity 3: A Victorian timeline

Start a timeline for Queen Victoria's reign, and add to it throughout the topic. There is so much material to include that it might be advisable to divide events into separate columns or topic headings, rather than allowing an integrated timeline to become unwieldy. The following chronological list of some of the events of the Victorian age could be subdivided under headings such as these: Entertainment and exhibitions, Inventions, Events abroad, Health and education, Publications, The Royal Family, Technology, Transport, Social issues. You can add to each category as work progress.

Main events

1819
Victoria born.

1837
Victoria crowned as Queen.

1840
First Co-operative shop opened in Rochdale.

1844
The working day restricted to 12 hours for women and young people.

1848
Prince Albert introduces the first Christmas tree.

Main events *continued*

1851
The Great Exhibition was held at the Crystal Palace.
Singer produced the first practical sewing machine.

1852
Morse Code was used in telegraphy.
Livingstone set off to explore the Zambesi.

1853
Anaesthetics became widely accepted after chloroform helped Queen Victoria in childbearing.
Vaccination against smallpox was made compulsory.

1854
Britain entered the Crimean War.

1855
Florence Nightingale brought hygiene to nursing.
The first iron Cunard steamer crossed the Atlantic.

1856
The Crimean War ended.

1859
De Lesseps began work on the Suez Canal.
Darwin published his *Origin of Species*.

1860
The first English horse-drawn trams appeared.

1861
Albert, Prince Consort, died.
The American Civil War began.

1862
The Revised Code of Education set up the system of Payment by Results.
Abraham Lincoln abolished slavery in America.

1863
Rules for Association Football were laid down.
Charles Kingsley published *The Water Babies*.

1864
The torpedo, and pasteurization, were invented.

1865
The American Civil War ended; President Lincoln was assassinated.
Overarm bowling was permitted in cricket.
Lewis Carroll published *Alice in Wonderland*.

1866
Dr Barnardo opened his home for waifs.

1867
Working men in towns got the vote.
Lister introduced carbolic antiseptic.

1868
Gangs Act forbade employment in farming of children under 8.
First Trade Union Congress was held in Manchester.

1869
The Suez Canal was opened.

1870
Forster's Elementary Education Act set up school boards.
The $\frac{1}{2}$d post was introduced.

1871
Full legal recognition was given to trade unions.
Stanley found Livingstone.

1873
Barbed wire was invented in the United States.
The first successful typewriter appeared.

1874
The Factory Act introduced a maximum 10-hour working day and raised the minimum age of child workers.
English lawn tennis began.

1875
Disraeli introduced social reforms; Public Health Acts.

1876
Bell's telephone, Edison's phonograph and Bissell's carpet sweeper were invented.
School attendance was made compulsory.

1877
Anna Sewell wrote *Black Beauty*.

1878
The 'Red Flag' Act restricted the speed of mechanical road vehicles.
Electric street lighting began in London.
The C.I.D. was established.

1879
Swan and Edison independently produced the carbon filament incandescent electric light.

1882
Cricket between England and Australia began the contest for the Ashes.

1883
The first skyscraper was built in Chicago, following the development of safety lifts by Otis.

1884
The right to vote was granted to workers in agriculture.

1885
Daimler developed lightweight, high-speed engines in Germany.

1886
The gas mantle was invented.

1887
The Golden Jubilee was celebrated.
The Coal Mines Regulation Act was passed. Boys under 13 were not allowed underground.

1888
Dunlop developed the pneumatic tyre.
The Kodak box-camera appeared.
'Jack the Ripper' murders took place in London.

1889
An Act was passed to prevent cruelty to children.

1890
Motion picture films were shown in New York.
The first 'tube' railway opened.

Main events *continued*

1891
Wireless telegraphy was developed.
Conan Doyle published *The Adventures of Sherlock Holmes.*

1892
Tinned pineapple was introduced.
The first automatic telephone switchboard was set up.

1893
Aspirin was introduced.

1895
Röntgen discovered X rays.
Gillette invented the safety razor.
The first motor-car exhibition was put on in London.

1896
The Red Flag Act was repealed, and the maximum speed was raised to 14 mph.
The first modern Olympic Games were held in Athens.

1897
The Diamond Jubilee was celebrated.

1898
Pierre and Marie Curie discovered radium.

1900
Cadbury established the Bournville Village Trust.

1901
Queen Victoria died.
Marconi transmitted wireless messages from Cornwall to Newfoundland.

Study Unit 3a: Victorian Britain – setting the scene.
Suggested levels of work involved in activities

Activity number	Level	Activity number	Level	Activity number	Level
1	2/3/4/5	2	2/3/4/5	3	2/3/4/5

CHANGES IN INDUSTRY AND TRANSPORT

Pupils should be taught about the following:

Economic developments

a Steam power, factories and mass production, *eg economic growth and the provision of jobs for men and women, the impact of mass production on living and working conditions*

b the growth of railways, *eg the work of Robert Stephenson and Isambard Kingdom Brunel, the impact of railways on everyday life*

Activity 1: The Industrial Revolution
Continue 'scene-setting' for an understanding of the Victorian age by learning about the background to the Industrial Revolution, which had such a dramatic effect on the lives of British people. Focus on specific developments, for example in steam power, mining or the cloth industry. Contrast them with the 'cottage industries' which had existed previously. Record these developments in 'before and after' diagrams, or paintings. A large series of such pictures could be mounted as a 'patchwork' wall-display, to reinforce the scale of the changes that occurred in industry (see overleaf).

Key words and concepts will inevitably emerge, these being industrialisation, mechanisation, mass-production, the building of factories, and the growth of towns. Help the children to appreciate the relationships between these developments: for example, consider why factories were built (machines were too big to fit into houses), and why towns grew up around them. Mention the work of Rowntree in York and Cadbury at Bournville, near Birmingham, in building housing estates for their workers.

Activity 2: Industrial sites
Find out where in the British Isles the earliest factories were established. If possible, visit the sites of original

industrial enterprises to sketch buildings, consider their legacy in the local area, and ascertain ways in which the environment has changed since the days of the Industrial Revolution. If your school is within easy access of an original industrial area, then fieldwork can be a major focus of the topic, leading to very detailed work on the particular industries concerned and their impact on the locality.

Annotate a map to show the location of the main industrial centres of Britain in the mid-nineteenth century. **Copymaster 37** provides the necessary outline, showing the major sites of three key industries – shipbuilding, iron and coal. Discuss the location of

these industries, and use an atlas or reference books to discover the names of the actual places indicated. Write the names of towns and counties on the map.

Starting in the north-west and travelling around the coast, the place-names are:

Glasgow	Southampton
Barrow	Portsmouth
Liverpool	London
Swansea	Hull
Cardiff	Newcastle upon Tyne
Bristol	Edinburgh
Plymouth	

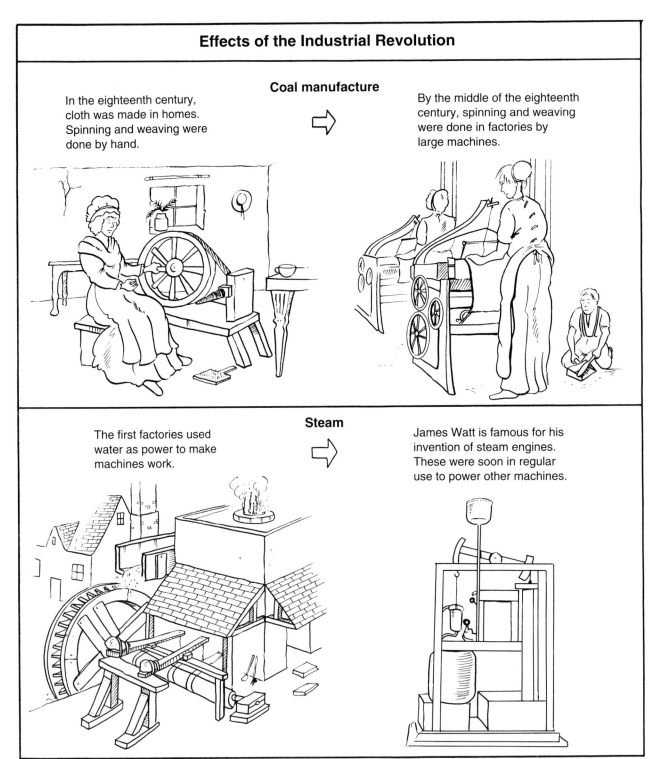

Effects of the Industrial Revolution

Coal manufacture

In the eighteenth century, cloth was made in homes. Spinning and weaving were done by hand.

By the middle of the eighteenth century, spinning and weaving were done in factories by large machines.

Steam

The first factories used water as power to make machines work.

James Watt is famous for his invention of steam engines. These were soon in regular use to power other machines.

Inland, the towns in the midlands are Birmingham, Stoke-on-Trent and Nottingham; and Denbigh (to represent the coal industry in North Wales).

Consider why industries grew up in these places, for example, why shipbuilding and coal were established in the area of Newcastle-upon-Tyne. This map can then be extended by adding to the key appropriate symbols for other industries of the day and indicating their distribution on the map. Some suggestions for industries/symbols are given opposite. This will produce a good picture of the pattern of British industry in Victorian times, and reasons for this pattern. Regional variations can be emphasised by structuring quiz-type questions for investigation from atlases and reference books, for example:

– Name the counties of England where many spinning and weaving factories were established.
– What metal was mined in Cornwall?
– Which county became the centre of the pottery trade?

Activity 3: Britain's industrial power

Write about why Britain was the world's leading industrial power at this time. Plot the expanding British Empire on a world map, and investigate the nature of British goods traded abroad (cotton, woollen goods, leather, hardware, iron, steel, ships, railway engines, coal, etc.). Find out which countries bought these things. Draw 'import and export' diagrams to show trade patterns, and consider why food became such a key import.

Talk about the impact of the British Empire and the expansion of trade on shipping and the shipbuilding industry. The greatest ports in the world at this time were London, Liverpool and Glasgow. Mark key ports

☕	pottery	T	tin
S	salt	🧶	wool
🌾	cotton	🌿	silk
🔲	slate	🐄	leather
L	lead	🧱	building materials

and shipyards on a map of the British Isles and discuss the nature of these places today. Why did shipbuilding decline in later years?

Activity 4: Railways in Britain

Develop an understanding of the Industrial Revolution in other forms of transport, notably the railways. Again, this would make a detailed sub-topic for a group of children to work on. Find out about the work of George Stephenson, the age of steam, and the hectic days of railway expansion between 1844 and 1847. Draw maps to show the main railway lines that were in existence by 1847. Collect and/or create pictures of well-known locomotives of the Victorian age, such as the *Rocket* or the *Locomotion*, and assemble them in a book or as a

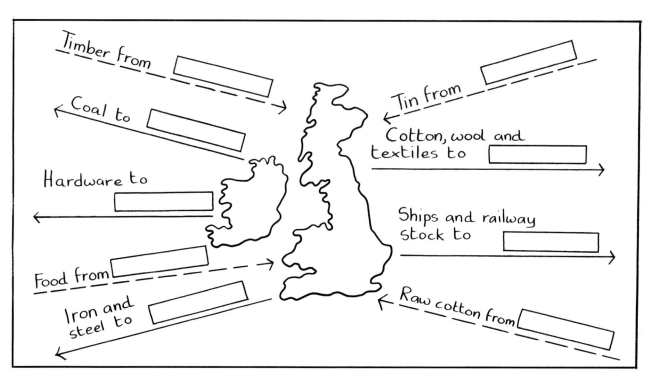

61

border to a wall-display on the 'Railway Revolution'. Write imaginative stories about what it might have been like to travel by train for the first time. What would the passengers have thought about it all?

Find out where the world's first modern passenger-railway was built. How much did it cost? And what has the name of William Huskisson to do with railway history?

Discuss the great interest in steam railways which still exists today. Ask the children to suggest why so many people pursue this hobby and spend so much of their spare time restoring and running locomotives. Find out about the work of individuals and societies in preserving the heritage of the steam age. If there is a railway preservation society near the school, try to arrange a visit to see one of these mighty locomotives in action: the children could sketch the engines, and record their experiences in vivid descriptive writing. Back at school, read the story of *The Railway Children*, and play pieces of music written to depict the sounds of steam engines.

What happened to the canals as the railway engine made its presence felt? Why?

Background information: *Railways in Britain*
The world's first modern passenger-railway was the Liverpool and Manchester Railway, completed in 1830 at a cost of £800 000. William Huskisson was a local Member of Parliament who was fatally injured by the locomotive during the opening ceremony.

Activity 5: Isambard Kingdom Brunel
Investigate the impact of the life and work of Isambard Kingdom Brunel on the industrial revolution. Perhaps a group could make a special research study on this man's contribution to the times, and its lasting impact – relating this to other research on the iron and steel industry.

Background information
Steel, i.e. iron with carbon added, was first produced by Benjamin Huntsman in the 1740s. The output of steel from Britain increased threefold between 1850 and 1880. Steel became extremely important in structural engineering. Ships were now made of steel rather than wood, and were powered by steam. The first Atlantic crossing ever made by a steam-driven ship was accomplished in 1838 in a vessel designed by Isambard Brunel, named the *Great Western*. Isambard Brunel was thus a famous engineer. He was born in 1806, and at the age of 23 designed the Clifton suspension bridge near Bristol. In 1833 he became engineer to the Great Western Railway Company. The *Great Western* ship, of 1340 tonnes (twice the size of any other steamship) was launched at Bristol in 1837. In 1839 Brunel built another ship, the *Great Britain*, which was two and a half times as big as the *Great Western*.

Activity 6: The Suez Canal
Look at Victorian shipping routes to help the children understand the significance of the opening of the Suez Canal in 1869. Draw sketch maps to show the

improvements in routes and travelling times brought about by the building of the canal.

Background information: *The Suez Canal*
The Suez Canal took ten years to build, and was the brainchild of a Frenchman, Ferdinand de Lesseps. It was financed largely by France and Turkey, at a cost of many millions. When the Suez Canal was completed, it was over a hundred miles long and ships took about fifteen hours to travel through it. The Canal lopped almost 4000 miles off the journey to India from Britain, and around 1200 miles off a voyage to Australia.

Activity 7: Canals in Britain
Consideration of the Suez Canal could lead into a sub-topic on canals in England, especially if your school is located in an area where practical fieldwork is possible. By 1830, canals crossed England, linking the great ports of Liverpool, London, Hull and Bristol (see opposite).

Ask the children to find out about the colourful lives of the 'navvies', whose hard labour built the canal system. The navvies had a special language of their own which the children might like to investigate.

Background information: *Canals in Britain*
The Waterways Museum at Stoke Bruerne, near Towcester, Northants NN12 7SE (Telephone: Northampton 862229) is a fascinating place to visit, displaying a collection of artefacts which bring to life over two hundred years of canal history. The Museum provides an illustrated questionnaire for children to complete, and has a supply of other informative material, including maps, guides, books, postcards, reproductions of unusual canal notices, narrow-boat pictures, and so on. Boat trips can also be arranged between Easter and the end of October.

Schools in the Birmingham area can conduct fieldwork and go on narrow-boat outings on the city's canal system: indeed, it is a little known fact that Birmingham has more miles of canal than Venice! Of course, anyone conducting a party of children on a canal visit should ensure that they are aware of safety precautions and appropriate behaviour at all times.

Visitors to the Black Country Museum, Tipton Road, Dudley, West Midlands (Telephone: 0121 557 9643) can also take a short canal trip with an opportunity of 'legging' the boat through a tunnel. In addition, they are able to visit a reconstructed village, built to show how people lived and worked in the Black Country during the latter years of Victoria's reign. The village includes a colliery, a general store, a chainmaker's house, a chemist's shop, a Methodist Chapel, a boat dock, a coal-fired bakery, and the 'Bottle and Glass' public house, amongst other attractions. Many of these buildings have been saved from demolition and painstakingly rebuilt and/or furnished with original fittings, in order to preserve the atmosphere of a nineteenth-century village. It is also possible to see chain-making and glass-blowing on the site. The Museum produces its own excellent work-books for children, together with numerous other items, and is well worth a visit.

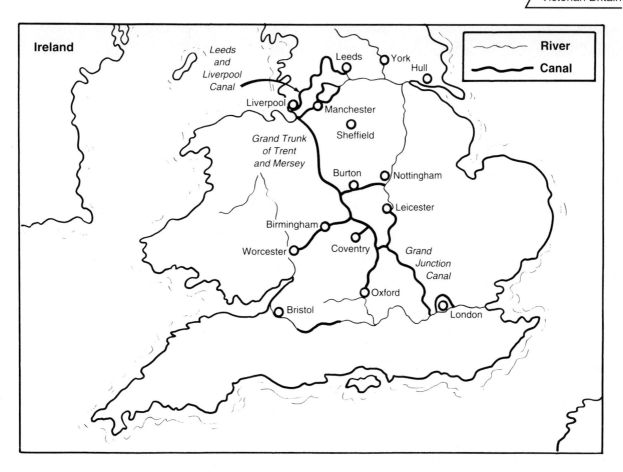

Victorian Britain

Study Unit 3a: Victorian Britain – changes in industry and transport. Suggested levels of work involved in activities

Activity number	Level	Activity number	Level	Activity number	Level
1	2/3/4/5	4	2/3/4/5	6	2/3
2	2/3/4/5	5	2/3/4/5	7	2/3/4
3	2/3/4/5				

THE LIVES OF PEOPLE AT DIFFERENT LEVELS OF SOCIETY IN TOWN AND COUNTRY

C38–45

Pupils should be taught about:

the lives of people at different levels of society in town and country

c at work, *e.g. factory life, Lord Shaftesbury and factory reform, Florence Nightingale and nursing, domestic service, agriculture, the armed forces, the merchant marine, workhouses*

d at home, *e.g. family life at different levels of society, Victoria and the royal family, the role of religion, public health and medicine*

e at leisure, *e.g. music, sport, holidays, the Great Exhibition*

f at school, *e.g. Sunday schools, voluntary schools, board schools, public schools*

VICTORIANS AT WORK ▶

Activity 1: How towns developed

Link the great growth in mechanisation, steam power and industry to the growth of towns. Design a large wall-frieze of an industrial town around 1850, showing back-to-back houses, narrow streets, a nearby railway line and, in the background, the inevitable smoking factory chimneys. Bring your frieze to life by adding cut-out figures of young children playing in the streets, people selling fruits and flowers on a street corner, a policeman chasing a thief, and horses and carts trundling by. Beneath the frieze, write the names of some well-known British towns and cities which developed as a direct result of the Industrial Revolution: Birmingham, Glasgow, Liverpool, Oldham, Sheffield, Bradford, etc.

Wherever possible, relate the above activity to local fieldwork and show how your town would have appeared in Victorian times. Consult paintings and sketches of the period in the local art gallery or museum, as well as reference books in the local-studies section of your library. It might even be possible to make a model or diorama of a street in a typical Victorian town or city.

Write stories about town life in Victorian times – streets lit by gas-lamps; different shops and markets; the people of the street (for example, chimney-sweeps, knife-sharpeners, butchers' boys, pickpockets, flower-sellers). Include details of the qualitative aspects of town life – streets were often dirty (consider why); the air was often polluted by factory smoke; smells were not very pleasant (consider the possible lack of toilets and running water); and nearby streams and rivers were often full of industrial pollution.

This paints a somewhat bleak picture, so it is necessary to consider also the positive aspects of developing towns: the availability of work, better housing, the growth of railways, access to new labour-saving machines for the home, and so on. Ask the children to debate the qualitative aspects of Victorian town life. What would they have enjoyed about 'growing up in a (for example, Lancashire) town', and what would they have disliked about it?

Activity 2: Working in a factory

Write and illustrate accounts about conditions in early factories. Ask pupils to imagine that they are factory workers, and to write about a typical working day. This activity can, of course, introduce the issue of child labour, as depicted on **Copymaster 38**. Collect and/or create pictures of scenes such as boys climbing into machines to mend them, children being whipped for falling asleep during a long day, and young boys struggling to carry materials that are clearly far too heavy for them.

Discuss why conditions for many Victorian workers were so primitive. Why is life in a modern factory so different? Make a list of differences between early factory life and industrial employment today. What has brought about these changes? This could lead into the consideration of fundamental issues, such as changing

legal aspects of health and safety at work, laws about hours of employment and age of employees, and the legal rights of working people. Find out what laws were passed in the reign of Victoria and add the dates to the timeline.

Background information: *Working in a factory*

In poor families, children were sent out to earn extra money at the age of seven or eight, sometimes even earlier. As they were small, many children were used in cotton or woollen mills to tie up threads which had broken, or to tidy up under the machinery – while it was still running: indeed, many children were the victims of accidents when they became trapped in the machinery. They were paid very low wages and often worked as many as twelve or fourteen hours a day. These factory children were always tired and often unhealthy; some of them grew up with lifelong handicaps and deformities caused by the work they had to do.

Activity 3: Factory reform

Ask the children to put themselves in the position of a campaigner arguing for reform of conditions in factories and mines. Write a campaigning speech, or design a poster to get the message across, giving due reasons.

Activity 4

Research precise details of factory reform, investigating key people and legislation involved.

Background information

At the turn of the nineteenth century, conditions of work and pay were extremely poor in factories and mines in Britain. Reformers began to campaign for improvement in the long working hours, unhealthy conditions and very low rates of pay. By the end of the century, a minimum age limit of 11 had been established for working in factories, there was far more regulation of working conditions, and factories were regularly inspected.

Activity 5: Fear of the workhouse

Explain to the children that there were no old-age pensions or welfare benefits in Victorian times. Ask them to speculate on what might have happened to someone who became ill, unemployed or too old to support themselves.

Copymasters 39 and **40** may help the children to gain an awareness of the pressures faced by many working-class families on low incomes. The game is competitive, though not in a negative way, since the aim is to survive for the longest time, and avoid a visit to the workhouse.

The rules of the game are simple. Players travel around the board by rolling a dice, avoiding or landing on the various chance squares and gaining or losing money according to the instructions. One circuit of the board is equivalent to the passing of a week in the life of each particular character. When a player who is still in work passes his/her starting point, he or she collects a week's wages and pays rent. Unemployed players continue in the game by moving round the board, but can collect no wages. Unemployment can only be halted and wages restored by throwing a six. Debts incurred whilst unemployed still stand, and must be paid off.

If a player does not have enough money or savings to pay any bills, he or she can sell items of furniture or pawn other belongings in order to stay in the game. Once players have no other resources left they are eliminated from the game and must take their place in the workhouse. The winner is the person who avoids this indignity!

The money element in the game could be notional, but it would be preferable to use plastic coins, bank-notes, etc. Modern currency is used for ease of operation, but this could be translated into pounds, shillings and pence if complete authenticity is required. If necessary, players can blank off any items that they have sold or pawned, in order to keep an accurate record of their situation.

Activity 6: Home affairs, health, public conditions, law and order
Ask pairs or groups of children to work together on an investigation into the life and work of famous people associated with health and working conditions of the period. Obvious names to research include Joseph Lister, James Simpson, Florence Nightingale, Lord Shaftesbury and Robert Peel.

Study Unit 3a: Victorian Britain – the lives of people at different levels of society in town and country: at work.
Suggested levels of work involved in activities

Activity number	Level	Activity number	Level	Activity number	Level
1	2/3/4/5	3	2/3/4	5	2/3/4
2	2/3/4/5	4	2/3/4	6	2/3/4

VICTORIANS AT HOME ▶

Activity 1: Tell me all about it
By far the best ways of learning about everyday life in Victorian times are by talking to people who have stories or accounts passed down from grandparents and great-grandparents, and by studying artefacts and photographic evidence of the period. A local history museum is the obvious starting point, followed by visits to relevant buildings or places in the neighbourhood. You may be fortunate enough to know someone who was born when Victoria was on the throne. If not, consult books for accounts of life and leisure.

Activity 2: Emily's story
Copymaster 41 gives a brief and genuine account of her childhood, told by Emily Cope as she approached her 90th year. She was born in Yattendon in Berkshire in 1896, and later moved to Birmingham, where she spent her adult life. The year of Emily's fifth birthday marked the end of Queen Victoria's reign, and her early childhood provides a vivid contrast with the upbringing of children nowadays. Ask the children to read Emily's account, and discuss the various ways in which her experiences differ from their own. For example, discuss the obvious influence of the church in her life, the idea of having only one birthday present, and the strict rule of going to bed at 7.30 p.m. every night. Talk about what can be learned about social history from her writing – about popular books and games, fashions and family routines.

In the space provided, ask the children to draw a picture of Emily as they imagine her, together with some toys and books she might have known.

Activity 3: Family trees
Ask the children to draw family trees of their own relatives, and to try to find the names of relatives who could have told stories about Queen Victoria and the Britain of her time, had they still been alive. Enlist the help of the children's parents, and try to find out where their Victorian ancestors lived. Do any artefacts of their lives and homes still remain? It is likely that enough objects will be loaned by willing families to organise a class museum. If so, discuss how to display these very precious items, and the vital importance of caring for valuable objects from the past.

Activity 4: Victorian households
Copymaster 42 shows, in outline, four rooms in part of a typical upper-class Victorian residence. Find out about the lives of such a family and their servants, and compare and contrast these with the lives of a poor family. Ask the children to draw lines on the copymaster, matching the household items to the correct rooms. Make drawings of other typical Victorian family houses and household gadgets, and write about how and when these various gadgets would have been used.

Compare life in terraced town houses with that in the splendid houses of richer people. Find out about the lives of domestic servants such as the butler, the cook, the housekeeper, the groom and the between-stairs maid. Ask the children to write about 'my life as a tweeny'.

Activity 5: Games

Find out about the toys and games Victorian children liked to play with, but remember, rich and poor children led very different lives in those days. If replicas of such Victorian toys as the whip and top, hoop and stick or cup and ball can be obtained, let the children try them out. Boardgames were also popular at this time. The book *Great Board Games*, compiled by Brian Love and published by Book Club Associates by arrangement with Ebury Press and Michael Joseph Limited in 1979, contains a number of games that were played in the late nineteenth century.

The children might like to find out what games and toys kept their parents and grandparents amused. If possible, draw or paint pictures of these activities.

Finally, the children could investigate the costume of rich and poor Victorian children, and draw pictures of themselves as they might have appeared, perhaps wearing pinafores or Eton suits.

Activity 6: Churchgoing

Consider the great importance of religion in the lives of Victorian people. Look for evidence of Victorian churches in your locality, and investigate their history and significance. What were the main church denominations and beliefs?

Write about the Victorian Sunday – the clothing worn, visits to Sunday School, tests on the church sermon, and family activities. What could the children do on Sundays, and which toys could they play with? Find out what 'signing the Pledge' meant. Ask the children to compare the Victorian Sunday with a typical Sunday nowadays. Let them write down what they and

their families do on Sundays. They may well be surprised (if not appalled) to discover that almost everything done today would have been forbidden in the days of Queen Victoria. Discuss the general shift in attitudes since Victorian times towards a more 'free and easy' family lifestyle. Ask the children why and how this change has occurred, and whether or not they feel it is a change for the better.

Visit the graveyard of a local church which dates back to the Victorian age, and see what can be learned about the lives and beliefs of Victorians from the inscriptions on their graves. Discuss appropriate behaviour with the children before the visit. This activity needs handling with sensitivity, especially if any child has recently suffered a family bereavement.

Activity 7: Public health

Diseases were common and serious in Victorian times. Discuss why, and find out the names of some of them. Ask the children to imagine that they are doctors and to write about some of the diseases they might have encountered. Illustrate these accounts with annotated paintings or cartoons of an imaginary 'surgery' (see opposite).

Find out what conditions in hospitals were like, about the lack of attention to sterilization, common factory accidents, and everyday domestic medical problems (largely relating to dirty cramped, slum-like conditions, and lack of modern drugs and hygiene). Write about advances that were made in the diagnosis, treatment and prevention of disease in Victorian times, and about the steps taken to make towns healthier places. In particular, find out about, and note the significance of, the Public Health Act, passed by Parliament in 1848. Remind children that there was no welfare state at this time – what might happen to poor families who could not afford to pay for a doctor to visit them?

Ask the children to research the lives and work of people such as Elizabeth Blackwell, Dora Pattison (Sister Dora of Walsall), Elizabeth Garrett Anderson, Joseph Lister, Humphrey Davy and Florence Nightingale. What contributions did they make to safety and medical progress?

Write imaginary interviews with key people of the time who dealt with public issues, for example, a policeman in the London Metropolitan Police force, a governor of a prison, and a hospital surgeon. Ask questions and construct replies that illuminate aspects of their work. Throughout this section of the topic, help children to understand how public welfare improved greatly during Victoria's reign. Towns, factories, hospitals, prisons and schools all became much better places in which to spend time.

Study Unit 3a: Victorian Britain – the lives of people at different levels of society in town and country: at home.
Suggested levels of work involved in activities

Activity number	Level	Activity number	Level	Activity number	Level
1	2/3/4/5	4	2/3/4	6	2/3/4/5
2	2/3/4	5	2/3/4	7	2/3/4/5
3	2/3/4				

VICTORIANS AT LEISURE ▶

Activity 1: Victorian entertainments
Find out about the major developments that took place in the entertainment world during Victoria's reign. Theatres flourished before the days of television. Help the children to discover the names of some famous dramatists of the period, such as George Bernard Shaw and Oscar Wilde.

Activity 2: Gilbert and Sullivan
Investigate the work of Gilbert and Sullivan, and remind the pupils that children have been singing 'Onward,

Christian Soldiers' (music by Sullivan) for many years. Listen to more of Sullivan's music, for example, the overtures to *The Mikado, Iolanthe, Yeoman of the Guard* and *The Pirates of Penzance*. Perhaps the children could learn some of the songs – the trio 'If You Go In' is lively and tuneful (and can also stimulate work on proverbs and their meanings afterwards!); whilst any teacher who can execute the 'Nightmare Song' should impress his/her audience considerably, if only for the mental and vocal dexterity required to remember and deliver the lyrics so swiftly. Both songs come from

Iolanthe, and scores/records of this opera are easily obtainable from good music shops.

Provided the story has been explained beforehand, and the children have been familiarised with some of the music, it may be worth while organising a visit to an amateur or professional performance of a Gilbert and Sullivan opera. If such a visit does take place, perhaps the children could afterwards write imaginary accounts of the exciting experience of attending a first-night performance of one of the works of Gilbert and Sullivan.

Activity 3: At the music hall

Paint pictures and write about Victorian music halls – the entertainment venues of the working classes, whose colour and flamboyance ensure the popularity of their songs even today. Learn some well-known music-hall songs, such as 'My Old Man said follow the van', 'Down at the old Bull and Bush', 'Burlington Bertie', 'Boiled beef and carrots', 'If it wasn't for the houses in between', 'Polly Perkins', and 'It's a great big shame'. If there is enough talent among the children, present a music-hall performance in your school. Perhaps members of the teaching staff could perform their 'party pieces' on this occasion?

Activity 4: Sports and pastimes

What sports did the Victorians enjoy? Pupils could investigate this and write illustrated reports of what they discover. What did the players look like in those days?

Background information: Sports and pastimes

Football was growing in popularity during Victoria's reign (the Football Association was formed in 1863, the F.A. Cup competition was first held in 1871, and the English Football League began in 1888). The first cricket Test Match was played in 1880, and lawn tennis started in 1874. Women played tennis, hockey, golf and cricket, usually clad in long skirts and dresses. Both men and women took up cycling, though women wearing trousers were considered to be most unladylike by many old-fashioned Victorians.

Activity 5: On holiday in Victorian times

Ask the children to find out how Victorians spent their leisure time – and particularly about their holidays. Could everyone afford an annual holiday? The children could produce paintings of a seaside scene, complete with bathing machines and ladies bathing dresses. What did the gentlemen wear?

Activity 6: Inventions and discoveries

This aspect of the topic could well be approached by writing illustrated biographies of well-known scientists, artists and writers of the time. Place an emphasis on finding out about achievements which significantly altered the lives of people, or which provide part of our rich cultural heritage, for example:

The discovery of 'wireless telegraphy' by Guglielmo Marconi.
The invention of coded messages by Samuel Morse.
The invention of the telephone by Alexander Graham Bell.

Investigation of the laws of electricity by Michael Faraday.
The theory of evolution propounded by Charles Darwin and supported by Thomas Huxley.
The 'penny post' system introduced by Rowland Hill in 1840.

Other improvements included matches, refrigeration, box-cameras, the phonograph, the bicycle, the steam turbine, typewriters, and (originally in Germany and France) the horseless carriage powered by the internal combustion engine.

Ask the children to make a list of things that have been discovered or invented in the past ten or twenty years, or perhaps in their own lifetime. Explain that these achievements will be part of history when they have children of their own.

Copymaster 43 provides children with full details of the Morse Code, and can be used in a variety of ways. First, explain the significance of the code in the history of communications. Letters and figures are represented by dots and dashes, as shown; dots are short signals, dashes are long ones. The Morse Code could be used with flashing lights, electric impulses, sound and flag movement, and was recognised and understood around the world. When radio was invented, urgent messages could be communicated quickly over long distances. This activity represents an international dimension to the topic, setting Victorian Britain in the context of developments in the wider world. Samuel Morse invented the code in America, and it soon made a significant contribution to the cause of international communications.

Ask the children each to write their name in Morse Code in a space at the foot of the copymaster, and then to write a message that can be decoded by a partner.

Activity 7: The arts

Visit an art gallery to find out about famous artists of the period, and research the names of Victorian writers and poets. Read extracts from the works of Charles Dickens (you could perhaps arrange a viewing of the film *Oliver!*), and explain how his writing helped to publicise some of the social evils of the day. Learn by heart prose extracts or whole poems, which could be recited during your Victorian school day, or during a class assembly which aims to share knowledge about the cultural legacy of the period.

Consider why women writers in Victorian times (such as Ann, Charlotte and Emily Bronte, and Mary Ann Evans) sometimes used men's names instead of their own.

From field evidence, sketch Victorian buildings, and find out more about their architecture and construction. What building materials were commonly in use for the erection of houses and public buildings?

Visit your local library and ask to see newspapers from Victorian times. These will reveal much about fashions, architecture, current affairs and everyday social life during the period. Ask the children to compare and contrast them with present-day newspapers, and to write down any observations they may care to make. The children could even produce

The Houses of Parliament

The Royal Albert Hall

**Nelson's Column
in Trafalgar Square**

their own newspapers about historical events which took place during Victoria's reign, complete with 'photographs', advertisements, editorials, etc.

Activity 8: The Great Exhibition, 1851

To set previous activities in the wider context of the growth of trade and the British Empire, tell the story of the Great Exhibition of 1851 in Hyde Park, London, and its royal opening by Queen Victoria. **Copymaster 44** provides a way of recording some of the items on display, and is a useful means of summarising the importance of British trade and industry at that time. Children can colour the background building, the huge Crystal Palace, made of iron and glass. Ask them to surround the fountain with drawings of objects that were on display, which could include railway engines, ships, agricultural implements, a huge variety of tools and household machines, clocks, and furniture of all kinds. Research on suitable 'gadgets of the day' can be done in museums and art galleries, as well as from books and other documents.

Ask the children to write an account of an imaginary visit to the Crystal Palace. They should tell of what they saw, who was there and what they were wearing, and what snippets of conversation they overheard. In preparation for this writing, discuss such phrases as 'Britain – Workshop of the World', or 'Showpiece of World Industry'.

Background information: The Great Exhibition

The idea for the 'Great Exhibition of the Works of Industry of All Nations' was mainly that of Prince Albert, Victoria's consort. Joseph Paxton designed the Crystal Palace building (1848 feet long and 408 feet wide), and even incorporated several on-site elm trees into his plans.

The Exhibition opened on 1 May, 1851. Admission was 1/-(one shilling) from Monday to Thursday, and 2/6 and 5/- (half a crown and a crown) on Fridays and Saturdays. There were over 100 000 different exhibits, including the Koh-i-Noor diamond, a model locomotive and a fire-engine from Canada, and Samuel Colt's revolvers from America. Queen Victoria wrote of the Exhibition, 'What used to be done by hand, and used to take many months doing, is now accomplished in a few instants by the most beautiful machinery'.

The Exhibition remained open for five months, and over six million people visited it. The Crystal Palace was dismantled afterwards and rebuilt in South London, where it remained until it was destroyed by fire in November, 1936.

The children might like to plan a Great Exhibition of today, or perhaps of the future, and draw pictures of what they think would be on display.

Study Unit 3a: Victorian Britain – the lives of people at different levels of society in town and country: at leisure.
Suggested levels of work involved in activities

Activity number	Level	Activity number	Level	Activity number	Level
1	2/3	4	2/3	7	2/3/4/5
2	2/3	5	2/3	8	2/3/4/5
3	2/3	6	2/3/4/5		

VICTORIANS AT SCHOOL ▶

Activity 1: Spare the rod and spoil the child

Education in Victorian times could be a major sub-topic in its own right. Indeed, the whole topic on Victorian Britain could begin with a comparison of school life today with that of a hundred years or so ago. It is a subject which the children can relate to easily, and one which will be remembered in stories passed down from grandparents and great-grandparents. Few 'Victorians' remain to be consulted, though this may be a possibility: if not, interview family members (of your own or the children's families) to find out about their schools and schooldays. Any information the children can glean will be helpful in comparing and contrasting schools 'then' and 'now'.

Consult a local museum for details of school-related artefacts and photographs. If you are fortunate enough to work in a Victorian school building, then the school itself will provide documentary, photographic and 'concrete' evidence. The illustration opposite gives some idea of what a Victorian classroom was like.

Write the story of a Victorian school child – say, Charlie – who lives in a back-to-back terraced house in any large town or city. Suppose Charlie is eight or nine years old. Describe his experiences in school: what subjects were taught, what teaching methods were used, what equipment was available, and what the discipline was like in those days. Illustrate Charlie's story with drawings of the schoolroom and its significant equipment (including the cane and dunce's cap!).

Find out about the laws which changed education, and the significance of the 1870 Education Act.

Read or tell the children the story of Wackford Squeers and Dotheboys Hall from *Nicholas Nickeby* by Charles Dickens. They could imagine being a pupil there, and write about life under such a harsh regime.

Activity 2: A Victorian day at school

Turn your own classroom into a Victorian schoolroom for a day. Arrange the desks in strict rows facing the teacher's, which should be raised on a dais, if possible. Imitate the traditional high windows, if necessary by partly covering modern windows with black paper so that the children cannot see out of them. It is perhaps best to undertake this activity when other work on the Victorian era has been completed, so that the classroom walls are covered with atmospheric displays of portraits of Victoria, industrial towns, and Britain's importance in international trade. Many local museums will lend artefacts to 'decorate' a Victorian schoolroom.

Use **Copymaster 45** to help the children dress appropriately for a Victorian school day (they should colour the drawings after consulting paintings and reference books). Boys should wear dark-coloured clothing, with long socks over trouser bottoms, and the heaviest shoes (or boots) they possess. Make 'Eton' collars out of thin white card. Girls should wear dark skirts or dresses, as full in length as possible. Make white pinafores (from paper, if necessary) to cover these dresses. Finishing touches for the girls are dark tights and boots or heavy shoes. Introduce vocabulary associated with this Victorian dress, including 'Eton collar', 'boater', 'blazer', 'cummerbund' and 'pinafore'. Don't forget that you should dress as closely to the Victorian style as possible, too. Long hair should be tied up in a bun, and a visit to a local theatrical costumier might well be a benefit, since it is important to set as high a standard of authenticity as possible. Perhaps another adult could be persuaded to play the part of the School Inspector.

Conduct your school day with appropriate lessons and routines. The children should be seated in alphabetical order, with boys and girls separated. They should stand to greet you with a chant of 'Good morning …' or 'Good afternoon …', and wait until they are asked to be seated. They should, of course, stand when any adult (such as the head teacher or the School Inspector) enters. Make sure the children sit still, upright and are quiet at all times. Lesson content could include writing on slates, counting with 'old' money,

70

chanting tables, handwriting practice, reciting poetry and doing 'drill'. Discuss which aspects of an authentic Victorian school day are not being put into practice (for example, having as many as fifty children in the room: caning them for misbehaviour or poor work: making individual pupils the class dunce, or tying them up in a sack!). If the school has access to a video camera, the proceedings could be recorded and become a useful resource for future work.

A typically moralising Victorian poem, which could be learned by heart or used for handwriting practice, is available on an activity sheet from Sudbury Hall Museum. Part of it is quoted opposite:

Background information: Victorian childhood
Teachers in the Midlands wishing to give their classes a fascinating glimpse into childhood would find a visit to Sudbury Hall and its Museum of Childhood a most rewarding experience. Sudbury Hall is situated in the village of Sudbury, near Derby. The museum contains exhibits of childhood memorabilia ranging from lead soldiers and boardgames to teddy bears and large dolls' houses. There is an Edwardian nursery and a school-room, and the Museum also produces an extremely stimulating and comprehensive teaching pack, crammed with activities and background information.

Obedience to Parents

Let children that would fear the Lord,
Hear what their teachers say;
With reverence meet their parent' word,
And with delight obey.

Have you not heard what dreadful plagues
Are threatened by the Lord,
To him that breaks his father's law,
Or mocks his mother's word?

But those who worship God, and give
their parents honour due,
Here on this earth they long shall live,
And live hereafter too.

Study Unit 3a: Victorian Britain – the lives of people at different levels of society in town and country: at school.
Suggested levels of work involved in activities

Activity number	Level	Activity number	Level
1	2/3/4/5	2	2/3/4/5

RESOURCES ▶

Non-fiction

Allen E. *Keeping Clean*, Turn of the Century Series, A & C Black, 1991.

Evans, D. *How We Used To Live: Victorians Early and Late*, A & C Black, 1991.

Lawrie, J. *Victorian Times*, Collins.

Shuter, J. *Victorian Britain*, Our World Series, Heinemann.

Stoppleman, M. *School Day*, Turn of the Century Series, A & C Black, 1991.

Tanner, G. *Rubbish* and *Breakfast*, both from the Turn of the Century Series, A & C Black, 1991.

Thomson, E. *In the Post* and *Washday*, both from the Turn of the Century Series, A & C Black, 1991.

Victorian Britain, History in Evidence Series, Wayland.

Family Life in Victorian Britain, Family Life Series, Wayland.

The Victorians, Look into the Past Series, Wayland.

A Victorian Christmas, Victorian Life Series, Wayland.

Victorian Britain, Primary History Series, Collins.

Victorian Britain, Oxford Primary History Series.

Fiction for younger readers

Goodall, J. *Victorians Abroad*, Macmillan, 1980. Pictures describe the customs and behaviour of Victorians on their travels.*

Ahlberg, *Mr Tick the Teacher*, Viking Kestrel, 1985. Turn-of-the-century story about a small village school. One of the 'Happy Families' series.

Avery, G. *Mouldy's Orphan*, Penguin, 1981. A small girl takes home an orphan ... but her parents have little enough to feed their own family.

Bull, A. *The Visitors*, Heinemann, 1986. Queen Victoria stays in a remote Scottish inn.*

Cresswell, H. *Time Out*, Lutterworth, 1987. Tweeny lives in a household in 1887, where her father is the butler. They are transported to 1987 for a holiday.*

Darke, M. *Kipper's Turn*, Blackie, 1976. A story of children struggling to survive in London in the 1880s.*

Darke, M. *Kipper Skips*, Blackie, 1979. Includes description of school life in Victorian England.*

Garfield, L. *Fair's Fair*, Simon & Schuster, 1983. Cold and hungry in the streets at Christmas, an urchin shares his pie with a dog – with happy results.

Lively, P. *Fanny and the Monsters*, Heinemann, 1983. Fanny is taken to the Crystal Palace for a birthday treat. Plenty of background on the proper behaviour for little girls.

*These books are out of print but are still available from libraries and second-hand bookshops.

Fiction for more competent readers

The following stories are more demanding in terms of reading stamina. They provide useful background, and selected passages could be read aloud.

Aitken, J. *Midnight is a Place*, Red Fox, 1991. Imaginative and evocative tale of children in early industrial Britain.

Burnett, F.H. *The Little Princess*, Puffin, 1984. Sara Crewe is a pupil at a Select Seminary ... until her fortunes change.

Burnett, F.H. *The Secret Garden*, Armada, 1988. Orphaned girl from India starts a new life in Victorian Yorkshire.

Burton, H. *The Henchmans at home*, OUP, 1970. Six stories centred around life in a small Suffolk town.*

Cross, G. *The Iron Way*, OUP, 1990. Conflict between the navvies and Sussex villagers, as the railways bring steam engines to previously peaceful countryside.

Edwards, D. *A Strong and Willing Girl*, Methuen, 1980. Domestic service during Victoria's reign.

Kingsley, C. *Water Babies*, Gollancz, 1986. Classic tale about child chimney-sweeps.

Scobie, *Twist of Fate*, OUP, 1990. Powerful story of children in the cotton mills.

Tomlinson, T. *Flither pickers*, Julia MacRae, 1990. Moving story set amongst the fisher-folk of the north-east coast, in the late nineteenth century. Illustrated by contemporary photographs.

Turner, P. *Steam on the Line*, OUP, 1968. A story about the coming of the railways. Not everyone welcomed the advance of this new form of transport.*

Poetry

First Golden Treasury of Children's Verse, Macmillan, 1989. Victorian and Edwardian rhymes.*

Stevenson, R. L. *A Child's Garden of Verses*, Gollancz, 1985. First published in 1885, this collection speaks of Victorian childhood, and includes poems such as *The Lamplighter*.

Blueprints links

You will find the following other Stanley Thornes books useful: *Investigating History: Life in Victorian Britain.*

STUDY UNIT 3b
BRITAIN SINCE
1930

Pupils should be taught about the lives of men, women and children at different levels of society in Britain and the ways in which they were affected by the Second World War and changes in technology and transport:

Changes in technology and transport	**a**	changes in industry and transport, including the impact of new technologies, *e.g. motor cars, computers, space travel;*
Britons at war	**b**	the impact of the Second World War on the people of Britain, *e.g. evacuation, the Blitz, the armed forces, rationing.*
The lives of people at different levels of society in different parts of Britain	**c**	at home, *e.g. family life at different levels of society, housing conditions, diet and health, changes in the roles of men and women;*
	d	at work, *e.g. the Depression, changes in employment, automation, men and women at work, emigration and immigration;*
	e	at leisure, *e.g. radio, cinema and television, the Festival of Britain, sport, holidays.*

TOPIC WEB

Changes in technology and transport

- Changes in industry and business
- The European Union
- Travel and transport
- New technologies

Everyday life

- At work
- At home
- At leisure

BRITAIN SINCE 1930

Britons at War

- The impact of WWII on the people of Britain
- Education and blitz
- The armed forces
- Rationing
- VE Day
- The first atom bomb
- The work of women

73

CHANGES IN TECHNOLOGY AND TRANSPORT

Pupils should be taught about the following:

Changes in industry and transport   **a** the impact of new technologies, *e.g. motor cars, computers, space travel*

Activity 1: Britain as a world power

Copymasters 46 and **47** will provide a dramatic presentation of Britain's changing role as a world power in recent years. The map on **Copymaster 46** shows the British Empire as it was in 1914. Ask the children to colour the areas within the Empire in red, and then to look them up in an atlas or on a globe. On the map on **Copymaster 47**, colour in red the areas still under the British crown. Consider the difference between the two maps. What happened to the other nations in the empire? Have some of them changed their names? If so, add appropriate labels on the second map, and discuss the reasons for the changes.

Investigate some examples of changing patterns in industrial production. Represent findings diagrammatically, for example:

Cotton and woollen   *because*   demand increased for
mills declined   man-made fibres, e.g.
                                  Bri-Nylon, Terylene.

Other examples could include the decline in iron and steel manufacture (due to increased demand for other materials, such as plastics); and the decline in the coal industry (due to the growing use of other forms of power, including electricity and nuclear power). Perhaps the children could be divided into small groups to research the changing patterns and fortunes of some of these traditional industries.

Activity 2: The technological revolution

Again, the scope is very wide indeed and any project must be selective. There is probably no better way of introducing this aspect of study than by using a calculator and/or a computer program. Set the children a number of increasingly difficult calculations (depending on age and ability) and use a stopwatch to time how long these take to complete using just paper and pencils. Then ask the children to do the mathematics again, with a calculator to help them, and time the operation again. How much time was saved by using the new technology –for one person? What does that imply for the entire class? How much time could be saved over the whole country? In a day? In a week? In a year?

Another demonstration involves explaining and setting up a simple spreadsheet on a computer, with the facility to total the figures automatically at the foot of each column. Type in several columns of figures (say, lists of marks for a fictional group of pupils), and let the children see how the computer automatically keeps a running total as each new number is added. Once again, the children could attempt to total the same lists of figures manually, and then by calculator, and compare the time taken to complete these tasks. It may be possible to demonstrate other aspects of information storage and retrieval. There are numerous computer programs currently available, ranging from databases and simulations, to a program that works like a cricket scoreboard and simultaneously keeps track of the batsmen's runs, the team total and the bowlers' analyses.

How many of the children have a computer or word-processor at home? What is it used for? Help them to realise that, while they have access to new technology and may be computer-literate, many of their parents and grandparents will not be so fortunate. Find out how long computers have been commonplace in schools, and about the impact of their use on the worlds of business, industry and commerce. Perhaps some of the children's parents work with computers. If so, invite them to describe their occupations, and explain how new technology has changed their work and working methods in recent years.

Remind the children that calculators and computers are not infallible, and explain the expression 'Garbage in, garbage out'.

Write about the silicon chip, its discovery, use and impact on our lives. Find out where 'Silicon Valley' is located, and how it got this unusual name. (Silicon Valley is in California, the heart of the United States' computer research and development industry.)

Activity 3: The rise of big business

Consider the trend towards the domination of industry by large international companies. Before 1930, it was far more common to find family businesses and very small manufacturing establishments. Find out who are the 'giants' of today and investigate where some of the multi-national companies (e.g. Shell and ICI) trade and have their headquarters. Introduce associated concepts and vocabulary, such as 'competition', 'take-over' and 'subsidiary'. (This aspect of the topic has excellent potential for links with the cross-curricular theme of economic and industrial understanding.) Help the children to understand that these have been key concepts in British industry in recent years, which have affected consumers, producers and the nature of Britain's role in world trade.

Activity 4: The European Union

Help the children to understand the significance of the European Union, and the effect that this has had on British trade and industry. Talk about why it was called a 'Common Market', and about its origins and development. Provide an outline map of Europe so that children can shade in and label member countries. Discuss the significance of 1992 in the history of Europe.

Activity 5: Travel trends

Help the children to appreciate that economic and industrial developments since 1930 are closely related to changes in transport. The increase in air travel, for example, resulted in a huge decline in the shipping of passengers, with a knock-on effect for the shipbuilding industry. Divide the class into working groups, each to research a different aspect of changes in transport since 1930. This work will include the rise of the family motor car as a common form of transport; the dramatic increase in air travel; and developments on the railways. In 1948, the railway companies of Britain – the Great Western Railway; the London, Midland and Scottish; the London and North Eastern Railways; and the Southern Railway – were nationalised and became British Railways. Ask each group to report back with details of general trends, and pictures of the latest developments, e.g. Concorde, high-speed intercity trains and the latest styles of family car.

Discuss how these changes in transport have affected many other aspects of our lives, both directly and indirectly. The list is a long one, and may include:

- Cars have altered the shapes of houses, most of which now have garages built alongside them.
- Holidays are now far easier to organise.
- Because of high-speed trains, people can live many miles away from their work and commute every day.
- Because of air travel, foreign foods are far more readily available.
- Far more people are killed or injured because of traffic accidents.
- Transport fumes increasingly pollute the natural world.

Illustrate the above list on posters, augmented with other facts suggested by the children, and arrange these in a display entitled 'On the move in modern times – Good News and Bad News'.

The children might like to try to imagine what transport and travel in the future will be like. Once again, encourage them to make intelligent predictions based on the latest scientific ideas and forecasts, together with trends and inventions. This is a subject which should stimulate a good deal of imaginative writing, and artwork of all kinds.

Activity 6: Space travel

Undertake a sub-topic on space travel, to include the exciting story of the Apollo XI mission, and the first man landing on the moon in 1969. Build up a space-flight timeline, together with illustrated accounts of space flights and astronauts. Below are some dates to start you off.

This sub-topic affords ample scope for creative writing and artwork of all kinds. A useful source of inspiration in terms of model-making is the book *Space-Age Craft* by B. R. M. Targett and M. C. Green, published by Harrap.

1957	Sputnik 1 (USSR) is launched.
1961	Yuri Gagarin (USSR) is the first man in space.
1963	Valentina Tereschkova (USSR) is the first woman in space.
1965	Aleksei Leonov (USSR) makes the first space walk.
1966	Luna 9 (USSR) makes the first soft landing on the moon.
1968	First manned flight of Apollo series – Apollo 7 (USA).
1969	Neil Armstrong and Edwin Aldrin are the first men to walk on the surface of the moon – Apollo 11.
1971	The Moon Rover is first used – Apollo 15.
1972	The last of the Apollo missions to the moon – Apollo 17.

Study Unit 3b: Britain since 1930 – changes in technology and transport.
Suggested levels of work involved in activities

Activity number	Level	Activity number	Level	Activity number	Level
1	2/3/4/5	3	2/3/4/5	5	2/3/4/5
2	2/3/4/5	4	2/3/4/5		

BRITONS AT WAR

Pupils should be taught about the following:

Britons at war

b the impact of the Second World War on the people of Britain, *e.g. evacuation, the Blitz, the armed forces, rationing*

Activity 1: A War 'museum'

By far the best way of tackling this dimension of the project is to collect together a 'museum' of artefacts which bring the days of wartime 'alive' for the children. It may be possible to establish your own collection of suitable objects, for example, photographs, a gas-mask, ration books, articles of clothing, a soldier's identity card, medals, tin helmets, weapons, etc. Be aware of safety at all times; and impress upon the children the need to take great care of precious items which have been loaned, and of the courtesy of returning them in perfect condition with a letter of thanks. If the establishment of such a display of treasures is not possible, then a local history museum may have a loan service for schools. War is a very difficult concept for children to grasp, and the great effect that wartime days had on home life will seem very remote from the freedom we enjoy today.

As well as collecting your own artefacts, see if your local museum has a wartime display. Ideally, take the children to see the wonderful displays of the Imperial War Museum in London. This museum also has a wide collection of postcards, wartime posters, transparencies, leaflets and other memorabilia available for purchase. During term-time, film shows and illustrated talks can be arranged, though children attending these should be aged ten years or older. The address of the museum is as follows: Imperial War Museum, Lambeth Road, London SE1 6HZ. Enquiries should be addressed to the Keeper of the Department of Education and Publications.

Study a map of Europe at the time of the war and compare it with a map of modern-day Europe. What, if any, changes can be noticed?

Europe at the outbreak of war in 1939

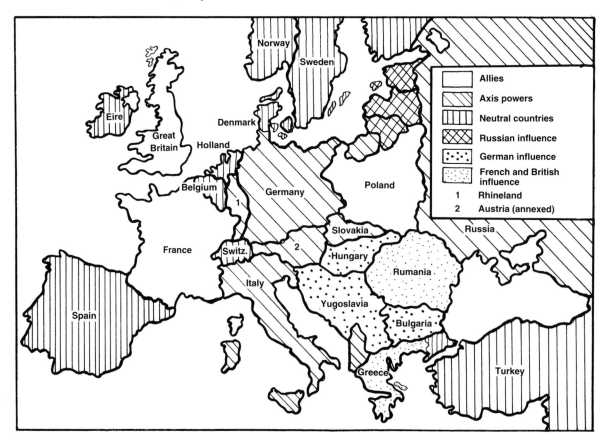

Activity 2: The local effects of war

Find out about the impact of the war on your local area. Visit your library and ask to look at wartime newspapers. Copy down some of the headlines and try to find out about some key events that happened locally. Here are ideas on what to look for:

- What is the name of the newspaper and does it still exist?
- What is the date of the edition you are studying?
- What is the main story or headline about?
- Are any famous people mentioned?
- What fashions were people wearing in those days?
- What sorts of goods were being advertised?
- How much did they cost? (How much is this nowadays?)
- What were schools like?
- How did children amuse themselves in those days?
- Who or what is mentioned on the sports pages?
- What sorts of entertainment are advertised?

As well as looking at newspapers for leads into stories, investigate the locality through fieldwork. Look for plaques commemorating soldiers who lost their lives, war memorials, and evidence from gravestones. Explain the significance of Remembrance Sunday and the sale of poppies every year.

Your local library may also have photographs of the area dating from before or during the war. Compare this evidence with the appearance of the locality today. Were any key buildings destroyed by air raids? Maps will also be helpful for this activity. Compare large-scale, pre-war maps with up-to-date ones. Note any significant changes, bearing in mind that other factors besides the war may have brought these about.

Looking at newspapers is an excellent way of introducing 'wartime vocabulary' – Nazi bombers, British Command, warning from Hitler, Japan surrenders, etc. Establish a 'Dictionary of World War II'. As the study progresses, note down key words, including the names of people, accompanied by suitable definitions and explanations. Assemble these into a loose-leaf book with illustrations. This will form useful reference material that the class itself has compiled. Children with access to technology could record the information in a World War II database.

Activity 3: Fighting talk

Talk to people who have memories of wartime and, if possible, invite some of them to come to school and share their reminiscences with the children. Ask if they have any objections to the use of a tape-recorder. Their stories will provide a wealth of facts and background material for both creative and factual writing, and a well-edited tape-recording of such visits can be a useful item of oral history for the future, too. Remind the children to thank your visitors afterwards.

If possible, the visitors should be from different backgrounds who spent time during the war in various areas of the country. This will help the children to gain a wider understanding of the effects of war on different parts of Britain, for example, the major cities were often subjected to heavy bombing raids, while more rural areas escaped this. And inevitably, no two people's experiences will be the same!

Prepare for these interviews by structuring questions or subjects for discussion, for example, housing, food and its rationing, evacuation, air-raids, clothing, education. Ask invited guests if they have any artefacts which they could bring and talk about, or perhaps lend to your classroom 'museum'. An activity such as this needs very careful preparation (of both children and guests), so that maximum benefit is gained from the experience.

Activity 4: You're in the army now!

Copymaster 48 will provide an introductory activity or a cover for topic books. After consulting reference books and photographs, the children can colour the drawing authentically. Then ask them to draw four important objects that a soldier needed during the war, in the blank spaced provided. Compare finished results – between them, the children should have drawn a wide range of artefacts associated with military life.

Taking each of the drawn objects in turn, ask the children to write a sentence about its importance and use. With luck, some of these things will be available in your classroom 'museum'. Add the work to the ongoing 'Dictionary of World War II'.

Write stories about 'A soldier at war' – his duties, his regime, his fears and hopes. The children could try to write a page or two from his diary, perhaps before and after a great battle. What emotions and events do they think those pages might contain?

Activity 5: Evacuation and blitz

Write and illustrate stories about evacuation. These can be entirely fictitious, or based on true stories told by classroom visitors and children's relatives. Ask the children to explain how they think they would feel if they were suddenly faced with the prospect of leaving home to be evacuated to the country. Some pupils may have been separated from their parents, perhaps for a stay in hospital, and may be able to remember how they felt at the time.

Imaginative stories can be written about 'The Raid'. Ask children to describe the hours spent in an air-raid shelter, listening to the sound of sirens and distant explosions. How was the time spent? What was in the shelter? They should try to describe the feelings of anticipation and gloom as people emerged from the shelter not knowing what the street outside would look like …

Draw pictures of a street scene before a raid, and the devastation left in its wake afterwards. Find out about the work of the bomb-disposal men, and the air-raid wardens. Why were people asked to 'Put that light out!'?

Many children will be familiar with the BBC TV comedy series *Dad's Army*. Whilst being a successful programme in its own right, the children may learn from it much about the 'home front' by careful observation of costumes, prices, settings and situations. In the interests of balance, a group of children could find out more about the real Home Guard (originally the Local Defence Volunteers), and what they intended to do had Hitler invaded Britain. The class could learn to sing the theme song of the series, 'Who do you think you are kidding, Mr Hitler?', and perhaps write a second verse of their own to fit the tune.

The *Dad's Army* theme is available on a LP record entitled *BBC Comedy Themes*, issued in 1980 on the BBC record label (Number REH 387); and also on an earlier record of *Angels and 15 other original BBC TV themes* (Number REB 236, from 1976). The sheet music was originally sold by the Southern Music Publishing Company Ltd, 8 Denmark Street, London WC2H 8LT.

Blitz	The bombing of British cities during the war. The word comes from the German 'blitzkrieg', meaning 'lightning war'.
Gas-mask	A mask to protect people from breathing in poisonous gases that might have been released by the enemy.

Activity 6: Get the message?

Copymaster 49 introduces children to the style and design of war-time posters, and can be coloured and discussed. The words needed to fill the gaps in the sentence at the foot of the sheet are 'waste', 'money', 'War' and 'swastikas'. What was the Squander Bug? Follow up this activity by asking the children to design other posters based on authentic messages of the time. For example, they could advertise the government's 'Dig For Victory' campaign, which aimed to encourage people to grow their own food.

Activity 7: Make do and mend

Relate a discussion on the 'Dig For Victory' campaign to the need for food rationing. Study authentic ration books and food coupons, and find out how the system of rationing was supposed to work. Talk about the implications of these measures. Look up war-time recipes and discover how people 'made do' with such a limited range of food. It may be possible to build up a class recipe/cookery book to explain and illustrate ingredients available, typical meals of the time, and unusual recipes designed to cope with the situation. Seek the help of relatives and classroom visitors, who may remember 'dishes of the war'. Who were Potato Pete and Dr Carrot?

Background information: *Food rationing*

Opposite is a basic list of food rations per person per week. The quantities varied during the war years, depending on availability.

Recipes for such delicacies as War and Peace Pudding, Carrot Croquettes, Carrot Soup, Carrot

Savoury and Chestnut Stew can be found in *How We Used To Live, 1925–1945* by Freda Kelsall, a book to accompany the excellent Yorkshire Television schools programme of the same name and first published by MacDonald Educational in 1976. Other recipes to look out for include Pilchard Layer Loaf, Fish in Savoury Custard and Woolton Pie (see below) which was named after the then Minister of Food, Lord Woolton.

Woolton Pie

Cooking time: about 1 hour

This is an adaptable recipe that you can change according to the ingredients you have available.

Dice and cook about 1lb of each of the following in salted water: potatoes (you could use parsnips if topping the pie with mashed potatoes), cauliflower, swedes, carrots – you could add turnips too. Strain but keep $\frac{3}{4}$ pint of the vegetable water.

Arrange the vegetables in a large pie-dish or casserole. Add a little vegetable extract and about 1oz rolled oats or oatmeal to the vegetable liquid. Cook until thickened and pour over the vegetables: add 3–4 chopped spring onions.

Top with potato pastry or with mashed potatoes and a very little grated cheese and heat in the centre of a moderately hot oven until golden brown. Serve with brown gravy.

This is at its best with tender young vegetables.

Play a record or tape of the song 'When can I have a banana again?', and explain the effect of war on Britain's merchant shipping. Why did the Germans attack allied convoys?

Food rationing per person

Food	Weekly allowance
Bacon or ham	4–8 oz
Cheese	1–8 oz
Butter	1–8 oz
Eggs	$\frac{1}{2}$–4
Milk	$\frac{1}{2}$–2 pints
Tea	2–4 oz
Sugar	8–16 oz
Sweets and chocolate	2–4 oz
National Dried Milk	1 tin (= 4 pints) every 4 weeks
Dried eggs	1 packet (= 12 eggs) every 8 weeks

Activity 8: VE Day

What do the letters VE stand for? When was VE Day? Can any friend or relative tell the children what they remember of the event? Did this mean that the war was really over?

Paint a large 'victory' scene, with street parties and celebrations to mark the end of the war. Prepare for this by reading newspapers of the time and consulting photographs and books. It may also be possible to obtain a videotape of cinema newsreel extracts for the year 1945, which would give the children a flavour of the nation's feelings of relief when the war was finally over. Parkfield have produced a series of one-hour VHS video cassettes featuring extracts from Pathe newsreels of years past, including the 1939–45 period. Help the children to understand the political dimensions, with reminders of who had been fighting whom and for what reasons, and who the victors were and why.

Add writing around your frieze to explain the nature of the victory and its significance; and decorate it with real flags (of Britain and the allies) and with strings of coloured ribbon or crepe paper. Discuss why street parties were held – why are such occurrences not common today? Can the children remember any events in the more recent past that have been celebrated in the streets?

Activity 9: The first atom bombs

This section of study could lead to a sub-topic on the atomic age, if time permits. Organise a class debate on nuclear weapons, or nuclear activity in general. Prepare for this by considering the dropping of the atomic bomb on Hiroshima and on Nagasaki in 1945, together with its effects, implications and significance in the course of events of World War II.

Construct pictures of the Hiroshima explosion, with its well-known 'mushroom' cloud: a 3-D effect could probably be created by using cotton wool and paint. Surround or superimpose upon the cloud words which the children feel are appropriate to describe the atmosphere such pictures create. Help them to understand the political significance of nuclear weapons in the world today, and the potential nature of a third world war. Be sure to maintain a balance of opinion, for the sake of objectivity.

Activity 10: The work of women

As a sub-topic leading neatly into the issue of wider social changes, the children could consider how the role of women in Britain changed with the outbreak of war. The work of men who had joined the forces still had to be done, and it was the women of Britain who led the way. Discuss with the children what 'reserved occupations' were in war-time. Ask the children to investigate the kinds of work that women did in those

> She's the girl that makes the thing that drills the hole that holds the spring
> That drives the rod that turns the knob that works the thingumabob.
> She's the girl that makes the thing that holds the oil, that oils the ring
> That makes the shank that moves the crank that works the thingumabob.
> It's a ticklish sort of job,
> Making a thingumabob,
> Especially when you don't know what it's for!
> But it's the girl that makes the thing that drills the hole that holds the spring
> That works the thingumabob that makes the engine roar.
> And it's the girl that makes the thing that holds the oil that oils the ring
> That works the thingumabob THAT'S GOING TO WIN THE WAR.

days. Armed with this knowledge, they can draw pictures of women doing 'war work' to complete **Copymaster 50**. Above are the words of a popular song of the Second World War, which could be sung by the children in parts.

Background information: *The work of women*

In war-time, women worked in both industry (making munitions, ships, bombers and fighter aircraft) and in agriculture (the Women's Land Army helped to grow more crops, to fell trees and to keep the sawmills working). They drove buses, fire-engines and ambulances. The Women's Auxiliary Forces worked in anti-aircraft batteries, drove and serviced army trucks, operated radio transmitters, repaired all sorts of military equipment, and even flew new aircraft from the factory to various R.A.F. bases. A fortunate few even got the same rate of pay as the men! Caroline Lang's short book *Keep Smiling Through: Women in the Second World War* (from the 'Women in History' series published by the Cambridge University Press in 1989) contains many fascinating snippets and accounts of personal experiences which would interest the children.

Study Unit 3b: Britain since 1930 – Britons at war. Suggested levels of work involved in activities

Activity number	Level	Activity number	Level	Activity number	Level
1	2/3/4/5	5	2/3/4/5	8	2/3/4/5
2	2/3/4/5	6	2/3	9	2/3/4/5
3	2/3/4/5	7	2/3	10	2/3/4/5
4	2/3/4/5				

THE LIVES OF PEOPLE AT DIFFERENT LEVELS OF SOCIETY IN DIFFERENT PARTS OF BRITAIN

C51–54

Pupils should be taught about:

the lives of people at different levels of society in different parts of Britain

c at home, *e.g. family life at different levels of society, housing conditions, diet and health, changes in the roles of men and women;*

d at work, *e.g. the Depression, changes in employment, automation, men and women at work, emigration and immigration;*

e at leisure, *e.g. radio, cinema and television, the Festival of Britain, sport, holidays.*

AT HOME

Activity 1: The times they are a-changing

This is a vast period of time to cover, and one which has seen dramatic changes in family life and the roles of men and women in society. One approach would be to consider each decade at a time and research the social scene. This could be done as a class activity, or groups of children could focus on a specific decade before reporting back to the class as a whole. Key conclusions can then be drawn on trends throughout the period.

Make scrapbooks for each decade since (and including) the 1930s, incorporating photographs, drawings, written accounts and details of stories from newspapers. Many of the research activities suggested for the war-time period are appropriate here: for example, visit the local reference library and/or the nearest museum and ask to see newspapers, maps and photographs of the area; go out into the neighbourhood and look for evidence of how houses, schools and other public buildings have changed in their styles, architecture and functions. Ask people to come into your classroom and talk about growing up in the 1930s (40s, 50s, 60s, 70s, 80s). As before, such interviews should be carefully structured.

Activity 2: Any questions?

Ask the children to devise a list of appropriate questions, based on **Copymaster 51**, which is an initial record sheet for the interviews mentioned in Activity 1. No date or decade is stated, so the sheet can be copied for use with a range of interviewees. Space is left for a 'portrait' of the person being interviewed. The children's own questions (a vital addition) can be written on the back.

This activity gives practice in the skills involved in recording the essential features of what people have to say. Help the children to understand that they should note 'key words' associated with each answer, rather than trying to write down everything the person says. The aim is brief recording, while listening carefully and

remembering. Detailed accounts can be written up later.

Compile a list of the aspects of life that the interviews might cover, for example, houses, school, work, neighbours, food, clothing, sport and games. If this is done, sensible comparisons can eventually be made between decades, and trends through time can be teased out. It is easy to fall into the trap of just asking people to come and talk to a class, without planning any structure for the session: the event will be far more useful if set within guidelines. Always ask the guest if he or she minds if the children tape-record the proceedings and take photographs.

Activity 3: Social changes timeline

Make a 'timeline of social change' by assembling a collection of photographs of men, women and children through recent decades. This will reveal substantial changes in clothing, houses, holidays, etc. A good way to begin is by showing the children photographs of yourself as a baby, as a young child and as a teenager, together with photographs of your own parents, grandparents, and perhaps your own children. This activity can be related to work in family trees, which will be useful for many of the Study Units.

Ask each interviewee what he or she considers to be the most significant changes or events in his/her life so far. Note the replies, and eventually build up an overall picture of trends and alterations in attitudes.

Make a collection of drawings/pictures of household objects in common use today, mounted individually on cards (see opposite). Ask single children, pairs or groups to select a card and trace the development of their object. Provide questions to guide this investigation, such as:

How long has this item been part of our everyday lives?
What did earlier versions of it (if any) look like?
Where did it originate?

Make outline drawings of a typical house of the period (1930s, 40, 50s, etc.) with cut-away walls. Sketch in objects that might have been located in each room. The example below shows a house of the 1950s. Line up a variety of these houses in chronological order on a long

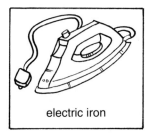

electric iron

tinned food

vacuum cleaner

freezer and frozen food

wall-frieze. This will demonstrate significant changes through time 'at a glance'. More ambitious children might like to make dioramas or other models of rooms or houses.

As children talk to people about decades gone by, read stories and consult record books, photographs and artefacts, the changes in British ways of life caused by immigration and emigration will begin to unfold. Help the children to understand that the multicultural atmosphere of the UK today has not always existed. This issue will be of more immediate significance to young learners in inner-city areas, who can trace the histories of families with a variety of ethnic backgrounds. If your school is not in a multicultural area, set up a pen-friend correspondence or make exchange visits with a suitable city school.

Consult reference books and produce a number of cut-out card figures of men, women and children dressed in costumes from each decade since 1930; or construct freestanding figures and 'dress' them appropriately. Line these up beneath your wall-frieze of

houses, and try to include as wide a cross-section of British society as possible. Costume through the ages is a fascinating and colourful topic that several groups may wish to investigate in greater depth.

Activity 4: Leaving school
Leaving school is another excellent topic for illustrating social change. Ask the children to write about what people in the various decades might have done after leaving school. What qualifications were available to them? What were their expectations and those of their families? This should lead to conclusions about the changing roles and aspirations of men and women in our society. Ask pupils to write illustrated accounts of what they hope to do upon leaving school. Read these out to the rest of the class, and discuss whether the ambitions are realistic. Would they have been possible twenty years ago? Fifty years ago?

Organise a class debate on 'Doing the housework'. No doubt, boys and girls will have very different points of view about whose job this is!

Activity 5: That's no job for a woman
Illustrate the changing roles of women in recent years with references to specific people and job opportunities. For example, consider the personality and significance of Margaret Thatcher as the first female Prime Minister, the ecclesiastical debate about women and the priesthood, and the gender-neutral language of job advertisements. Look at newspapers from the past and compare the wording of advertisements in the employment sections with modern equivalents (see mock-ups below).

Activity 6: Many faiths, one God
Relate earlier discussions on immigration and the nature of our modern multi-ethnic society to the concept of multi-faith Britain. Religious change cannot be separated from social and cultural change. If your study of this unit follows that of the Victorian period, remind the children of the very significant influence of religion on the everyday lives of the Victorians, and then ask for their views on whether religion still exerts the same influence today.

Find out about the churches and other places of worship in your neighbourhood, their names and

---

BARMAN WANTED

to work lunchtimes and evenings in our busy, friendly hostelry.

Apply to **Barney's Bar**

BAR PERSON WANTED

to work lunchtimes and evenings in our busy, friendly hostelry.

Apply to **Barney's Bar**

**MANAGER REQUIRED
for busy
car-hire business**

The man we are looking for . . .

**MANAGER REQUIRED
for busy
car-hire business**

The man/woman we are looking for . . .

---

denominations. If possible, visit one or more of them and discover more about their services and activities.

Children could debate the rights and wrongs of Sunday trading.

Activity 7: Matters for concern

Pose the question: what are people most concerned about in the world these days? (This question could be considered for each decade.) Answers for the 1990s will inevitably include the threat of nuclear war and damage to the environment. Discuss why environmental concern is a fairly recent issue, connecting it to scientific and ecological discoveries, and increasing public awareness of global problems. Integrate work on specific environmental issues with cross-curricular environmental studies.

Use **Copymaster 52** as a record sheet to highlight some of the key problematic issues that people have had to face during this period. Ask the children to colour the pictures, read the 'bubbles', and then write in each box the year or years that they think are applicable. Reading across each row from the left, the relevant years are 1939–1945, 1974, the 1950s, 1982, the 1990s and the 1960s.

Activity 8: Transplant surgery

Consider the tremendous advances that medical science has made in recent decades. Make a study of the work of Professor Christian Barnard, who replaced a human heart for the first time in 1967. Discuss the ethics and implications of this.

Activity 9: A royal timeline

Copymaster 53 can be introduced at the beginning of this unit for ongoing recording, or used as a summary 'quiz' at the end. It provides a way of listing key events, and setting them in the context of the royal succession. Use the narrow centre column to insert selected dates. Ask the children to record the related events on the left hand side of the page, and to draw small pictures as space permits. On the right-hand side they should write significant events in the life of the Royal Family. The events included will obviously need to be carefully selected (a skill worth encouraging), so ask the children to record only events which they consider to have has a very substantial influence on the course of history. These might include:

Abdication of Edward VIII
Accession of George VI
Second World War
Festival of Britain
Accession of Elizabeth II
First landing on the moon
Entry of Britain into the EEC
The first woman Prime Minister
Marriage and children of the Prince of Wales
First flight of Concorde

Study Unit 3b: Britain since 1930 – lives of people at different levels of society in different parts of Britain: at home. Suggested levels of work involved in activities

Activity number	Level	Activity number	Level	Activity number	Level
1	2/3/4/5	4	2/3/4/5	7	2/3/4/5
2	2/3/4/5	5	2/3/4/5	8	2/3/4/5
3	2/3/4/5	6	2/3/4/5	9	2/3/4/5

AT WORK

Activity 1: Factory life – then and now

Discuss parallel changes that have taken place in factory life and working conditions. Talk to people who work on factory production lines today, and ask them to describe their duties and environment. If possible, visit a modern factory. Compare the light, pleasant atmosphere of modern industrial buildings with the grim, airless establishments of days gone by. Write about a day in the life of a factory worker – which will, no doubt, include regular breaks, access to a canteen, and adherence to strict guidelines about health and safety procedures, including protective clothing.

Organise a class debate on the motion that 'Modern British workers are better off, with longer holidays and shorter hours'. This should give rise to valuable discussion of social issues, such as unemployment, the use of leisure time, and the advantages and disadvantages of early retirement schemes.

Relate the trend towards large companies and 'big taking over the small' to one aspect of life with which all the children will be familiar – shopping. Carry out a class survey of where families buy their groceries and other household goods. Obviously, results will depend on the location of your school, but generally they will demonstrate the recent move towards supermarket shopping and away from small corner shops. Record, in pictorial form, the advantages and disadvantages of shopping in super/hypermarkets (see opposite).

Find out what are the main industries in Britain today, and locate key industrial areas on a map. Look for industries in the locality of your school and undertake a special in-depth study of them, to find out what recent

changes there have been to the companies and their products.

Activity 2: The Great Depression

Debate reasons for the deterioration of the world economy in the 1930s. Write accounts expressing causes, concerns and consequences from the points of view of (a) a ruined businessman, (b) a poor family, and (c) a politician.

Background information

The deterioration of the world economy may be attributed to a number of complex factors including the effects of World War I and the Wall Street crash or failure of the American money market in 1929. Many businesses were ruined as a result. The establishment of new industries in Britain in the mid-1930s helped to restore the economy, but in many places, notably the north, recovery was extremely slow.

Activity 3: The Jarrow March

A classic example of the hard times of recession can be revealed by a study of the reasons for the Jarrow March (1936). Ask the children to find out who was marching, and why? How did the story end?

Background information: The Jarrow March

Jarrow is some seven miles from Newcastle-upon-Tyne, and in the 1930s most of the men worked in the

shipbuilding industry. However, with the depression, fewer and fewer ships were built. By 1936 only 100 of the 8000 shipbuilders were still in work. The government did little to help them, and so 200 men marched to London to present a petition to Parliament. Despite great sympathy from onlookers and the press, the march did not achieve any real improvement in Jarrow's fortunes.

Activity 4: Immigration, emigration and race relations

Research and discuss reasons for the great increase in movement of people in and out of Britain in recent years. Look up on world maps the countries of origin of some of the leading (in terms of size) immigrant groups. Consider the various impacts of this on British society. Sensitively introduce the subject of the Race Relations Act, and reasons for this.

Background information

As the British economy revived in the 1950s, the country suffered from a shortage of labour. People, especially from the Commonwealth countries of India, Pakistan and the West Indies, were encouraged to come and work. Their presence caused early resentment and often such people were discriminated against in such matters as housing and jobs. An Act of Parliament designed to protect people from racial prejudice was passed in 1968.

Study Unit 3b: Britain since 1930 – lives of people at different levels of society in different parts of Britain: at work.
Suggested levels of work involved in activities

Activity number	Level	Activity number	Level	Activity number	Level
1	2/3	3	2/3/4/5	4	2/3/4/5
2	2/3/4/5				

AT LEISURE

Activity 1: The good old days

As with work on social changes, a suitable way of dealing with the cultural dimension is the decade-at-a-time approach, finding out how people spent their leisure hours in each period. Alternatively, choose a theme, for example, cinema, music, food, sport, fashion, and research significant issues and developments through the period as a whole. Then draw, paint or make large montage pictures or collages to illustrate the changing scene over the years – film-stars and screen images, pop groups, fashions, sporting events, leisure clothes and so on.

Organise a class fashion-parade. The children will have tremendous fun trying to obtain/make costumes appropriate to the 'Oxford bags' days of the thirties, the teddy-boy image of the fifties, the flower-power/ hippie look of the sixties, and so on.

Activity 2: That's entertainment!

Follow the development of entertainment through the decades, including sub-topics on radio, television and the cinema. Make 'then and now' drawings, as shown below. Groups could work independently on the different topics; for example one group could research the story of radio, produce some illustrated writing and report back to the class as a whole. To complement this, try to find some early *Children's Hour* programmes or popular radio broadcasts for the children to hear: possibilities include *Toytown; Journey Into Space*; and *Dick Barton, Special Agent*.

Make a list of popular TV programmes enjoyed by children today. No doubt some of the 'soaps' will feature high on the list. Find out when *Coronation Street* started, and discuss how early episodes of such programmes can be a valuable source of information about life in days gone by. Which other programmes have stood the test of time, and why? As with popular music, a number of surveys can be carried out and statistics presented in graphic form, decade by decade.

Follow the development of the cinema, focusing on 'all-time greats'. Investigate the well-known movies of the 1930s, such as *Gone With The Wind* and *Snow White and the Seven Dwarfs*. Discuss why these are 'legends' of cinema history. As before, lists of the top ten films and film-stars can be collected for each decade, and compared with current ones. These lists could be approached thematically, in terms of action films, thrillers, musicals, comedies, science fiction, horror, and so on.

Let the children consult family and friends in order to compile lists of favourite actors, actresses, comedians, singers, dancers, etc., for each decade. The 1930s, for instance, might well include names like Laurel and Hardy, Errol Flynn and Bette Davis; the 1940s might include James Cagney, Humphrey Bogart and Lana Turner; the 1950s Marilyn Monroe, Burt Lancaster and Robert Mitchum; and the 1960s and 1970s Peter Sellers, Sean Connery and Clint Eastwood.

Another research project that the children will enjoy is collecting old comics and children's annuals from years gone by. Which of the current comics has been on the market for the longest time? If the children can find some comics from the forties and fifties, they might like to draw their own pictures of some of the characters.

Activity 3: Top of the pops

Listen to the music of various eras, and perhaps learn some popular songs from the 1930s, 1940s, 1950s, etc. Possibilities might include 'The Sun has got his hat on', 'Run, Rabbit, run', 'Happy days are here again', 'Rock around the Clock', Living Doll' and 'Simon Smith and his Amazing Dancing Bear'. Expose the children to different styles of music, such as light classical, big-band and traditional jazz. There is an ever-increasing mass of recorded music from these periods, so there should be no lack of material to choose from.

As you approach the 1960s, listen to Beatles music ('Yellow Submarine', 'All you need is Love', 'Michelle', 'Octopus's garden', etc.) and records by The Who, The Rolling Stones, Cliff Richard, and others. Discuss the 'swinging sixties' with their open-air concerts, early discotheques, and *Top of the Pops* on television. Consider reasons for 'Beatlemania', and discuss why the impact of this group was so dramatic.

Find out which have been the 'all time greats' in terms of leading number-one musical 'hits' of the past 60 years, and listen to as many of them as possible. Resources such as *The Guinness Book of Hit Singles* will be useful here. **Copymaster 54** can be used to record these titles in the appropriate spaces on the Wurlitzer. Alternatively, copies of the sheet can be used by parents, relatives and adult friends to list their all-time 'Top Twenty' records (perhaps a decade at a time?), and the children can then compile a class list of favourites according to the 'votes' cast – an activity which offers interesting possibilities for the graphic representation of results.

Similar activities could be undertaken to discover favourite male and female vocalists, pop groups, big

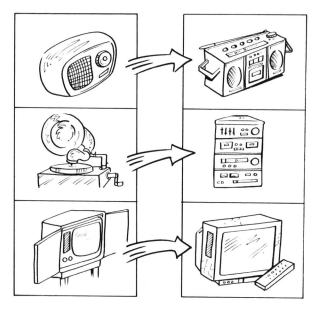

bands, instrumentalists, and so on. It may be possible to make a collection of concert programmes lent by family or friends who have seen these artists 'live'; and some fans may even possess precious autographs which can be photocopied. Let the children contact fan-clubs (using school notepaper, and under your supervision to avoid them being asked for money to join such clubs) and involve them in your topic. Collect, draw/or paint pictures of the pop-music heroes and heroines of the past 60 years.

To finish, it might be interesting for the children to review the current popular-music scene and find out how many artists have consistently recorded hit songs in past decades. Who is the longest-established living pop-singer/group of them all? Is there any way of calculating this? (Parents and grandparents should be able to help here.) And which of the current singers/groups do the children think is likely to survive into the twenty-first century?

Activity 4: Television
Another notable technical development is television. The first television service was opened in Britain by the British Broadcasting Corporation on 2nd November 1936. Colour television is a comparatively recent innovation. Ask the children to find out when their own family first acquired a television set and/or a video recorder, and discuss the impact that these objects have made on family lives. There is plenty of scope here for class and school surveys, with statistics being portrayed in graphic form.

Activity 5: A dedicated follower of fashion
Illustrate the changes that have taken place in hair-styles, and jewellery and shoe designs over the years. A border of shoe pictures would make an interesting surround to a wall-frieze entitled 'Fashions of the Twentieth Century'. The children might like to speculate what people will be wearing in the twenty-first century, and/or create their own designs.

Activity 6: Sporting highlights
Make a sports scrapbook, to illustrate leading sporting events and personalities, perhaps singling out three or four key players or teams for each decade. Events which spring to mind include Roger Bannister running the first four-minute mile, and England winning the World Cup for football in 1966.

Study Unit 3b: Britain since 1930 – lives of people at different levels of society in different parts of Britain: at work.
Suggested levels of work involved in activities

Activity number	Level	Activity number	Level	Activity number	Level
1	2/3	3	2/3	5	2/3/4
2	2/3/4/5	4	2/3	6	2/3/4

RESOURCES ▶

Non-fiction

Haigh, G. *Britain since 1930*, Collins.

Kelsall, F. *How We Used To Live 1954–1970*, A & C Black, 1991.

Lawrie, J. *Modern Times 1930–1960*, Skills and Resources for History Series, Collins Educational.

Rees, R. *Britain since 1930*, Heinemann.

The Twentieth-Century World, Oxford University Press.

Family Life in the Second World War, Family Life Series, Wayland.

History Makers of the Second World War, History Makers Series, Wayland.

The Blitz, Evacuation, Prisoners of War, Propaganda, Rationing, Women's War, The Home Front Series, Wayland.

Fiction

Easy-reading and picture books

Farmer, P. *The Coal Train*, Heinemann, 1977. Post-war London, and hardship in the terrible winter of 1947.*

Farmer, P. *The Runaway Train*, Heinemann, 1980. The excitement of an excursion after the war.*

Gavin, J. *Kamla and Kate*, Methuen, 1983. Two girls from different cultures become friends and learn about each other's customs.

Keeping, C. *Adam and Paradise Island*, OUP, 1989. A picture-story book about development in the urban landscape.

Kemp, G. *The Well*, Faber, 1984. Tales of a childhood in the Midlands in the 1930s.

Miles, *Crisis at Crabtree*, Lutterworth, 1986. Whimsical story of houses fighting for survival against the threat of a new motorway, demolition and preservation orders.

Rogers, P. *From me to you*, Orchard Books, 19087. Grandmother tells of her life, marrying in the 1930s, being widowed in the Second World War, and then enjoying her child and grandchildren.

Smith, N. *Will you come on Wednesday?*, Julia MacRae, 1987. Stories about children from a variety of cultural backgrounds. In particular, how they take their school play to the home of one mother who never goes out.

*These books are out of print but will be available from libraries and second-hand bookshops.

Books for better readers

The following stories are more demanding in terms of reading skills. They provide background detail, and selected passages could be read aloud.

Anderson, R. *Paper Faces*, OUP, 1991. Set in 1945, a story about the difficulties of adjusting to post-war realities, and a father who is almost a stranger.

Bawden, N. *Keeping Henry*, Puffin, 1987. Children evacuated to a Welsh farm.

Carus, Z. *Hunted!*, Blackie, 1989. Two young people try to help their Jewish friend, as the Germans invade the Channel Islands.

Magorian, M. *Back Home*, Viking Kestrel, 1985. A girl returns from spending the war years in the USA, and finds her old lifestyle restricting, made more difficult by parents who have problems in readjusting to one another.

Morpurgo, M. *Friend of Foe?* Magnet, 1984. Evacuees meet a German soldier in wartime Britain.

Rowlands, A. *Milk and Honey*, OUP, 1989. Set in 1958, against a background of race riots. Nelson, a Jamaican immigrant to Britain, finds it cold and unfriendly. A story for discussion.

Townsend, J.R. *Goodbye to Gumble's Yard*, Puffin, 1981. A family moves to a brand-new housing estate in the 1960s, with mixed success.

Walsh, J.P. *Fireweed*, Penguin, 1972. A story of the blitz.

Westall, R. *The Machine-gunners*, Macmillan, 1975. A gripping story with a Second World War background.

Poetry

Betjeman, J.A. *Ring of Bells*, selected by I. Slade, John Murray, 1964. Several poems in this selection give strong impressions of Britain in the 1930s and after.*

Orme, D. (compiler) *Toughie toffee*, Armada, 1989. A selection of poems about twentieth-century city life – shops, flats, streets – full of life.

Reilly, C. *Chaos of the night: women's poetry and verse of the Second World War*, Virgo, 1964.

*This book is out of print but will be available from libraries and second-hand bookshops.

Blueprints links

You will find the following other Stanley Thornes books useful: *Investigating History: Life in Britain Since 1930*.

STUDY UNIT 4 ANCIENT GREECE

Pupils should be taught about the way of life, beliefs and achievements of the ancient Greeks, and the legacy of ancient Greek civilisation to the modern world:

The ancient Greeks

a Athens and Sparta, *e.g. everyday life, citizens and slaves;*
b arts and architecture, *e.g. pottery, sculpture, theatres, temples, public buildings, and how these help us to find out about the ancient Greeks;*
c myths and legends of Greek gods and goddesses, heroes and heroines;
d relations with other peoples, *e.g. Persians, such as the stories of Marathon, Thermopylae and Salamis, the Greeks in Southern Italy, the campaigns of Alexander the Great, the influence on the Greeks of other civilisations, such as Egypt or Rome:*

The legacy of ancient Greek civilisation

e influence on the modern world, *e.g. politics, language, sport, architecture, science.*

TOPIC WEB

Athens and Sparta

- Setting the scene
- The city states
- Athens and Sparta
- Everyday life
- Trade
- Databases

Relations with other peoples

- Greeks and Persians
- The Greeks in southern Italy
- Alexander the Great
- The impact of Egypt and Rome on Greece

ANCIENT GREECE

Influence on the modern world

- Politics
- Language
- Sport
- Art and architecture
- Philosophy and science

Myths and legends

- Myths and legends
- Fables
- Gods and goddesses
- Heroes and heroines

Arts and architecture

- Architecture
- Pottery
- Theatre
- Drama
- Poetry
- Music
- Literature

THE ANCIENT GREEKS

Pupils should be taught about:

the ancient Greeks

a Athens and Sparta, *e.g. everyday life, citizens and slaves*

b arts and architecture, *e.g. pottery, sculpture, theatres, temples, public buildings, and how these help us to find out about the ancient Greeks*

c myths and legends of Greek gods and goddesses, heroes and heroines

d relations with other peoples, *e.g. Persians, such as the stories of Marathon, Thermopylae and Salamis, the Greeks in Southern Italy, the campaigns of Alexander the Great, the influence on the Greeks of other civilisations, such as Egypt or Rome*

SETTING THE SCENE

Activity 1: Where is Greece?

Look at **Copymaster 55** and observe the shape and position of Greece on a map of Europe. Study photographs of its natural landscape and terrain and make a list of words and phrases to describe these features, for example:

mountainous	divided
rocky	isolated
stony	finger-shaped
barren	surrounded by sea
cut-off	countless islands

This basic geographical thinking will help to explain why ancient Greece did not become a nation like other European countries.

Using **Copymaster 55**, children should note the positions of key cities, including Athens, Sparta, Pylos, Argos, Thebes and Corinth. In ancient Greece such towns were isolated, divided by mountains, with only rugged pathways between them. Towns, surrounded by farmland and barren countryside, formed the city states. Talk about why the cities and towns often fought each other (economic reasons? envy? pride? fear?), and what occasions would bring them together (sports and games, fear of enemy attack).

Activity 2: A timeline

Begin an illustrated timeline that can be elaborated and extended as the project as a whole progresses. Write key dates across the length of a classroom friezeboard or wall, leaving space beneath for a written statement of events and suitable illustrations (see below).

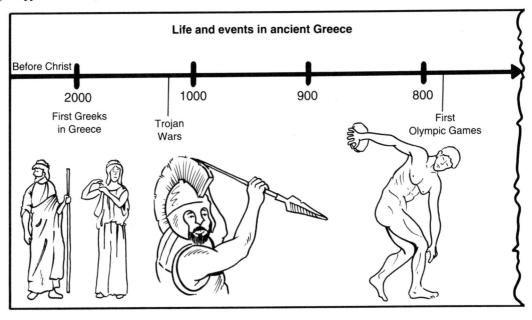

Life and events in ancient Greece

Before Christ

2000 — First Greeks in Greece

1000 — Trojan Wars

900

800 — First Olympic Games

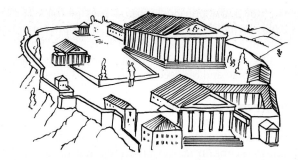

Activity 3: The city states

Find out about the government of the city states, and the origin of the word 'democracy' or 'people's rule'. Divide the class into groups, each to represent a different sector of city-state society – citizens (free adult males who could discuss and vote on city matters), women, foreigners, slaves. Organise a debate on the justice, or otherwise, of the democracy. Was government truly democratic in the sense that we know it today? Ask each group to argue its case for being included in decision-making.

Introduce the Greek word *politikos*, meaning 'of the city'. Use dictionaries to research the common English words deriving from this source – politics, political, politician. Investigate the differences between Greek state 'politics' with citizen involvement, and our own system of party politics.

Background information: *The city states*

The Greek word for a city state was *polis*. Nowadays, we have words like metropolis and metropolitan, derivations from the original Greek. Each polis included the city and the countryside around it. There was often a temple dedicated to the patron god of the city, built on high ground, called an *acropolis*. This word means 'highest city'.

Study Unit 4: Ancient Greece – setting the scene.
Suggested levels of work involved in activities

Activity number	Level	Activity number	Level	Activity number	Level
1	2/3	2	2/3/4/5	3	2/3/4/5

EVERYDAY LIFE IN ATHENS AND SPARTA ▶

Activity 1: Athens

Undertake a detailed study of Athens, the largest and by far the most famous of all the city states, as depicted on **Copymaster 56**. This copymaster could be used as an introduction to the entire topic on Greek life in ancient times. Pupils can colour the drawing of the Acropolis and Parthenon, thus familiarising themselves with the famous townscape and its architecture. The boxes are to be filled in. Depending on ability levels, either provide answers to be inserted into appropriate slots or expect children to conduct their own research to discover the answers: Acropolis, Parthenon, Sacred Way, Agora, Piraeus. The completed sheets could be stuck onto larger sheets of paper for pupils to decorate with suitable illustrations, perhaps of people of the city or Greek-style art.

Athens had roughly 2500 kilometres of territory making up its polis. The great majority of the city states were much smaller in size, with only a few thousand citizens in each.

Activity 2: Law and order

Examine the role of the citizens in carrying out duties of law and order. City states had no lawyers. Courts were places for the people, who argued their own cases. These cases were judged by a jury of fellow citizens, who displayed discs to signify their verdict.

Use **Copymaster 57** to make a pair of juror's discs. Colour in the circles to make them appear like natural stone, and then cut out the discs and mount them on similar sized discs of stiff card. Pierce a small hole in the centre of each and insert a short wooden stick (or length of drinking straw).

Use the discs in dramatic role-play. Act out jury scenes with children playing the parts of people presenting their cases, and of jurors arriving at a decision and each displaying the appropriate disc.

Activity 3: Sparta

Compare the more democratic ruling of Athens with what we know of life in Sparta, another significant city. This was the chief settlement of the Dorians, who invaded Greece from the north in about 1200 B.C. Only here did 'kings' exist. Find out and write about the duties of Spartan kings. Make a wall-painting of the council of elders and of the city magistrates or 'Ephors'. Ask pupils to debate the relative merits of the Athenian and Spartan systems of government. Find out what the expression 'a Spartan lifestyle' means.

Research the life of Draco, a Greek statesman who

wrote down the previously vague laws of the city of Athens. Write about the nature of the punishments which often accompanied these laws. Look up the meaning of the word 'Draconian', which is associated with this man and his deeds.

Background information: *Sparta*
The Spartans were noted as courageous warriors: indeed, every Spartan man had to undertake a harsh training regime to make him strong and fit. All male babies were examined at birth, and any sickly children were left in the open air to die (you could write a story about a Spartan boy child who was left to die, but managed to survive and make his mark in the world).

Activity 4: Citizens and slaves
The children could do some research into the lives of Greek citizens and their slaves, and look for contrasts in their separate and very different lifestyles. Could a slave ever become a free man and, if so, how? Ask the children to write about 'My life as a citizen in ancient Greece'. What rights and privileges do they enjoy? Then ask them to consider the life of a slave in those days and write a similar account of life from this very different viewpoint. Compare the two lifestyles that emerge through these accounts.

Background information: *Citizens and slaves*
There were two main ranks of people in ancient Greece – free men and slaves. In Athens, for example, only men born of Athenian parents were recognised as citizens: free men who had come to live in Athens from elsewhere were known as *metics*. A slave who was skilful enough to be paid for his services could sometimes save enough money to buy his freedom, but even then he could never become a metic or a citizen. The status of a woman depended on the rank her husband or male relatives had attained. Women were not allowed to play any part in the government of the city state.

In Sparta, only men born to Spartan parents were granted the status of citizen. Other free men were called *perioikoi*, or 'neighbours'. Citizens and perioikoi rarely mixed, unless they were serving in the army.

Activity 5: The status of women
Find out about the lives of girls and women in ancient Greece. How were girls educated in those days?

Activity 6: Trade
Provide a large wall-map of Greece to show the children its position in relation to other nations with which the Greeks traded. Include and label Britain, Spain, Italy, Russia, the Holy Land, Egypt, Africa, the Mediterranean Sea and the Black Sea. Affix pieces of red string or ribbon to link Greece with places which received its exports, and green string or ribbon to connect Greece with places which provided imported goods. Annotate these trade links by sticking on cards illustrating the produce concerned.

Background information: *Trade links*
Greek exports included oil from olive trees, wine, silver and pottery; imports included grain (from colonies around the Black Sea and from Russia), metals, furs and leather hides.

Activity 7: Across the oceans
Draw or paint pictures of Greek cargo vessels used to transport goods across the seas. Write about the dangers of sea travel at this time, when there were no sophisticated aids to navigation. Discuss the geographical problems Greece had in relation to communication and trade.

Ask the children what essential item of ships' equipment they think was invented by a Greek called Anacharsis. (Answer: the anchor.) Give them a clue – the first ones were large stones.

Activity 8: Money management
Ask the children to think about why money changers and bankers became important at this time. Why were they known as *trapezitai* ('table men')?

Background information: *Money management*
Most of the trading was done by private merchants who were allowed to roam the seas freely, provided they paid customs duties to the city states. Different city states became associated with different goods – Athens was known for its pottery, silver and honey; Macedonia for its horses; and so on. Many city states minted their own coins, usually of silver or gold, and often bearing pictures of the gods or mythical heroes.

Activity 9: Vines and olive trees
Find out more about the two key crops of Greece – vines and olive trees. What are the ideal conditions in which these plants grow? The children could draw them, and write accounts of how their fruits are harvested and processed.

It is possible to obtain vine leaves in delicatessens and some large supermarkets in this country. Discuss their present-day culinary use, and perhaps cook a typical Greek dish which employs them, such as vine leaves stuffed with a rice and herb mixture.

Porridge and bread made from barley was the staple diet for many people in ancient Greece. They also ate lots of fruit, vegetables, fish, eggs and cheese. Some wild animals were hunted for their meat. Wealthier families could afford bread made from wheat.

Activity 10: Rural life
The majority of people in ancient Greece derived their income from the land. Rich Athenians often owned farms near to the city: they lived in town and relied on slaves and labourers to do the hard work on the farm. Rural communities depended on the land for survival.

Use **Copymaster 58** to help the children to appreciate the fundamental importance of rural life. Ask them to imagine they are slaves and to write accounts of toiling under the hot sun to harvest olives, treading grapes to make wine, or ploughing the dry soil to prepare it for planting seeds. They should then write parallel accounts from the point of view of the estate owner, visiting to inspect the work of the slaves and drinking the fruits of the vine harvest.

The illustrated crossword puzzle on **Copymaster 58** teaches basic vocabulary related to rural life and associated aspects of the economy. Depending on ability levels, either leave all answers completely blank allowing for individual research, or fill in key letters to assist completion. The answers are as follows:

Down	Across
1 Labourer	1 Plough
2 Grapes	2 Broadcasting
3 Barley	3 Olive
4 Vines	4 Soil

Background information: Rural life

Farming in ancient Greece was often hard work, due to the lack of good soil and the hot weather – most crops were grown during the wetter months, between October and April or May. Most Greek farms grew olive trees, grape vines and crops such as beans, lentils and barley. Olive oil was used for lighting and for cooking: indeed, olive trees were considered so important to the economy that in Athens they were protected by law.

Activity 11: Town life

Write accounts of everyday life in Athens. Help the children to appreciate the atmosphere of the city with its open-air restaurants, workshops and theatres, and the importance of the Agora (town square or meeting place for discussion and trade).

Activity 12: Greek costume

Study and illustrate the clothing worn in those days. How were these clothes made, and what were they made of? What were a 'chiton' and a 'himation'? (A chiton was a loose woollen tunic worn knee length by men and full length by women; a himation was a cloak that was draped around the body.) What different fashions were there for men and women? Find out about footwear, jewellery and hairstyles too. Make figures from papier mâché and 'dress' them in the style of the ancient Greeks – men and women, rich and poor.

Jewellery such as brooches and pendants can be fashioned from scrap materials and sprayed with paint.

Activity 13: How do we know?

Ask the children to consider how we know all these things about everyday life in ancient Greece. If possible, visit a museum and study relics of Greek civilisation. Show how pottery and paintings are a valuable source of illustrative evidence of day-to-day activities, festivals and customs.

Activity 14: A young ancient Greek

Ask the children to imagine what it was like to be a child growing up in ancient Greece. Find out and write about schooling, with its emphasis on learning history, writing, Greek literature, arithmetic, geometry, music, dancing and athletics. What might a typical day in school have been like? Boys were educated from the age of seven. Girls stayed at home!

Activity 15: Alpha to Omega

Learn the letters of the Greek alphabet. **Copymaster 59** is designed to show the shape of each letter and allows space for the children to write in the names. Depending on the ability of the children, the sheet can be photocopied with the letter names as written at the bottom inserted into the boxes; or the letter names can be covered, leaving a blank space for writing, and the children research the names themselves.

Activity 16: Greek coins

Investigate ancient Greek coins. Study and collect pictures of authentic coins and, if possible, compare them with coins in use today. Make replicas of coins in the classroom, using stiff card, scissors, cocktail sticks and aluminium foil. Cut circles out of the card, to form the bases for the coins, and cover these with foil. Using a cocktail stick or similar sharp object, gently etch appropriate designs into the surface of the foil. Be aware of safety at all times.

Activity 17: Cookery in ancient Greece

Plan an ancient Greek menu. Research typical dishes from books on international or Greek cookery, selecting those with ingredients that were readily available at the time, for example, olive oil, vine leaves, grapes, barley, bread, beans, lentils, herbs, fruit, vegetables and poultry. Cook one or more authentic Greek dishes, and eat in typical Greek style – females sitting on stools and males lying on low couches. PE benches covered with material make useful couches.

Activity 18: Databases

If your school has access to information technology, perhaps the children could research and produce databases on different aspects of ancient Greece. The process of constructing such a resource would be useful, since the children will have to consider the type of database they intend to use (a simple card-index system, or something more detailed and complex), and how they intend to categorise and index the databases while designing the programs, as well as inputting the information accurately. A database entitled 'Pantheon' could include all the children's research notes and creative writing on the gods and their various powers; another called 'Fables' could contain their versions of Aesop's tales as well as new stories of their own; a third – 'Mythbase' – could include the wealth of legends about the Greek heroes and heroines. Teachers interested in desktop publishing might be able to help children produce their own computerised illustrations, since facilities do now exist to scan and reproduce line drawings effectively. The experience of recording and retrieving this information will not only reinforce learning about ancient Greece, but also provide a child-centred database for future reference.

**Study Unit 4: Ancient Greece – everyday life in Athens and Sparta.
Suggested levels of work involved in activities**

Activity number	Level	Activity number	Level	Activity number	Level
1	2/3/4	7	2/3	13	2/3/4
2	2/3/4	8	2/3	14	2/3/4
3	2/3/4/5	9	2/3	15	2/3
4	2/3/4/5	10	2/3/4	16	2/3
5	2/3	11	2/3/4	17	2/3
6	2/3	12	2/3/4	18	2/3/4/5

ARTS AND ARCHITECTURE

Activity 1: Leisure time

Find out from pictures or museum evidence more about how the ancient Greeks occupied their leisure time. Apart from eating, drinking and going to the theatre, sport played an important role in everyday life. Paint pictures of the common sports learned in school and enjoyed in adult life, including wrestling, running, boxing, javelin and discus throwing. If a museum visit is possible, find out what toys Greek children may have played with.

Activity 2: Greek architecture

Pay some attention to the architectural detail of Greek columns with their decorated tops. Such columns were usually built to support temple archways and colonnades.

Reproduce them as paintings or in 3-D from corrugated card, and display them along the classroom wall.

Investigate the area around the school for evidence of buildings which reflect the Greek 'classical' style of architecture: older local town halls, such as that in Birmingham, often reveal signs of Greek influence. Take photographs or sketch the buildings and then model them back at school.

Activity 3: The Acropolis

Make a model of the Acropolis, with its Parthenon and other buildings. Try to ensure accuracy as far as possible – the Parthenon had 17 pillars along each side and 8 along the front and back. Its original measurements were:

Investigate the building materials used in the Parthenon (stone pillars and slabs, and a wooden roof with tiles on top). Write accounts of its technology and construction, including the difficult task of levelling the top of the rock of the Acropolis.

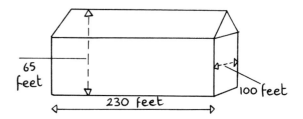

If possible, pay a visit to the British Museum to view the sculptures from the Parthenon walls. Failing that, study pictures of these and discuss what we can learn from them about life in ancient Greece.

Corinthian style   **Ionic style**

Activity 4: Greek pottery

Make replicas of the well-known craft product of Athens – pottery – using either clay, papier mâché over wire, or card. Study original Greek work first, if possible in a museum, or through photographs and reproduction pieces. Using ideas for designs and colours based on these, paint the surfaces of your replicas with Greek-style art.

If a study of genuine Greek pottery is possible, discuss what we can learn about everyday life in ancient Greece from such ordinary objects. Is this true of pottery today? Are such objects reliable evidence? What sort of artefacts will our civilisation leave behind for future generations to puzzle over?

Activity 5: The Greek theatre

Draw plans, make models or draw pictures of a Greek theatre, showing the position of the skene, 'orchestra', altar and audience. The word 'orchestra' originally meant 'dancing floor' – can the children find out why? What modern theatrical word derives from the word 'skene'?

Ask the children to imagine that they are ancient Greeks and to write about a visit to the theatre. They should describe what they would see and hear, the costumes that were worn, and the common themes of the plays. How was a Greek 'chorus' different from what we understand by the word today?

Parts in Greek plays were taken by actors in masks, wearing costumes designed to make them look much bigger than they really were. Ask the children why they think this was so. Classical Chinese actors today

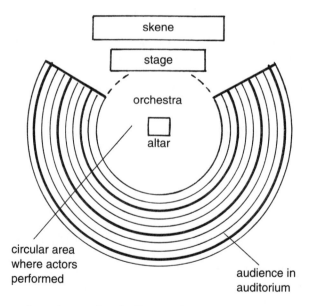

skene

stage

orchestra

altar

circular area where actors performed

audience in auditorium

perform in masks similar to those worn in ancient Greece. Make your own masks in the classroom. **Copymaster 60** provides a general outline, which can be coloured, mounted on thin card and cut out. Staple it to a 3-cm wide strip of thin card that will fit around a child's head. Elaborate on this basic idea by designing other masks. Many Greek plays feature the same characters – king, queen, soldier, old man, drunkard, messenger, clown, slave, hero, heroine, glutton – and these would be appropriate designs for the children to attempt. Even if you have not got the copymaster, you

only need to draw oval shapes on strong card, and cut openings for eyes and mouth. Card noses and hair can be glued on later. Let the children decorate the masks appropriately, turning them into faces of comedy or tragedy, and then use them for re-enactment of Greek theatre. If appropriate, tell the stories of some classic Greek plays such as *Oedipus Rex*.

Help the children to understand the differences between comedy and tragedy. If possible, listen to the record and/or obtain the sheet music to the song 'Comedy Tonight' from *A Funny Thing Happened On The Way To The Forum* by Stephen Sondheim (available from Chappell & Company Ltd, London). The children will enjoy singing the lively tune, and the tongue-twisting lyrics will aid vocabulary work. Perhaps the class could create an accompaniment of 'comedy effects' using glockenspiel, wood blocks, bells, horns, swanee whistles, etc.

Introduce the Greek word *hypokrites*, meaning 'actor'. How is this related in meaning to a word we use today?

Background information: The Greek theatre

The tradition of theatre in ancient Greece began in the form of a yearly festival of songs and dances held to honour Dionysus, the god of wine. In Athens, this developed into an annual play-writing competition, and soon the Athenians were enjoying theatrical performances of tragedy and comedy. Tragic plays had serious themes such as mortals defying the will of the gods; or concerned human emotions such as love, hate, anger, jealousy, revenge. Comic plays, by contrast, contained lots of knockabout slapstick and jokes. Only men were allowed to perform in these plays.

Activity 6: Greek playwrights

The Greek theatre has already been mentioned. Relate study of this to the lives of famous Greeks associated with the dramatic arts. Aristophanes wrote over 50 comedies for the theatre; Euripides wrote 90 plays (of which 18 are still in existence); and Aeschylus is a well-known writer of tragedies. Investigate the titles and themes of some of their works.

Activity 7: Greek music

Investigate the music of early Greece. Music was commonly studied in the schools and the children might like to make paintings of musicians with their flutes, harps, pan-pipes, lyres and cymbals. Discuss why we do *not* know what the music of the time sounded like (no tape-recorders, records or compact discs). How are we able to guess about early music? Listen to tapes or records of modern Greek music (readily available to tourists in Greece, and also in good music shops in this country). What instruments are commonly played in Greece today? Perhaps Greek musicians could visit and play traditional music in your school?

Activity 8: Apollo and the Muses

Apollo was the god of poetry and music, but can the children find out who the Muses were? They should write down and illustrate their findings.

MYTHS AND LEGENDS

Activity 1: Myths and legends

Many Greek myths and legends concerned the gods and their adventures, or the brave deeds of heroes and heroines. Homer wrote classic tales of adventure in the *Iliad* and the *Odyssey*, and there are many other stories which can still be enjoyed today. Read or tell some of these legends to the children including, for example:

Jason and the Argonauts,
Perseus and the Gorgon,
Bellerophon and Pegasus,
The story of King Midas,
Theseus and the Minotaur,
The story of Persephone,
The Labours of Hercules,
Daedalus and Icarus,
Arion and the Dolphin,
Phaeton and the Horses of the Sun,
Orpheus and Eurydice,
Prometheus and the Gift of Fire,
Pandora's Box.

These legends offer considerable scope for creative work, particularly in art and craft. Many of the stories contain fearsome monsters with strange magical powers, which can be depicted in paintings, models and/or collages. The children might like to write 'legends' of their own and create new and even more terrifying creatures. What other phenomena in our modern world might be said to have been inspired by mighty gods? Perhaps the children could create a Pantheon of twentieth-century 'gods', some good and others evil.

Discuss the significant role of the Greek language in the spread of Christianity. The gospels were originally written in Greek.

Activity 2: Aesop's fables

Another interesting aspect of Greek literature for children to investigate is the contribution of Aesop and his fables. Ask the class how Aesop became famous for his stories without ever writing them down. Read or tell some of the fables, and perhaps the children could illustrate them: most will have heard of *The Tortoise and the Hare*, but there are many others, including:

The Miller, his son and their Donkey
The Shepherd Boy who cried Wolf
The Ant and the Grasshopper
The Fox and the Stork

Explain the moral of each story. Many of the sayings in the tales have become part of our language and tradition – you could ask the children to find out which of Aesop's fables have given us: 'a dog-in-the-manger attitude'; 'look before you leap'; 'sour grapes'. Perhaps the children could write and illustrate modern fables of their own.

Background information: *Aesop's fables*

Aesop is said to have been a slave who lived in ancient Greece. He gained great renown for telling stories about animals, many of which illustrate the wise or, more often, the foolish behaviour of mankind. It is said that, because of the wisdom of these fables, Aesop was set free from slavery and became a respected guest at the royal court.

Activity 3: Gods and goddesses

Greeks 'worshipped' or talked to a huge range of gods. Find out the names of the well-known ones and how their festivals were celebrated, and read/tell stories associated with them. Include Zeus, Hera, Apollo, Poseidon and Athene (after whom Athens was named). What connection does Cronos have with time? Who were the Titans? What was an oracle? Design pictures, posters or collages to represent these gods and illustrate their significance. Use these for a 'gallery of Greek gods', otherwise known as a Pantheon (see below).

Background information: *Gods and goddesses*

Explain to the children that, in common with other ancient peoples, the Greeks created tales from their own imaginations to try and explain the phenomena of the natural world, such as the changing seasons of the year, sunrise and sunset, the winds and the tides, life and death. They did not have the scientific knowledge of our modern world, and so they believed that these events occurred as a result of the all-powerful will of the gods. To disobey or anger the gods was to court disaster.

Columns can be made of corrugated paper, painted white.

| Zeus | Poseidon | Dionysus | Ares |
| King of the gods and god of the weather | God of the sea | God of wine | God of war |

Study Unit 4: Ancient Greece – myths and legends.
Suggested levels of work involved in activities

Activity number	Level	Activity number	Level	Activity number	Level
1	2/3/4/5	2	2/3/4/5	3	2/3/4/5

RELATIONS WITH OTHER PEOPLE ▶

Activity 1: Wars against Persia
Investigate the extent of the Persian Empire, the nature of the Greek rebellion against the Persian invasion, and the significance of 'the Persian Wars'.

Introduce the children to the well-known story of Marathon. In 490 B.C. the Persian king Darius I invaded Greece and was defeated at the battle of Marathon, a town north of Athens. A messenger called Pheidippides, despite his weariness after the battle, carried news of the Greek victory on foot to Athens, a distance of over 40 kilometres. After delivering his message, Pheidippides collapsed and died from exhaustion. The Olympic marathon race derives its name from this historical event. Draw or paint pictures of Pheidippides arriving in Athens, crying out his news, and collapsing in the crowd. Find out how Miltiades' battle plan enabled the Greeks to defeat a numerically superior Persian army. Produce an historical newspaper dealing with this story, including 'eyewitness accounts', latest news, 'expert' opinion, maps, etc.

Background information: *Wars against Persia*
The Persian army, in a fleet of 600 ships, landed in the bay of Marathon, planning to attack Athens. The Greek general Miltiades sent Pheidippides to ask the Spartans for help. When he arrived, he was told that the Spartans were engaged in a religious festival and could not send reinforcements until the festival was ended. Pheidippides raced back to Miltiades with the news (a return journey of over 100 miles on foot), and new battle plans were laid. When the battle was over, some 6000 Persian soldiers had been killed, compared to only 192 Greeks. Pheidippides survived the battle, but unfortunately not the final run to Athens.

Activity 2: The defeat of Persia
Tell the story of the ending of the Persian Wars – by the land battle at Thermopylae, and the sea battle off the coast at Salamis in 480 B.C. Draw a map to show the position of both Thermopylae and Salamis, with illustrations of the ships that would have gone into battle. More ambitious would be a model of the sea battle, using junk materials, card and papier mâché. How were sea battles conducted at this time, when ships could not fire missiles at each other? Paint pictures of the battles and write about them.

Background information: *The defeat of Persia*

Ten years after Marathon, Darius's son Xerxes marched again on Greece. He crossed the Hellespont, a mile-wide stretch of water between Asia Minor and northern Greece, by lashing hundreds of ships together to make a boat-bridge for his soldiers to march across. The Persians met a force of 300 Spartan warriors, led by King Leonidas, at a narrow mountain pass. The Spartans fought bravely, and the Persians were unable to break through until a Greek traitor showed them another route which brought them to the rear of the Spartans. Attacked from both sides, the Spartans fought on until the last man had fallen.

The Greeks, meanwhile, left a small force to defend the city and took to their ships. The garrison at Athens kept the Persians out for two weeks, thus buying enough time for the Greeks to regroup. The Greek leader, Themistocles, lured the Persians into attacking at Salamis by sending a 'double agent' to convince Xerxes that the Greeks were afraid and disorganised. When the battle was over, the Persians had lost almost half of their ships.

Another battle took place at Plataea in 479 B.C. Once again the Persians were defeated and this brought their invasion plans to an end.

Activity 3: Fall of the city states

Write about the fall of the Greek city states, and the eventual conquest of Greece by the Romans.

Research, write and illustrate the life of Alexander the Great. Get the children to describe his military tactics and battle campaigns. Ask them what a 'phalanx' was? And who or what was Bucephalus? Let them draw maps showing Alexander's journeys and conquests.

Background information: *Alexander the Great*

Alexander the Great was the son of Philip of Macedonia. Born in 356 B.C., he became king at the age of twenty when his father was murdered. A priestess once told Alexander that he would never be defeated in battle: such was his courage and military skill, her prediction proved to be true. By the time he died of a fever at the age of 32, Alexander had conquered half of the known world.

Study Unit 4: Ancient Greece – relations with other peoples. Suggested levels of work involved in activities

Activity number	Level	Activity number	Level	Activity number	Level
1	2/3/4/5	2	2/3/4/5	3	2/3/4/5

THE LEGACY OF ANCIENT GREEK CIVILISATION

C63

Pupils should be taught about:

the legacy of ancient Greek civilisation • influence on the modern world, *e.g. politics, language, sport, architecture, science*

Activity 1: What did the ancient Greeks leave behind?

Design an illustrated wall-map to summarise the great legacy we have acquired from ancient Greece. Draw the country of Greece in the centre, with coloured strings or ribbons radiating out to connect with illustrations of the key areas of this legacy (see page 97).

Divide the class into groups, each to do a detailed investigation of one aspect of the legacy. Some aspects have already been alluded to, for example, the classical style of architecture, the meaning of 'democracy', the writings and thinking of philosophers and authors.

Above all, help the children to appreciate how we know that these things/ideas are derived from ancient Greece. Consider the nature of the evidence. Record this work by extending the wall-map with examples of each area of the Greek legacy, and an explanation of how we know about it.

Draw the children's attention to the wide range of words deriving from Greek that are part of our 'classical' language today, for example: orchestra, scene, epic, stadium, politics, marathon, harmony, rhyme, athlete, odeon, geography, democracy, theatre, discus,

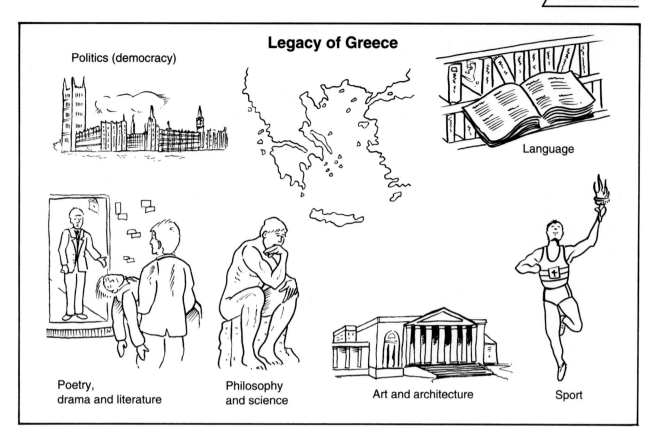

Legacy of Greece

Politics (democracy)

Language

Poetry,
drama and literature

Philosophy
and science

Art and architecture

Sport

geometry, lyric, pentathlon, decathlon. Put these and other words into sets along thematic lines (for example, sport and theatre) – a very useful exercise in reinforcing the scope of the powerful legacy of ancient Greece.

Activity 2: The Olympics

The Olympic Games would make an extremely valuable sub-topic, especially in an Olympic year. They can be used to investigate many aspects of ancient Greece, including everyday life, the Persian Wars, and the legacy of sport and language.

Copymaster 61 can be a basic introductory sheet for a sub-topic on the Olympics or part of your work on Greek sport. Let the children colour each picture, thus familiarising themselves with some of the common games. Discuss and write about how the athletes prepared themselves and what they wore for their sport (many were naked).

Read or tell the legend of Pelops, in whose honour the first games are said to have been held, and his courtship of Hippodamia, daughter of King Oenomaus. These games are said to have developed eventually into the Olympics we know today.

Make paintings or collages of the dramatic sport of chariot-racing, part of the ancient Olympics which took place on the 'hippodrome' (horse track). Might this name be connected with the bride of Pelops? Ask the children where they might see the word 'hippodrome' today?

Find out about the many other events in the early games and what prizes were won by the athletes. What is a pentathlon? A decathlon? A *Victor Ludorum*? Ask the children to try to find out the name of the earliest known Olympic champion, imagine themselves in his

place and tell the story of the race. It seems that Olympic records were first kept during the games in 776 B.C. An athlete called Coroebus appears to have been the earliest known winner of an Olympic event.

Background information: The Olympics

The earliest Olympic Games were held in honour of Zeus every four years, at a site in the south-west of Greece known as Olympia. They lasted for five days, at the end of which prizes such as olive wreaths or palm branches would be awarded to the winners. Successful athletes might even have a statue set up in their honour, and some were sponsored by city states.

Activity 3: The modern Olympics

Compare the events of the Greek Olympic Games with those of modern Olympics. Have the Olympic Games ever been held in this country? Explain the significance of the Olympic flame and let the children draw or paint pictures of it being carried to the stadium or round the track. How many different sports are included in the Olympics nowadays? Compare records of achievement over the years (*The Guinness Book of Records* and/or similar athletics record books are useful sources of information), and discuss reasons for the improved performance of modern athletes.

Collect stamps bearing an Olympic sporting theme or motif – these are often issued in an Olympic year by the country hosting the games.

Draw or paint pictures of famous sporting Olympians taking part in their chosen activities – it may even be possible to show the children video recordings of thrilling competitions from recent Olympic Games.

They could write imaginative stories about 'The day I won the race', 'My Olympic medal', and so on. Perhaps a visit could be arranged to a local athletics club to watch a meeting in progress. The children could learn about using stop-watches to time the athletes.

Other activities could include holding a class or year Olympics competition within the school. Perhaps a series of ten events in a decathlon could be arranged – the inclusion of some light-hearted contests (e.g. marbles, conkers, sack race, skipping, egg-and-spoon race), in which results are usually decided by an element of luck, might encourage more children to take part than only those who are naturally gifted at sport. Points should be given for finishing positions in each event, with the overall winner being the competitor with the highest aggregate score over the ten events. The children could also help to organise the meeting, providing race numbers, judging the events, recording times and results, updating the scoreboard, making medals or other prizes, and so on.

Explain to the children the words which embody the Olympic spirit, dictated by Pierre de Coubertin when he organised the first modern games in 1896;

The most important thing in the Olympic Games is not to win but to take part, just as the most important thing in life is not to have conquered but to have fought well.

Activity 4: Scientists and philosophers
Help pupils to appreciate the importance of 'thinking' as developed by the Greeks – the basis of the study we know today as philosophy. Find out about the lives of two of the greatest philosophers the world has ever known, Socrates (470 to 399 B.C.) and Plato (427 to 347 B.C.), both of whom lived in Athens. Plato was a disciple of Socrates and was once sold as a slave. After his master killed himself by drinking hemlock, Plato carried on the work that Socrates started.

Some great Greek thinkers are famous for their ideas on medicine and science rather than on morals and religion. Find out more about the life and work of Aristotle (384–322 B.C.) who originated what might be called the methodology of science – looking, thinking, and formulating a theory; and Hippocrates (460–377 B.C.) a physician and surgeon who wrote on medical matters and is regarded as the 'father of modern medicine'. What is the Hippocratic Oath?

Make a large illustrated class book on the life and work of famous men of Greece. Different individual children or groups can choose which outstanding lives to research and illustrate. In addition to the people already mentioned, the biographies could include those of the authors Sophocles and Euripides; the mathematician, Pythagoras; and the builder and architect Kallikrates.

Activity 5: Dorian invasions
Investigate the impact of Dorian invasions on Greece, and the train of events set off by these, giving rise to Greek influences on other cultures and lands, such as southern Italy.

Background information
The Dorian invaders of Greece were so called because they were believed to have come from a place called Doris in northern Greece. Their conquering of the Achaean people began before 1100 B.C. and was accomplished with crude weapons made of iron. As a result of the Dorian invasions, Achaean people fled elsewhere, giving rise to the establishment of Greek colonies in places such as nearby islands, and Asia Minor. The first Greek colony in the western Mediterranean was established at Cumae in Italy. The Dorians captured most Greek cities, with the notable exception of Athens. Their principal town was Sparta.

Activity 6: Friend or foe?
Organise a discussion on what it would have been like to be a member of a city state elsewhere, such as in southern Italy. Debate the tensions that inhabitants would have experienced. On one hand they would have had a strong sense of 'belonging' to a race, a culture, promoted by the getting together of Greeks at events such as festivals and Olympic Games. On the other hand, there were frequent tensions and wars between the states in Greece and those elsewhere.

Background information
Greek city states in southern Italy were autonomous. They were not ruled by Greece, hence there were tensions between them and states in Greece itself. Syracuse in Italy was one of the largest city states. There was frequent warfare and hostilities between the Sicilians and the southern Italian Greeks.

Activity 7: 'Wise men' of Greece
When debating the legacy of Greece and the links between mainland Greece and the influence of Southern Italy, note that some of the best known 'wise men' were actually southern Italian Greeks. These included Pythagoras and Archimedes. Find out more about the lives and influence of these people.

Activity 8: Influence on other civilisations
At the conclusion of your topic, discuss the impact of the dividing up of the empire, and the significant influence of Greek thought, ideas and language on other places in the ancient world.

Background information
When Alexander's empire broke up, some of his leading generals had great influence in other places. Antipater took over the government of the European part of the empire, and General Seleucus took power in Persia and Babylon. General Ptolemy began to reign as king in Egypt, as well as over part of the North African coast and the Holy Land. The new 'kings' fought each other as they went about their business of protecting and enlarging their kingdoms.

Many cities had of course already been influenced by Alexander, including Alexandria in Egypt. Thus Greek thought played a powerful role in the development of city life and culture of the ancient world.

**Study Unit 4: Ancient Greece – legacy of Ancient Greek civilisation.
Suggested levels of work involved in activities**

Activity number	Level	Activity number	Level	Activity number	Level
1	2/3/4/5	4	2/3/4/5	7	2/3/4/5
2	2/3/4/5	5	2/3/4/5	8	2/3/4/5
3	2/3/4/5	6	2/3/4/5		

RESOURCES ▶

Non-fiction

Burrell, R. *The Greeks*, Oxford University Press, 1990.
Knott, B. *Ancient Greece*, Oxford Primary History Series.
Taylor, P. *The Ancient Greeks*, Heinemann.
Ancient Greece, Primary History Series, Collins Educational.
The Greeks, Look Into the Past Series, Wayland.
Greek Cities, Beginning History Series, Wayland, 1991.
Ancient Greece, Everyday Life Series, Usborne.
Greek Legends, The Stories: The Evidence Wayland.
Ancient Greece, Jump! History Series, Two-Can.
Ancient Greece, See Through Series, Heinemann.
The Greeks, What Do We Know About Series, Wayland.
Ancient Greece, Collins Primary History Series.

The British Museum has published an activity book on The Ancient Greeks (British Museum General Enquiries – Tel: 0171-636-1555)

Fiction

Goscinny, *Asterix at the Olympic Games,* Knight, 1976. Cartoon-style; an old favourite.
Sutcliff, R. *Truce of the Games,* Hamish Hamilton, 1971. Story about a friendship between two boys who meet at the Olympic Games.
Walsh, J.P. *Crossing to Salamis,* Heinemann, 1977. A story that describes the restrictions on women in ancient Athens.*
Walsh, J.P. *The Walls of Athens,* Heinemann, 1977. Rebuilding the fortifications of Athens.*

Myths and legends retold

Gates, D. *Golden Gold: Apollo,* Penguin, 1984.*
Gates, D. *Fair wind for Troy,* Penguin, 1984.*
Gates, D. *Mightiest of the mortals: Heracles,* Penguin, 1984.*
Gibson, M. *Gods, men and monsters from the Greek myths,* P. Lowe, 1977.
Green, R.L. *Heroes of Greece and Troy,* Bodley Head, 1960.
Green, R.L. *Luck of Troy,* Penguin, 1990.
Green, R.L. *Tale of Troy,* Penguin, 1989.
Lines, K. *Faber book of Greek legends,* Faber, 1986.
Oldfield, P. *Stories from ancient Greece,* Kingfisher, 1988.
Snelling, *Greek myths and legends,* Wayland, 1987. Simple collection of a few Greek myths.
Storr, C. *King Midas and his gold,* Methuen, 1985.*
Storr, C. *Theseus and the minotaur,* Methuen, 1986.*

*These books are out of print but are still available from libraries and second-hand bookshops.

Blueprints links

You will find a valuable geographical unit of work on modern Greece (Corfu) in *Blueprints: Distant Places*, and relevant ideas in technology in *Blueprints: Technology Key Stage 2*. The following other Stanley Thornes books will also prove useful: *Investigating History: Ancient Greece*.

STUDY UNIT 5
LOCAL
HISTORY

Pupils should be taught about an aspect of local history. This should be ONE of the following:

a an aspect of the local community over a long period of time, *e.g. education, leisure, religion, population change, settlement and landscape, law and order, the treatment of the poor;*

──────────── OR ────────────

b an aspect of the local community during a short period of time or the local community's involvement in a particular event, *e.g. Viking York, the impact of the Norman Conquest on a local area, deserted medieval villages in an area, the local area during the Civil War, how the land was enclosed, the impact of the First World War on the locality;*

──────────── OR ────────────

c an aspect of the local community that illustrates developments taught in the study units, *e.g. local fortifications, the Romans, Anglo-Saxons or Vikings in the local area, life in the country house, child labour in the Industrial Revolution, new towns in the twentieth century.*

TOPIC WEB

Aspects and issues through time – religion

- Survey of places of worship
- Former religious buildings
- The parish church; the significance of the parish
- Maps/models of a parish
- Study of a church – architecture and furniture
- Bells, the organ, church music
- Church buildings – shape, outside features, building materials
- Evidence from gravestones and other churchyard features
- Written records, artefacts, collections
- Other places of worship
- The national scene
- Key dates to remember

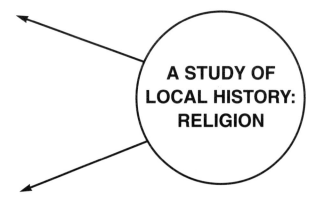

A STUDY OF LOCAL HISTORY: RELIGION

Approaches to study through time

- Use people; conduct interviews
- Consult biographers and diarists
- Investigate sources of evidence, e.g. maps, manuscripts, newspapers, photographs, books, artefacts, other archive material
- Consult the experts – librarians, museum and art gallery staff, archivists, archaeologists
- Ascertain which field sites and buildings to visit

INTRODUCTORY NOTE

Unlike the other topics covered in this book, the local history unit is, inevitably, 'content free'. Your focus will be determined by a variety of individual factors, including the historic 'wealth' of your own specific locality and your choice as to how you will relate this to other Study Units. The ideas for approaches to study that follow are therefore transferable to a variety of situations. They introduce a range of research and recording skills. Religion is then examined as an example of one specific aspect of the local community that is well worth studying. It raises important issues, spans a long period of time, and can be related to national trends and developments taught in other study units.

APPROACHES TO STUDY THROUGH TIME

C62

Activity 1: Let's talk about it

Involve people in the local community in your research. Interviews and less formal discussions are two of the best ways of collecting information, both of a factual and an anecdotal nature. Seek out individuals who have lived in the neighbourhood all their lives, and who can remember significant changes that have taken place or have had personal involvement in the event/issue you are researching. Invite appropriate people into the classroom, or visit them in their homes. The grandparents and great-grandparents of the children (and of yourself!) may well be willing to participate: otherwise, seek advice from your local vicar, librarian or shopkeepers who are likely to know of long-established residents who would oblige.

It is essential that conversations are structured, otherwise general reminiscences may be without focus and the children will find it very difficult to be selective in their recording. In addition, the interviewee will generally be much happier with a pre-decided focus and a list of specific questions. Always ask your guest whether s/he minds the use of a tape-recorder. Recordings have great value for two reasons: firstly, it is almost impossible for the children to listen to every word said and make worthwhile notes at the same time, and secondly, the recording will be a very valuable resource that can be kept and used on many future occasions. Indeed, as the years go by, it will become an historic artefact in its own right.

Be sure to position the tape-recorder and guest speaker carefully before recording starts. Check that the recording level is adequate. Operate the recorder from the mains whenever possible, and have spare tapes and batteries available in case they are needed. A machine with built-in microphone(s) is less inhibiting for someone unused to public speaking. Leave the tape running during pauses, 'fluffs' or other interruptions rather than constantly stopping and starting – you can always edit the tape afterwards.

Design a questionnaire for use with your guests. This is a key skill in itself (see also the activities suggested on pages 77 and 80, which contain an outline questionnaire).

Activity 2: Do you remember?

Copymaster 62 provides some basic questions which can be elaborated upon. It will help children to appreciate the need for structure, and the importance of distilling answers into succinct phrases. Help them also to understand that it is the key facts that should be recorded, not every word an individual says. The sheet should be filled in with as few words as possible – words that will jog memories about the wider conversation. The space at the bottom of the sheet allows for the children's own questions about the specific event/issue under investigation. These could, of course, be decided by the class as a whole and added before the sheet is photocopied.

If possible, take photographs of your interviewees. As with tape-recordings, they can be used 'today' to illustrate accounts and wall-displays, and will form valuable artefacts of tomorrow. Ask your interviewees to bring photographs along with them if they can to show the class, or ideally to lend. Precious photographs could of course be photocopied (and enlarged, if the school has access to a suitable copier) if the visitor would rather not part with them. It is most important to emphasise that what appears merely to be an old photograph to the children is a valuable possession to its owner, and must be respected accordingly. If such items are loaned, they should be well protected (perhaps behind glass or in clear polythene/plastic envelopes) before being displayed, and returned intact with a letter of thanks from the children. Never pin through such items when displaying them – a plastic paper-clip attached to each corner and suitably adjusted will provide a small loop through which to pin, thus avoiding needless damage.

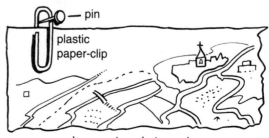
document or photograph

Activity 3: A visit to the library

Extend this use of oral evidence by seeking out the work of local biographers or diarists. Your local librarian will be a valuable source of information about suitable authors of personal observations, and many other resources. Pay a visit to the local-studies department of your library before the study commences, and ascertain the availability of maps, newspapers, photographs, books, manuscripts and other artefacts. Enquire about loan services and the organisation of visits to the library by your pupils. (See below.)

Activity 4: Mapping it out

Make a collection of maps of your area – both recent and historic, and study maps in the local-history department of the library. Look for differences in street names, and location and use of buildings and open space through time. Walk around the area to view apparent changes in land or building use. Ask the children to suggest why certain industries/shops/housing estates have been established in particular places.

Take photographs of the present-day locality, and compare them with photographic evidence of days gone by. As with maps, these will form useful evidence for discovering changes in street layout, transport lines, use of buildings and space. Ascertain whether it is possible to obtain aerial photographs of the neighbourhood – a valuable source of evidence, as well as a means of developing skills of map interpretation.

Activity 5: Using other resources

Make a study of other original sources: documents and archives (a visit to the city or county Records Office will be necessary if you wish to consult certain original documents). Various publishers have made collections of printed and archival sources (including copies of newspapers, posters, manuscripts, maps, parish registers, inventories and letters) which are available for purchase as history-teaching packs (see *Resources* on page 110).

Find out if any audio-visual and/or computer-software materials are available about your local area – perhaps focusing on a nearby site or building of historical interest. If not, then many general tapes/programs will be relevant as background information to an issue or event you are investigating, for example, life during World War II.

BBC network and local radio stations may be able to help you with recordings of historical documentaries, oral history and other sources of material. A weekly copy of *The Radio Times* and a supply of audio/video cassette tapes would be a useful investment.

Activity 6: Consult the experts

The head of the local-studies department of your library has already been mentioned as a key person to contact. There are others: the chief librarian, the Education Officers at the museum and art gallery, the director of the city or county Records Office, the local archivist, local archaeologists.

Talk to all of these people as you plan your study. Enlist their help in locating original and secondary resource material and in organising visits. Key questions to ask are:

- How could you help in providing access to artefacts and other materials for research?
- Can the pupils visit the library/Records Office/museum/art gallery?
- Are there sites of archaeological interest/discoveries nearby?
- Would you be willing to come to school and talk to the children?

– What other places in the locality can you recommend for a visit? (Perhaps National Trust, English Heritage or privately owned buildings or sites of antiquity.)
– What are the most worthwhile aspects of the locality to study from an historical point of view?

The result of these investigations should be to illuminate the potential of the local area for sound historical study, both from the point of view of original material to investigate, and the availability of sufficient back-up material to make it meaningful and worthwhile.

Study Unit 5: Local History – approaches to study through time. Suggested levels of work involved in activities

Activity number	Level	Activity number	Level	Activity number	Level
1	2/3/4/5	3	2/3/4	5	2/3/4
2	2/3/4/5	4	2/3/4	6	2/3

COMMUNITY RELIGION THROUGH TIME

C63–68

This aspect of the project will inevitably incorporate discussion of personal views, beliefs and other controversial issues, which must be handled in a very sensitive way. Activities centred around graves and churchyard evidence may not be appropriate if any children in your class have suffered a recent family bereavement.

Activity 1: An area survey
Begin with a survey of places of worship in your locality. Walk around the area and note the names and positions of any churches, temples, meeting houses, etc. Ask the children to say what places of worship they attend, and where these are. This survey will obviously vary a great deal depending on the location of your school, which may be in a village with one parish church, or in an inner-city area with numerous different buildings for the practice of many faiths. Plot your results on a map of the area (see also Activity 15).

As you survey the locality on foot, look for evidence of any buildings that were formerly religious meeting houses and are now used for other purposes. Test out your hypotheses about change in use by consulting the various forms of evidence discussed previously – maps, photographs, archives and the memories of local people. If you do find such buildings, make 'before' and 'after' pictures, if possible using photographic evidence to draw the original building.

Discuss reasons for the alteration in use of religious buildings – changes in population size and distribution, in religious beliefs, and in the significance of religion in people's lives through time.

Activity 2: Choose a church
Undertake an in-depth study of one or more of the religious buildings still in use today. If a large number exist, you may wish to be selective or divide the children into groups to carry out certain activities. No doubt

pupils and their parents who worship in a particular building will be able to provide further information and personal contacts. Begin with the parish church and help the children to understand the significance of the fact that their school is situated in a particular parish. This will provide links into a study of the history of the church through a long period of time. Make a preliminary visit to the church yourself and arrange to meet and talk to the vicar. Ask him or her:

– What is a convenient time for the class to visit?
– Would you be able to spare time to answer children's questions and provide information?
– What are the most interesting features of the building?
– What guide books/literature/photographs are available for sale and consultation?

Assure the vicar that the children will be well prepared and well behaved, and that the emphasis of their work is on practical investigation rather than on 'lecture-style' transmission of facts.

Activity 3: Work on the parish
Undertake background work in the classroom by finding out the name of the parish that the church is in. Investigate the history of the English parish system, which dates from around A.D. 600. Find out if the school is in the same parish as the church you are studying. Draw diagrams to show the present-day hierarchy of the Church of England, divided into dioceses (see next page).

This could be expanded to show junior clergy and lay readers of the church responsible to the vicar, and the bishop in turn being responsible to an archbishop. Ask the children to find out who is the ultimate head of the Church of England, and the names of the Archbishops of York and Canterbury. They could also find out the name of the bishop of their own diocese, how many

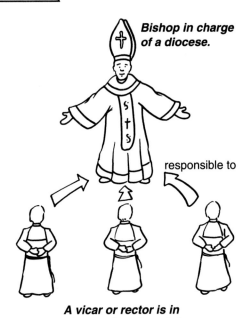

Bishop in charge of a diocese.

responsible to

A vicar or rector is in charge of each parish.

parishes he oversees, and the names of the bishop's own church/cathedral. Vocabulary will improve once the children are aware of what words like 'vicar', 'rector', 'diocese', 'parish', 'bishop', 'archbishop' and 'lay/laity' mean.

Find out more about the tithe system, and the origin of the term 'tithe barn'. From the year 1285 rectors were paid by tithes – one tenth of each villager's crops and livestock from within his parish.

Consult the vicar for details of the parish boundaries. Locate these on printed maps, then draw your own map of the parish, using appropriate symbols to show the church, the school, key roads (especially those leading to the church), and any other religious buildings or significant landmarks.

Activity 4: Do you live in this parish?

Work out which children in the class live within the parish boundary and plot their homes on your map. A great deal of worthwhile mathematics and mapwork can be done by considering such questions as 'Who lives nearest to the church?' (as the crow flies, and by road); 'Who lives nearest to the parish boundary?' etc.

Find out the practical significance of the parish boundary, in terms of such things as eligibility to appear on the electoral roll, or to be married in the church. In certain parts of the country, particularly in the north, there is a ceremony known as 'beating the bounds' which the children could investigate.

Progress from a map to a model of the parish. Construct the boundary out of corrugated card or wood and wire. Add model buildings of the church and school and paint the roads on the 'floorscape'. It will probably not be possible to depict every house on your model – perhaps you could add those of children in the class. Help the children to appreciate that a real parish boundary does not exist as a physical barrier: it is an imaginary line on the ground.

Find out the approximate size of the parish – what area of ground does it cover? How many houses are in

it? How many people? How many of those people are on the electoral roll/attend church services regularly?

Activity 5: Visiting the church

Prepare children for visits by talking about the function of the church – it is a 'house of God' that has probably withstood the test of time better than any other building in the community. Discuss why – it was built with care, and has always been maintained with care. Talk about the 'atmosphere' of a church, and the expectations of peace and tranquillity of its visitors. This will lead into a discussion of appropriate behaviour in and around the church, and sensible reasons why the children must behave respectfully during any visit.

Visit the church for study purposes: indeed, a series of visits may be necessary in order to investigate fully both inside and outside the building. Compile and take along with you an 'at-a-glance' dictionary of architectural terms the children may hear from the vicar or be asked to identify.

Activity 6: Inside the church

Copymaster 63 can be prepared from research in the classroom, then taken along and used as a recording sheet on the visit. Ask pupils to fill in the correct name for the feature being described, and then to tick the box when they have located the feature in the church. Appropriate sketches can be done on separate sheets of paper. Correct 'answers' for the copymaster, in order, are: aisle, altar, chancel, crossing, nave, piscina, reredos, transept. Space at the bottom of the sheet allows you to add a few additional words applicable to your church (e.g. tower, spire, chapel) before the sheet is photocopied.

Make a similar sheet to explain the 'furniture' of the church. Appropriate words for inclusion are pews, font, choir stalls, lectern, pulpit, banners, hassocks, organ. Ask the children to locate each of these features in the building and to make sketches of them, noting any interesting details (carving, lettering, etc). Discuss the use of this furniture.

Prepare a plan of your church building to take along on the visit. A typical plan is provided on **Copymaster 64** as an aid to explaining the 'standard layout' of a church. It will also help to locate such features as the chancel, crossing and transept. Depending on the age and ability of the pupils, these features can be labelled on your plan in advance, or the children can label a blank outline.

Ask the children to whom the church is dedicated. Perhaps they can find out more about the life of the particular saint.

Activity 7: A closer look at the windows

Study the church windows and sketch any pictures in the stained glass. Note down the details of the scenes depicted, and try to date the windows as accurately as possible. The children could make 'stained-glass' window scenes on their return to school. Display the finished work on any available classroom windows. Ask the children which Bible stories they think will make good stained-glass window designs.

Norman grotesque corbels

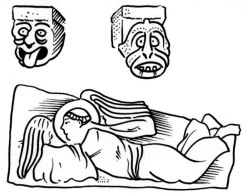

A misericord

One of the angels above a
Saxon chancel arch

A corbel

Activity 8: Other decorative features
Sketch any interesting pillars, doors or stone/wood carvings inside the building (see below and next page). These drawings can be used later as an aid to identification of the church architecture. Are there any carved bosses or coats of arms to be seen? If so, try to find out their significance. And does your church have any misericords?

Copymaster 65 introduces the art of brass-rubbing. With the permission of the vicar, make rubbings of stonework or brasses. You will need: 'heel ball' or cobblers' wax (like crayon, but softer), or perhaps oil pastels if cobblers' wax is not available; plenty of good quality plain white paper (perhaps in a roll); a reel of adhesive tape, as wide as possible, with which to tape down the paper over the brass before rubbing begins.

A typical
Norman
column

Late Norman
decorated capital

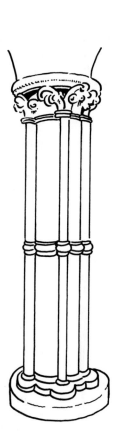

Early English column

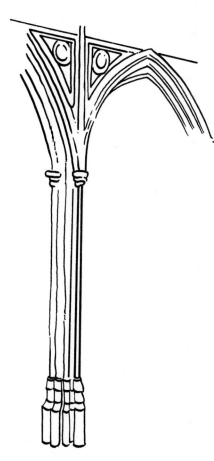

A nave column of the
Perpendicular style

Brasses are often valued for their antiquity, and it is possible to damage them unintentionally by using the wrong materials when rubbing. For example, it is wise to avoid the usual crayons found in school: they may scratch the brass. In fact, before launching the children on any brass-rubbing, consult a good handbook for practical advice and detailed instructions on how to carry out the activity effectively.

Ask questions about the people depicted on the brasses – often members of rich local families, benefactors of the church, or knights. Can the children find out the names of these people? Do the brasses include any birds or animals, and if so what do they tell us? The children could write a story about one of the people, making up an imaginary life history or particular adventure set in the appropriate period. Some typical brasses are shown below.

Activity 9: Music, memorials and records

Find out whether the church has bells. If so, it might be possible to arrange for a demonstration ringing, or to visit the bell-tower. This could lead to a fascinating sub-topic, on bell-ringing, to include when and how bells are rung, where the bells were 'cast', how many there are, and the names of different peals.

Sketch the church organ. Again, this may have a fascinating history. Who designed it, and when? Who plays it now? A sub-topic on ecclesiastical music would make a wonderful link between history and music in the curriculum. Find out if the organist would be prepared to play the instrument for the class to hear.

Look for historical evidence provided by memorials, both plaques and effigies. Write down the wording on

plaques, and discuss the significance of effigies – only rich people would have been buried inside the church. What can they tell us about such things as fashion, armour and lifestyle?

Find out about the written records kept by the church. Most old buildings will have details of weddings, christenings and burials, perhaps dating back to 1538, in the reign of King Henry VIII, when a parish register became a requirement. These registers provide a wealth of information about local people, as well as social and cultural changes.

Ask whether the church has any particularly valuable or interesting artefacts locked away for safe-keeping. Some churches have individual items, others have a 'museum' or special collection of objects or documents. The children may not be able to handle these, but the vicar will no doubt be prepared to talk about them and suggest how they are valuable evidence of the church's history and role in the wider community.

Activity 10: Outside the church

Walk around the outside of the church building. Make a sketch of its shape as a whole, noting obvious features such as the tower, spire, lich-gate and weather-vane. (See also **Copymaster 66**.) The illustrations on page 107 show the various features outside a typical parish church, and a common pattern of development for a church building of some antiquity.

If the church has a tower, sketch this accurately and note whether it is square, round, triangular or octagonal. Research the significance of the tower shape (round towers are particularly common in East Anglia). This activity could give rise to lots of opportunities for mathematics work, in terms of estimation and measurement. (See page 108.)

Note the materials used for the construction of the church. **Copymaster 66** introduces the subject of building materials. The top section of this sheet has been left blank for the children to sketch the outline shape of the church building. The space provided is not large, but it is sufficient to make a field-sketch which can be elaborated upon later. It is best to economise whenever possible on the number of sheets of paper children are carrying out into the field, and fastening them into a simple workbook is probably a good idea. The lower half of the sheet provides space to record details of the materials, information which is useful when dating parts of the building and discussing architecture. Questions to be asked could include:

- Is the stone local, or does it come from some distance away?
- Have tiles or bricks been used as well as stone, or perhaps instead of it?
- What is the roof made of – is it wood, slate, stone, tile, thatch? Or something else?
- Have extra parts been added to the original building over the years? If so, how do you know?
- Are there any stonemason's marks to be found? Some masons liked to 'autograph' their work when it was finished.

14th century armour

A titled lady of about 1460 to 1470

weather-vane
pinnacle
tower
gargoyle
bell louvres
parapet
buttress
scratch dial
table tomb
tombstone
west door
churchyard cross
lich-gate
gravestone
niche
porch
corbel

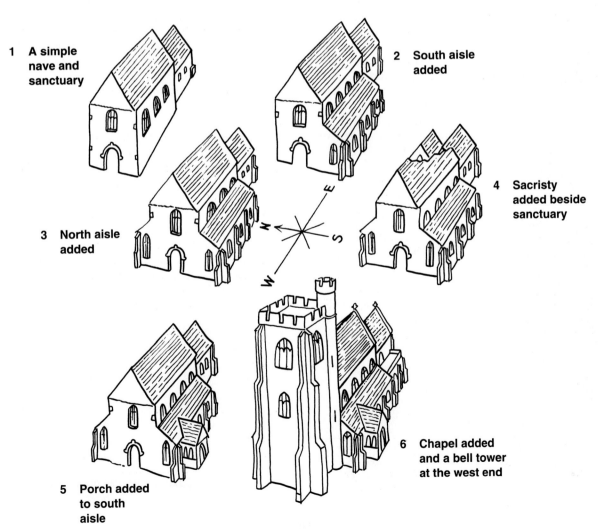

1 A simple nave and sanctuary

2 South aisle added

3 North aisle added

4 Sacristy added beside sanctuary

5 Porch added to south aisle

6 Chapel added and a bell tower at the west end

107

Some of the many shapes of church towers.

Background information:
Church buildings can generally be categorised into nine different periods or styles, as follows (though these dates are approximate):

pre–1066	Saxon
1066–1190	Norman
1160–1300	Early English
1270–1350	Decorated
1350–1580	Perpendicular
1600–1712	Jacobean
1700–1820	Georgian
1830–1900	Victorian
1900 onwards	Twentieth-century

If a survey of various churches in the neighbourhood is envisaged, perhaps the children could compile a wall-chart or do some graph work in order to record what periods the buildings belong to. Doorways and window-arches sometimes give clues as to when churches were built.

Activity 11: Gargoyles, corbels and lich-gates

Look for gargoyles – decorated waterspouts which take rainwater from the roof. Discuss why these are often fierce, evil-looking creatures (see above). Back in the classroom, make a painted or collage gargoyle frieze, or perhaps attempt some 'real' gargoyles using clay or papier mâché.

Ask the children to find out the difference between a corbel and a gargoyle. (A corbel is a projection from the face of a wall, supporting a weight. Often corbels are carved to represent heads or whole figures.) Are there any carved bosses or coats of arms to be seen on the outside of the building? If so, try to find out their significance.

If your church has a lich-gate, sketch this and investigate its history and significance. 'Lych' or 'lich' is the Saxon word for 'corpse', and the gate was an important focal point in the funerals of days gone by.

Activity 12: Information from the churchyard

Observing appropriate behaviour, and keeping to the pathways, investigate the churchyard. Graves and tombs can yield a wealth of historical information, giving details of local family names, occupations, life-spans and sometimes the causes of death.

Copymaster 67 serves a two-fold purpose. Ask pupils to 'fill in' the gravestones with details of the oldest grave they can find, a family grave, and one they consider to be the most interesting. (Back in the classroom, ask them to explain their reasons for identifying the latter.) Read the various inscriptions carefully since they will reveal a great deal about the significance of religion in people's lives. Around the edge of the copymaster sheet sketch any other interesting aspects of the churchyard, perhaps yew trees, a sundial or some special memorial. Make a separate inventory of all the gravestones, and dates of the births and deaths recorded.

From the results of this gravestone research, discuss how life-expectancy has increased through the years and try to find reasons for this. Consider each century (or perhaps a fifty-year period) and suggest the average life-expectancy of people during that period. Raise the related question of infant mortality, and investigate whether this seems to have changed through time.

Activity 13: Church architecture

Use your field-sketches as the basis for a sub-topic on church architecture. Consult reference books to find out about key features of particular periods. Some examples are shown below and opposite.

It may be that your parish church is made up of a variety of architectural styles, and was not completed in one period of history. Relate this to the wider 'national' picture of church building and architectural styles.

**A Saxon chancel arch
showing 'long and short' work.**

Norman doorway

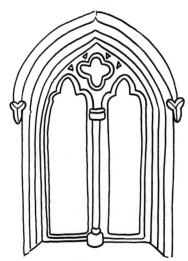

Early English window

Decorated window

Regency window

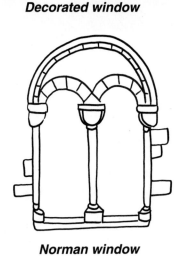

Norman window

Victorian gothic window

Activity 14: Classroom follow-up

Follow-up work in the classroom will, of course, involve elaborate art and craft work (brass-rubbings, stained-glass windows, gargoyles, pictures of the church, etc.) and detailed factual writing about the church as a whole – its past and its present. Once again, a tape-recording of the visit can assist in recall as well as being a useful resource for the future. You could even relate back to the introductory work on parishes by extending the church project to include a visit to, and an investigation of, your nearest cathedral church.

Activity 15: Other places of worship

The emphasis thus far has been on your local parish church, undoubtedly a worthwhile starting point. No unit on religion would be complete, however, without listing (or preferably visiting) other places of worship in the local community, and finding out about their activities and significance. A large number of the preceding activities are transferable to other places of worship. Compare and contrast the buildings, their architecture and furniture.

Activity 16: The wider context

Set your church studies within a much broader framework of national trends. Various activities already described have suggested how this might possibly be done. The role of religion in people's lives can be viewed alongside cultural, social and economic changes in Britain, and the beliefs and actions of certain monarchs.

A background knowledge of key dates will be helpful throughout the project, and **Copymaster 68** is designed to assist in this. Ask pupils to match each event with the appropriate date. Depending on the age and ability of the children, either give background information about each event (perhaps on prepared cards), or encourage open research from reference books. The sheet can be used as a basis for writing about significant happenings in the history of religion and beliefs, and to start off an illustrated timeline on 'Religion in Britain'. To save you time, the correct matching is

597	St Augustine's mission. Beginnings of the Christian church in England.
600s	Start of the church parish system.
800s	Vikings, who worshipped pagan gods, attacked Christians in Britain.
1285	Payment by tithes became law.
1534	Henry VIII became head of the Church of England.
1538	Parish registers had to be kept by law.
1649	Puritans in power under Oliver Cromwell.
1878	William Booth founded the Salvation Army.

Study Unit 5: Local History – community religion through time.
Suggested levels of work involved in activities

Activity number	Level	Activity number	Level	Activity number	Level
1	2/3/4/5	7	2/3/4	12	2/3/4/5
2	2/3/4	8	2/3/4	13	2/3/4/5
3	2/3/4	9	2/3/4/5	14	2/3/4/5
4	2/3/4	10	2/3/4/5	15	2/3/4/5
5	2/3/4	11	2/3/4	16	2/3/4/5
6	2/3/4				

RESOURCES ▶

Summary of historical sources

Maps (street maps, village and town maps, Ordnance Survey maps).

Newspapers local and national (also facsimile reproductions).

Periodicals/magazines of local societies and parishes.

Parish records registers, ratebooks, chapel records, etc.

Other records of private businesses, deeds, family and estate documents, letters.

Electoral registers

Directories, e.g. 'Kelly'.

Photographs, paintings, posters, drawings, prints, postcards.

Legal records for example, census returns, school log-books.

Reference books

Braun, H. *Parish Churches*, Faber, 1970.

Iredale, D. *Local History Research*, Phillimore (Chichester), 1974.

Jones, L. *The Beauty of English Churches*, Constable, 1978.

Pluckrose, H. *Look around – Outside*, Heinemann, 1984.

Rider, P. *Local History – A Handbook*, Batsford, 1983.

Smith, E. et al. *English Parish Churches*, Thames and Hudson, 1976.

Stephens, W.B. *Sources for Local History*, Manchester University Press, 1973.

Watkins, P. and Hughes, E. *Here's the Church*, Julia MacRae, 1980.

'Religions of the World' series, Simon & Schuster Educational, 1991. Titles include *The Muslim World, The Hindu World, The Jewish World, The Christian World, The Buddhist World, The Sikh World, The New Religious World.*

Blueprints links

You will find the following other Stanley Thornes books useful: *Local History Detectives: Churches; History Timeline: A Local Study*

STUDY UNIT 6
A PAST, NON-EUROPEAN SOCIETY

Pupils should be taught about the key features of a past non-European society chosen from the following list:

■ Ancient Egypt;
■ Mesopotamia, *e.g. Ancient Sumer or the Assyrian Empire*;
■ the Indus Valley;
■ the Maya;
■ Benin;
■ the Aztecs.

This unit should cover:
a key features, including the everyday lives of men and women;
b the use of archaeology in finding out about the people and society.

TOPIC WEB

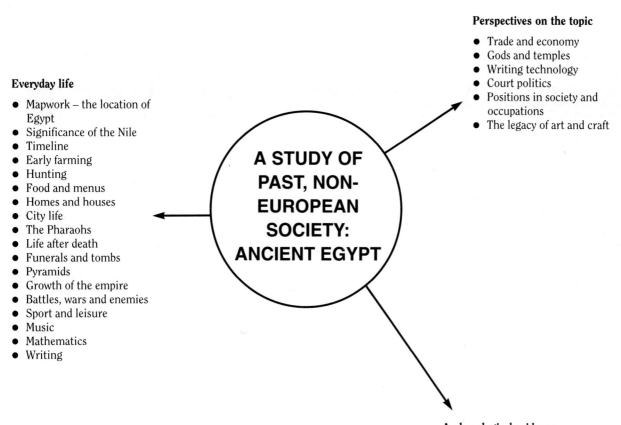

Everyday life

- Mapwork – the location of Egypt
- Significance of the Nile
- Timeline
- Early farming
- Hunting
- Food and menus
- Homes and houses
- City life
- The Pharaohs
- Life after death
- Funerals and tombs
- Pyramids
- Growth of the empire
- Battles, wars and enemies
- Sport and leisure
- Music
- Mathematics
- Writing

A STUDY OF PAST, NON-EUROPEAN SOCIETY: ANCIENT EGYPT

Perspectives on the topic

- Trade and economy
- Gods and temples
- Writing technology
- Court politics
- Positions in society and occupations
- The legacy of art and craft

Archaeological evidence

- Importance and nature of evidence
- The role of archaeologists

KEY FEATURES AND EVERYDAY LIFE

Activity 1: Where is Egypt?

Consult an atlas or globe to locate Egypt in the modern world. Explain how the civilisation of Ancient Egypt began some 7000 years ago on the banks of the River Nile. Consider the position of the Nile in relation to the Mediterranean Sea and Red Sea. Use **Copymaster 69** both to study the position of Egypt, and as an ongoing worksheet to which other items of information can be added as the topic progresses. In the first instance, ask the children to colour in blue the Mediterranean Sea, the Red Sea and the rivers; and to add these labels; Mediterranean Sea, Red Sea, River Nile, White Nile, Blue Nile. Then, at appropriate stages of the topic, ask the children to draw dots for and label the main towns (Giza, Memphis, Thebes, Khartoum, Sakkarah); and to colour in, as accurately as possible, the areas of Egypt and the Egyptian Empire.

Activity 2: The early settlers

Talk about why the great River Nile attracted early settlers. What did these people do? How did they live? This discussion provides an excellent link with the geographical study of a distant country. Explain how, over a period of time, the surrounding land had become dry, barren desert, and people had to search for a water supply. Write about the dangers and adventures involved in entering this territory – the Nile valley was marshy and full of dangerous wild creatures. Paint pictures of this formidable swampy jungle, complete with crocodiles and hippopotami.

Activity 3: A timeline

Begin a timeline of key events in the history of Egypt, large enough to go on the classroom wall. The children can add to this and include suitable illustrations as the topic progresses. Here are a few dates to start you off.

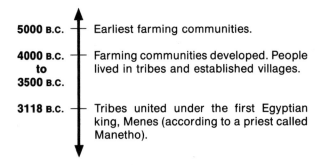

5000 B.C.	Earliest farming communities.
4000 B.C. to 3500 B.C.	Farming communities developed. People lived in tribes and established villages.
3118 B.C.	Tribes united under the first Egyptian king, Menes (according to a priest called Manetho).

Activity 4: The early farmers

Write accounts of early attempts at farming on the fertile muddy banks that resulted from the annual flooding of the River Nile (known as the inundation). Why do the children think Egypt was sometimes known as the 'Black Land'? Find out what crops were grown and which animals were reared.

Grow your own 'Egyptian crops' – barley and wheat. Sow seeds of these plants in the classroom, and set up experiments to investigate their ideal conditions for growth – light/dark? wet/dry? warm/cold? Discuss why such grains flourished on the banks of the Nile. Would they have survived away from the river?

Background information: *The early farmers*

The annual flooding of the Nile was caused by a combination of melting snow in Ethiopia and rainfall from Central Africa, usually between late June and September. The floods left a layer of rich mud over the land which enabled the Egyptians to grow crops. Planting could begin around November when the floods had subsided. Egypt even had the nickname of 'Kemi', meaning the 'Black Land', as a result of these rich deposits. The main crops were wheat and barley, also onions, garlic, lentils, beans, figs, olives, grapes, dates and pomegranates. The Egyptians tamed cattle, sheep, donkeys, goats and pigs.

Activity 5: Egyptian irrigation

Consider the key issue of availability of water all through the year – if the Nile flooded only once, surely there were problems. Ask the children to suggest how these problems might have been solved. Draw pictures or plans of the Ancient Egyptians' solution (see overleaf). Compare this with the irrigation methods used in Egyptian agriculture today. Have there been dramatic changes in technology in 5000 years?

Discuss how we know about ancient methods of irrigation in Egypt. Look for evidence on reproductions of contemporary paintings. You could try making a shaduf – a splendid project for design and technology.

Background information: *Egyptian irrigation*

Egyptian farmers stored the annual flood waters in elaborate systems of canals which could be dammed when water was plentiful, and then released through channels in the fields when water was scarce.

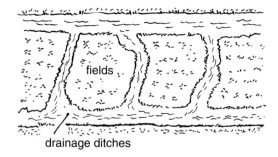
fields

drainage ditches

Activity 6: The farming year

Construct circular or triangular diagrams to illustrate the three seasons into which the Egyptian farming year was divided (see top of next page).

Each section can be illustrated with collage or paintings, and specific months of the year added for increased detail.

Make up word puzzles associated with the seasonal pattern. Consider a list of words, for example,

The Egyptian farming year.

'inundation', 'silt', 'till', 'hoe', 'scatter', 'plough', 'sickle', 'threshing', 'flail'. Locate these in the appropriate section of the diagram.

Write stories about hunting in the surrounding desert or in the waterways. Describe the mode of transport (for example, papyrus-stem boats); the equipment needed (spears, nets, harpoons, ropes); and the object of the expedition (fish, wild birds, animals) and how they were caught.

Make illustrated charts, like the ones shown below, to show how the crops were used. Similar charts can be developed for flax (used to make linen) and barley (used to make beer).

Background information: The farming year
The farming calendar consisted of three seasons, known as 'Flooding', 'Growth' and 'Harvest'. The soil was sometimes fertile enough for farmers to grow two crops before harvesting was over. The hot weather began again in April.

Activity 7: Food for the family
Design a menu for a typical rural family (perhaps bread, cheese, fruit and salad). Compare this with the variety of foods that would have been eaten by the wealthy (far more meat, including pork, beef, antelope, goose and duck, together with fish and a much wider range of breads and fruits). Act out an Egyptian meal in the classroom, with appropriate foods, seating and eating styles. Adults sat on basic stools. Children sat on mats. Utensils were knives and fingers.

Activity 8: A house in rural Egypt
Investigate the details of a typical house of rural Egypt. Using evidence derived from other books and photographs, ask the pupils to make a drawing as accurately as possible and to label building materials. Suggested additions include people (on the upper storey), grain bins and animals on the ground floor, and vegetable plots in the surrounding space outside the walls.

Construct houses like this out of boxes. A rectangular box, such as a shoebox, is ideal for the base and ground floor. Add a cardboard stage for the upper storey, supported by corrugated-card pillars and steps. The boxes can be painted or, ideally, covered with beige-coloured paper. Use scraps of straw to give an authentic appearance to the courtyard, strewn alongside dome-shaped storage bins.

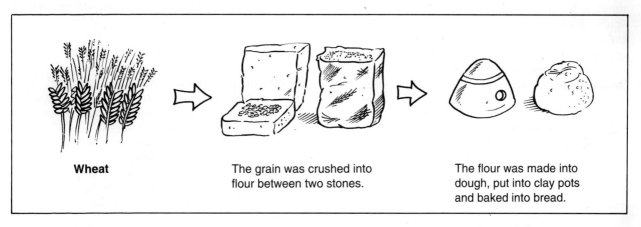

Wheat — The grain was crushed into flour between two stones. — The flour was made into dough, put into clay pots and baked into bread.

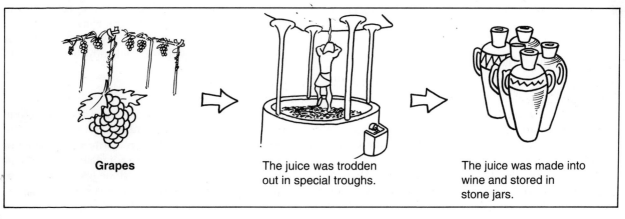

Grapes — The juice was trodden out in special troughs. — The juice was made into wine and stored in stone jars.

Compare these simple country houses with their more elaborate counterparts owned by the wealthy, and also with town houses. Paint pictures of larger dwellings, and make a list of comparisons, some of which are given here.

Homes of rural workers	Homes of the wealthy
Exterior – the original sun-dried mud or brick.	Houses plastered and painted.
Bare floors and walls.	Floor-rugs, wall-paintings.
No bathroom.	Bathroom and lavatory inside the house.

Background information: *Houses*
Most houses were made of mud bricks, baked in the hot sun. Windows were usually small, set high into the wall to cut down direct sunlight and keep the house cool. Wealthy Egyptians may also have owned a garden with shady trees and a pool, enclosed by a high wall. Poorer people made reed or mud huts, with bundles of reeds serving as a thatched roof.

Activity 9: A city street in Egypt
Make a large collage of a street scene from a city in the days of the Egyptian Empire (*c.* 1000 B.C.). Houses were often four or five storeys high because of scarcity of land. Roof space was used for living and sleeping.

Activity 10: The Egyptian pharaohs
Introduce the word 'pharaoh' or king. Discuss how the pharaoh was viewed as a god by the people, who believed his personal powers caused the annual flooding of the Nile. Find out and write about a king's life – his work, duties, family and privileges. This will lead into a major aspect of the topic as a whole – temples and tombs – which were built for the pharaohs. Ask the children to find out what they can about pharaohs like Akhenaten (and his queen Nefertiti), Cheops and Rameses.

Background information: *The Egyptian pharaohs*
The word 'pharaoh' means 'great house' (perhaps 'palace'?). Out of respect, the Egyptians would not refer to their god-king by name, and so they used the word 'pharaoh' – for example, to explain that 'the palace has ordered' something to be done.

The king had absolute power over the land and the people. He commanded the Egyptian army, and was also the chief priest. As he was a god, the king could not marry an ordinary woman, but only someone of royal blood: hence, many kings married their half-sister or sister.

Activity 11: Queen Hatshepsut
Find out as much as possible about Queen Hatshepsut, one of the few women pharaohs of Egypt.

Background information
The temple building of Queen Hatshepsut, one of the few women pharaohs, is at Deir el Bahari. The temple architect was Senenmut. It still stands today, though much of the original decoration has worn away. Hatshepsut's dates are 1503–1482 B.C. Her stepson,

Tuthmosis III, became the greatest of Egypt's warrior pharaohs.

Activity 12: Ruling the land
Ask the children to investigate how the people were governed, how taxes were collected, and how law and order was maintained. (Egyptian methods could be compared and contrasted with those of the Greeks and Romans.)

Background information: *Ruling the land*
The most important official under the pharaoh was the vizier. He upheld the law and commanded the royal treasury. Administration was carried out by the educated class of scribes, who kept records, collected taxes, and so on. Taxes were not paid in money, but in crops, livestock or other goods.

Activity 13: Life after death
Link work on tombs and pyramids to the beliefs held about life after death. Find out about customs and practices associated with the death of a king or nobleman. Write about the work of an embalmer, and draw pictures of mummies after the completion of the embalming process.

Copymaster 70 can be used for recording in pictorial form the details of a funeral procession. Ask the children to colour in the drawing of the coffin with the embalmed body being carried along to the tomb, and then to draw in other members of the funeral procession. This would include priests and mourners, as well as slaves carrying goods to accompany the deceased to the grave. Discuss the nature of these goods (everything that would be needed in the next world).

Compare the ceremony of a funeral procession for a member of the nobility with the simple arrangements made for the poor. Such people were buried in simple graves with a limited array of 'grave goods'.

Background information: *Life after death*
The mummification process took 70 days to carry out. The embalmer would draw out the brain through the nose with a wire hook, and remove the internal organs by cutting open the left side of the body. These organs were then dried out and stored in four jars. The heart was left in place. The body was covered in natron, a form of salt, which dried it out after about 40 days. It was then washed, anointed with perfumes and oils, and wrapped in layers of linen bandage.

The Egyptians believed that Osiris, ruler of the underworld, had the power to grant eternal life. The heart of each dead person would be weighed on a pair of scales: a heart heavy with sin would not balance, and its owner would be condemned.

Activity 14: The Pyramids
Design, construct and paint models of the huge stone pyramids that were built to enclose the tombs and the treasures of the dead pharaohs. Write about pyramid building at every stage – the detailed planning and architectural design, quarrying stone from the ground, cutting and moving the stones, constructing the walls, locating the tomb and burial chamber.

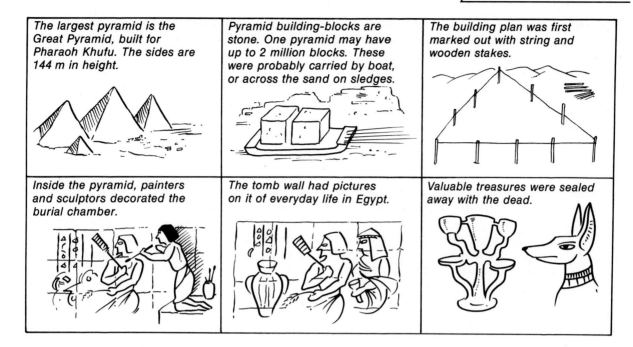

The largest pyramid is the Great Pyramid, built for Pharaoh Khufu. The sides are 144 m in height.

Pyramid building-blocks are stone. One pyramid may have up to 2 million blocks. These were probably carried by boat, or across the sand on sledges.

The building plan was first marked out with string and wooden stakes.

Inside the pyramid, painters and sculptors decorated the burial chamber.

The tomb wall had pictures on it of everyday life in Egypt.

Valuable treasures were sealed away with the dead.

Write a 'pyramid dictionary' to explain key words associated with these wonders; and make up a class book or display of 'pyramid facts' (see above).

Discuss pyramid security, i.e. how the tombs and treasures were hidden from thieves. Ask the children how they would have resolved this problem. Consider the appropriateness of the Egyptians' solutions, which included a maze of passages, false burial chambers, and the strength of huge stone slabs.

Draw plans of the inside of a pyramid, showing the burial chamber, ante-chamber, false chamber, and passages. Reproduce pictures of artwork that may have been painted on the walls and ceiling of the tomb and burial chamber. This may have taken some years. The rough stone was covered with a limestone plaster and marked out in squares. The scene to be depicted was worked out in miniature on a flat stone, which was 'squared up' in the same way as the wall. It was then a comparatively easy task to transfer the scene, square by square, to the area to be decorated.

Write about 'burying the pharaoh', following the work done on **Copymaster 70**. Include details of the 'opening the mouth' ceremony conducted at the entrance of the pyramid.

Find out what remains of the pyramids today. Point out to the children how they are able to tell us so much about the history of Ancient Egypt. Consult books, travel brochures and (where possible) museum evidence. Locate the sites of the pyramids on a map. There are about thirty pyramids in Egypt, the largest of which are at Giza. Tell the children about the Valley of the Kings.

Ask the children to find out about the construction of the Aswan Dam, and the operation to rescue the temple of Rameses II at Abu Simbel. Use the story as a problem-solving exercise – describe the situation and ask the children to propose solutions. They could frame their suggestions in written or pictorial form.

Activity 15: The Pyramid Game

The Pyramid Game on **Copymaster 71** can be cut out and mounted on stiff card. If appropriate, the bonuses and penalties on the gameboard could be blanked out before photocopying, so that the children can write in ideas of their own. For more permanent resources, ask the children to colour the boards and cover them with clear plastic. The game is intended to be played in pairs, with the aid of suitable counters and a dice. Players must land on the steps of the tomb entrance with an exact throw before proceeding into the pyramid itself. The winner is the first to land on the sarcophagus in the inner chamber.

Activity 16: Tutankhamun

Many tombs in the Valley of Kings had been stripped of their valuables by the time archaeologists excavated them. Tell the story of Tutankhamun, a boy-king whose tomb survived the activities of thieves. This exciting story offers much scope for artwork and creative writing. Ask the children to write the page(s) of Howard Carter's diary recording his feelings and impressions on discovering the treasures of Tutankhamun.

The children could make miniature 'mummies' from papier mâché and decorate them in the style of the Egyptians. They might even undertake the building of a life-size 'golden coffin' and mummified body, complete with death mask, in one corner of the classroom, and/or make some of the treasures from scrap materials such as tin-foil, ring-pulls, card and string. Incidentally, the humble fruit gum makes a convincing 'precious stone'!

Background information: Tutankhamun

The tomb was discovered by an archaeologist called Howard Carter. His expedition was financed by Lord Carnarvon, a wealthy man whose hobby was the study of Egyptian history. Carter had been digging in the Valley of the Kings, with the permission of the Egyptian government, since 1917. In that time he had found little of value, but all this was to change dramatically. In November, 1922, Lord Carnarvon received a cable which read:

Have made wonderful discovery in Valley. Magnificent tomb with seals intact. Recovered same for your arrival. Congratulations. Carter.

Carter had made perhaps the finest archaeological discovery in Egyptian history – the tomb of Tutankhamun, still untouched after more than three thousand years. Workmen broke through an outer door, sealed with the cartouche of Tutankhamun, and then took two days to clear a way through a dark passage before eventually reaching a second sealed door. Carter made a hole in this door. Peering through the hole, he saw statues and other objects, many of them made of gold. When he drew up an inventory of these items and sketched them all, he found that there were over six hundred altogether.

When Carter finally reached the burial chamber, he found a large shrine made of wood and covered with gold-plate. This shrine held three smaller wooden shrines, one inside the other. Inside the last shrine Carter found a chest or sarcophagus carved from quartzite. The sarcophagus contained a wooden coffin shaped like a human being, and plated with gold. This coffin contained two other jewel-encrusted coffins, also one inside the other, with the last one made of solid gold. In the last of the three coffins lay the mummified body of Tutankhamun, 'Lord of Lords, King of South and North, son of Ra', a young man of about eighteen years of age, wearing a magnificent funeral mask of beaten gold wrought in his likeness.

Carter found more treasures – they included bangles and bracelets, rings, models of ships, perfume caskets, gilt statuettes of the gods, decorated chests and other furniture, as well as chariots with golden wheels, a gold-bladed dagger in a golden sheath and a royal throne. The tomb was even guarded by a life-sized statue of Tutankhamun himself.

Activity 17: The death mask of Tutankhamun

Use **Copymaster 72** as a template for making masks of Tutankhamun. Study photographs of the death mask and colour the outline picture accordingly, then cut it out and mount it on card. Secure 3-cm wide strips of card at each side of the mask to go around the wearer's head. Use these masks in dramatic role-play, for example, acting out the funeral procession, or create a Tutankhamun wall-display. Find out where the actual treasures recovered from his tomb are now located, and what happened to the body of the king. Discuss the key role of evidence such as this in finding out about civilisations of the past.

Activity 18: The Sphinx

Write about the role of sphinxes in guarding the tombs of the pharaohs. Paint pictures of these huge stone sculptures alongside the pyramids.

Activity 19: The warrior pharaohs

Introduce the children to the concept of progression from the 'old' Egyptian civilisation into the New Age, or New Kingdom of Egypt as it is often referred to by historians and archaeologists. This New Age began around 1560 B.C. and was the time when warrior pharaohs went into battle to win an empire. It was the age of war and religious conflicts, which saw the building up of huge wealth, as indicated by the temples, pyramids and treasures already discussed. Indicate the growth of the empire on your timeline.

Paint or use collage to produce a large frieze across the classroom wall depicting the establishing of the empire. Include details of a fort, defending the frontier, the pharaoh riding into battle with horses and chariot, and soldiers on foot with bows, arrows, swords and spears. This could be extended to include a coastal scene, with fighting ships defending the coast from enemy attack.

Activity 20: The enemies of Egypt

Read more about the enemies of the Egyptians, such as the Hittites who settled in Anatolia (Turkey), and the Mitanni people, also from the north. Locate the direction of attack on a map of the area.

Activity 21: Leisure time

Find out as much as possible about how Egyptian people occupied their leisure time – perhaps beginning with the sports and entertainments in which they engaged. Analyse the evidence for these leisure activities. What does it tell us, and what does it not tell us? Make an 'evidence analysis chart', laid out like the one shown here.

Things we know	How we know	What we do not know from this source
People played instruments	Paintings on tombs	If these were the only musical instruments. If the music was written down. How people learned to play. (and so on)

116

Background information: *Leisure time*
The Egyptians were very fond of sports such as archery, ball games, boxing and wrestling. They also enjoyed hunting hares, gazelles, lions, ostriches, wild bulls, hippos and even crocodiles. Music, dancing and singing were very popular, as were reading and playing board games.

Activity 22: Children and their toys
If a museum visit is possible, look for evidence of how children played. If not, consult reference books. Did they have toys? What were these made of? Did toys go to the grave of a dead child?

Background information: *Children and toys*
Many Egyptian children had to work in the fields and had little time for play. Boys had to learn about farming, while girls were taught cooking and weaving. Some toys have been found in tombs, usually carved wooden animals whose mouths could be opened by pulling strings, model horses on wheels, or dolls.

Activity 23: What was school like in those days?
Find out and write about how the children of wealthier families were educated in Ancient Egypt, and illustrate this work. The children could compare the Egyptian way of education with that of Greece and Rome, as well as with their own education today. Ask them why Egyptian teachers used to say that a pupil's ear was 'on his back'!

Activity 24: Count like Egyptians
Learn to count in the same way as the Egyptians did. **Copymaster 73** provides the children with information about Egyptian numbers and some 'historical mathematics'. In order to understand this and be able to do the sums, they will need to be told that the numbers were written from right to left. For example, 15 was written as 5 ... 10, i.e. units on the left and tens on the right.

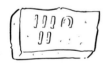

When this principle of writing and place value is understood, the mathematics becomes comparatively straightforward and fun. The children can complete their sheets individually, and then work in pairs or groups to devise further calculations or questions requiring a numerical answer.

Extend the activity into a discussion of how accomplished the Egyptians were at mathematics. Think of the complexities of planning and constructing pyramids and temples, with all of the calculations involved. This links to a general discussion on the importance of mathematics in everyday life, and of the role of early civilisations in the development of the subject.

Ask the children to find out what obelisks were and how they were constructed.

Activity 25: Inventions in Ancient Egypt
Investigate Egyptian inventions relating to mathematics and science, for example, a water-clock. This was basically a container from which water could drip. The correct time was indicated by the level of water left in the container. Refer to books on time and historic clocks and then design and construct your own water-clocks.

Activity 26: Hieroglyphics
Use **Copymaster 74** to introduce a study of Egyptian 'writing', called hieroglyphics. The children can trace the outlines of those provided and copy them carefully into workbooks, or use them as ideas for decorating margins. Look through other books showing examples of hieroglyphics and analyse the sorts of symbols that were used. On the scroll provided on the sheet, the children can draw other Egyptian words discovered from books, and/or make a list of symbols that were used in this picture-writing.

Print some hieroglyphics. Carefully cut out of polystyrene the outline shapes of some picture words, or make potato printing-blocks. Print on to fabric to make Egyptian-style wall-hangings.

Can the children find out about the Rosetta Stone and its connection with Egyptian hieroglyphics? What was a 'cartouche'? What does it tell us about an Egyptian manuscript?

Pupils in groups could devise their own modern picture signs, and write 'messages' for others in the class to interpret. To make this more difficult, ask them to write in a different direction from the one they are used to – for example, right to left.

Background information: *Hieroglyphics*
Hieroglyphics were picture signs, often used to help spell out words. There were over 700 of these symbols. Some hieroglyphics are read from top to bottom, while others can be read from left to right, or vice-versa. A Frenchman, Jean-Francois Champollion, solved the code of these hieroglyphics in 1822 with the aid of the Rosetta Stone (a stone bearing the same message in two different languages, Egyptian and Greek).

A cartouche was a frame, often rounded at the corners, drawn around a number of hieroglyphic symbols. It usually signifies a royal name.

Activity 27: Egyptian cosmetics
Research some of the interesting differences between traditional male/female roles and customs of Egyptian times, compared to the present day. For example, find out more about Egyptian cosmetics, that were worn by both men and women.

Background information
Both men and women in Egyptian times used oils and perfumes on the skin. They painted their lips, and green and grey kohl were used to outline the shape of the eyes. Kohl was made from minerals, ground to a powder and mixed with oil.

Study Unit 6: A past, non-European society – Ancient Egypt: key features of everyday life.
Suggested levels of work involved in activities

Activity number	Level	Activity number	Level	Activity number	Level
1	2/3	10	2/3/4	19	2/3/4
2	2/3	11	2/3/4	20	2/3/4
3	2/3/4	12	2/3/4/5	21	2/3/4
4	2/3/4	13	2/3/4	22	2/3/4
5	2/3/4	14	2/3/4/5	23	2/3/4
6	2/3/4	15	2/3	24	2/3/4
7	2/3	16	2/3/4	25	2/3/4
8	2/3/4	17	2/3	26	2/3/4
9	2/3	18	2/3/4	27	2/3/4

USES OF ARCHAEOLOGICAL EVIDENCE ▶

Activity 1: How do we know?

Emphasis has been placed throughout this topic on the nature of evidence. Talk with the children about the vital role of 'digging up the past', and the work of archaeologists. If possible, invite an archaeologist to talk about his/her work, stressing its delicate nature and the importance of the precise location of every find, no matter how tiny it might be. Analyse the role of specific archaeological evidence that has helped us to understand more about the Egyptian Empire, for example, fragments of stone with Egyptian writing on them, pieces of pottery, etc.

Activity 2: A time-capsule of today

If you were leaving a time-capsule behind for archaeologists to discover thousands of years from now, what would you put into it to help future generations understand modern life? Ask the children to list the items they would include – you may have to limit the number of items allowed in the capsule. The children might like to draw large cross-sectional diagrams of their time-capsule, showing some of the items they have included.

If your school has its own grounds, you could consider actually creating and burying a time-capsule containing a representative selection of items from or about contemporary society. Check whether any sort of planning permission is needed beforehand. Perhaps a helpful parent could provide a suitably secure container.

Study Unit 6: A past, non-European society – Ancient Egypt: archaeological evidence.
Suggested levels of work involved in activities

Activity number	Level	Activity number	Level
1	2/3/4/5	2	2/3/4/5

PERSPECTIVES ON THE TOPICS

The National Curriculum requires that the study of a topic such as this one is undertaken from a variety of perspectives (see page 111), and all of these have been covered in the activities already suggested. However, you may wish to highlight a particular perspective (e.g. economic, religious) and focus attention on this as a starting point. Such an approach would be suitable if, for example, you wished to integrate an historical topic on the Egyptians into a cross-curricular theme of economic and industrial understanding. The following ideas are examples of activities which reinforce one or more of the suggested perspectives from this general point of view.

Activity 1: Trade with other nations

Undertake a study of Egypt's trade with other nations (economic perspective). Find out what the Egyptians had to trade with (for example, gold, rope and grain), and what they needed in exchange (for example, copper and timber, silver, slaves and horses). On a map of the area, locate and draw lands that regularly traded with the Egyptians. These should include Crete, Greece, Sinai and Africa.

Paint pictures of Egyptian cargo boats (from small papyrus skiffs to larger merchant vessels) and write about the hazards of transporting valuable goods across the empire.

Activity 2: Gods and temples

Use **Copymaster 75** to launch a sub-topic on 'Gods and Temples' (religious perspective). The Ancient Egyptians worshipped hundreds of gods and goddesses and each had a temple. Make a display of statues of the gods, annotated with information about each of them.

Turn a corner of the classroom into an Egyptian temple. Make columns out of corrugated card painted gold, paint suitable religious pictures for the walls, and construct a statue of a god or goddess in its shrine. Act out a visitation to the temple. Only the pharaoh and priests were allowed in the shrine area. Priests offered daily prayers, food, drink and clothing to the statue.

Activity 3: Writing materials

Find out more about the writing equipment of ancient Egypt (technological perspective). Investigate the making of papyrus from reeds (see below), and present findings in illustrated note form. Display the children's written work on 'papyrus' scrolls: art paper will become suitably parchment-like if it is soaked for a time in cold tea and allowed to dry slowly.

Reeds were harvested. The stalks were peeled, sliced thinly and soaked. Two crossed layers were hammered under linen and then smoothed with a stone.

Activity 4: More about hieroglyphics

Hieroglyphics were painted on to papyrus sheets with brushes and inks, and the sheets were often rolled up. Make your own imitation papyrus rolls covered with hieroglyphics and pictures. Why not leave a message for others in the class to translate? Find out from a museum or secondary resources what we can learn about Ancient Egypt from the few original papyrus rolls that still survive.

Activity 5: A day in the life of a pharaoh

Ask the children to write autobiographical accounts of 'My Life as Pharaoh' (political perspective), telling perhaps of a day in court life, the receiving of ambassadors from lands in the great empire, and of trade negotiations.

Activity 6: Everyday life

Make a study of everyday clothes, including those worn by the poorer people as well as the wealthy scribes and the royal household. This will provide ample scope for art and craft work of all kinds.

Egyptians of both sexes used cosmetics such as eye paint. If you have access to stage make-up (greasepaint), the children might like to design elaborate eye make-ups (see page 120), either on paper or on each other. (I would suggest that you discourage the children from bringing make-up from home, and have plenty of cold cream and tissues available afterwards.)

Activity 7: Different points of view

Discuss a particular situation and then ask the children to write about it from the different viewpoints of certain people involved (social perspective). For example, consider the building of a pyramid from the point of view of:

– the pharaoh for whom it is intended;
– the chief architect;
– a worker dragging stones to the site;
– the king's inspector of the proceedings.

Activity 8: Egyptian art and craft

Undertake a sub-topic on the legacy of art and craft from Ancient Egypt (aesthetic perspective), perhaps using **Copymaster 76** as a starting point. Discuss the sheer elegance and beauty of the work of sculptors, artists and craftsmen. Consider the enormous artistic wealth of the Egyptian civilisation, as reflected in the discovery of the treasures of Tutankhamun.

Make imitation vases, bowls and plates from clay. Decorate these appropriately and display them in an 'Egyptian Gallery' in the classroom, surrounded by appropriate paintings and hieroglyphic hangings – perhaps even palm leaves, real or imitation.

Reeds were harvested. The stalks were peeled, sliced thinly and soaked. Two crossed layers were hammered under linen and then smoothed with a stone.

Activity 9: Biblical connections
The children could explore Old Testament stories with Egyptian connections. If possible, let them hear or attend a performance of *Joseph and His Amazing*

Technicolor Dreamcoat: they would enjoy singing some of the songs and acting out the story. The tale of Moses and the plagues of Egypt also has great scope for drama, creative writing and artwork.

gold eyelids,
green shadow,
blue vertical line

Study Unit 6: A past, non-European society – Ancient Egypt: perspectives on the topic.
Suggested levels of work involved in activities

Activity number	Level	Activity number	Level	Activity number	Level
1	2/3/4/5	4	2/3/4	7	2/3/4/5
2	2/3/4	5	2/3/4	8	2/3/4
3	2/3/4	6	2/3/4	9	2/3/4

RESOURCES ▶

Non-fiction

Defrates, J. *What do we know about the Egyptians?*, Simon & Schuster, 1991.

Fleming, S. *The Egyptians* Young Researcher Series, Heinemann.

An Egyptian Pyramid, Inside Story Series, Simon & Schuster.

The Egyptians, Look into the Past Series, Wayland.

Egyptian Pyramids, Beginning History Series, Wayland.

See Through: Ancient Egypt, See Through History Series, Heinemann.

Ancient Egypt, Jump! History Series, Two-Can.

Ancient Egypt, Everyday Life Series, Usborne.

The British Museum has published an activity book on The Ancient Egyptians (British Museum General Enquiries – Tel: 0171-636-1555)

Fiction

Books for younger readers

De Paola, T. *Bill and Pete go down the Nile*, OUP, 1987. A fun story about a school trip for crocodiles – they see the Sphinx and the pyramids.

Hutchins, P. *The Curse of the Egyptian Mummy*,

Bodley Head, 1983. An Egyptian statue has been stolen ... leading to an adventure.

For older readers, or for reading aloud

Green, R.L. *Tales of Ancient Egypt*, Penguin, 1989. Useful retelling of Ancient Egyptian myths and legends.

Harris, R. *The Moon in the Cloud/Shadow on the Sun/Bright and Morning Star*, Faber, 1972–89. A trilogy full of observation and information about life and customs in Ancient Egypt.

Storr, C. *Moses of the Bulrushes* and *Moses and the Plagues*, Methuen, 1984 and 1985. Two bible stories, set in Ancient Egypt, told in simple language for children. (Although this book is out of print, it will still be available through libraries.)

Blueprints links

You will find a valuable geographical unit of work on Egypt in *Blueprints: Distant Places*, and work on the Nile in *Blueprints: Junior Geography Resource Bank*. You will find relevant ideas in technology in *Blueprints: Technology Key Stage 2*. The following other Stanley Thornes books will also prove useful: *Investigating History: Ancient Egypt*; *History Timelines: Ancient Egypt*.

APPENDIX 1
FOOD AND FARMING

TOPIC WEB

Important historical issues

- Why farm? What is farming?
- Beginnings of farming – the Stone Age
- Beginnings of farming – international dimensions
- The Saxon three-field system
- Enclosures
- Growth of the woollen industry
- The Agricultural Revolution
- Mechanisation

Time-span

- A farming timeline
- A changing village
- Rare breeds – the breeding of livestock
- Farming today – the old and the new

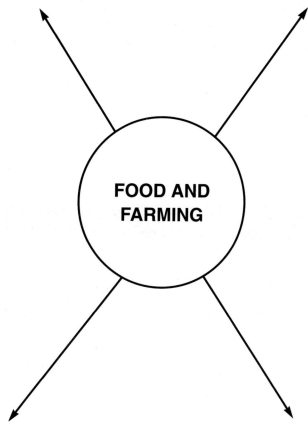

FOOD AND FARMING

Developments in different periods

- Key inventions/significant events
- Food and cooking through the centuries
- Ingredients – international dimensions

Links between local, British, European and World history

- An international timeline
- Farming around the world
- Farming areas today
- Factors affecting the siting of agriculture

IMPORTANT HISTORICAL ISSUES

C77–80

Activity 1: In the beginning …

As one of the important aims of this study unit is to cover a very wide time-span by comparing developments in food and farming during different periods, it would seem essential to 'begin at the beginning'. No doubt many children take food and the methods by which it is produced for granted. Remind them that farming and food production, like everything else in our lives, have undergone dramatic changes through time.

Discuss the vital importance of food production – without regular supplies of food we could not possibly stay alive. Food is a basic human need: the need to find it has always been a priority, right from the earliest days of people on our planet. This unit will, of course, integrate extremely well with aspects of the topic food and farming that may be tackled from the perspectives of other areas of the curriculum, notably science, geography and environmental education.

Find out how the first people on earth kept themselves alive. Draw annotated pictures of Stone Age settlers and their food-related activities (see below).

Activity 2: How do we know?

Discuss how we know about the farming activities of the Stone Age. If possible, visit a museum or consult books on this period to see the forms of reliable evidence we have – including flint tools, and the bones and tusks of animals which were hunted. Discuss the key role of archaeologists in digging up such important objects. Talk about how archaeological evidence suggests that the earliest people were nomads, that is wanderers from place to place in search of animals.

Activity 3: A Stone Age pit

Draw a cross-section of a Stone Age pit, dug out and used to trap wild animals (see overleaf).

Activity 4: Early farming communities

Explain that archaeological evidence reveals that, after a time, people formed tribes or groups. They settled in more permanent villages, learning the earliest and most basic skills of farming. Ask the children to suggest what these basic skills might have been, for example, learning how to tame animals and keep them together in groups; discovering that seeds put in the ground grow into

Stone Age people hunted and trapped animals.

They wore animal skins for clothes.

They collected berries, roots, leaves and nuts from plants.

With simple nets, they caught fish.

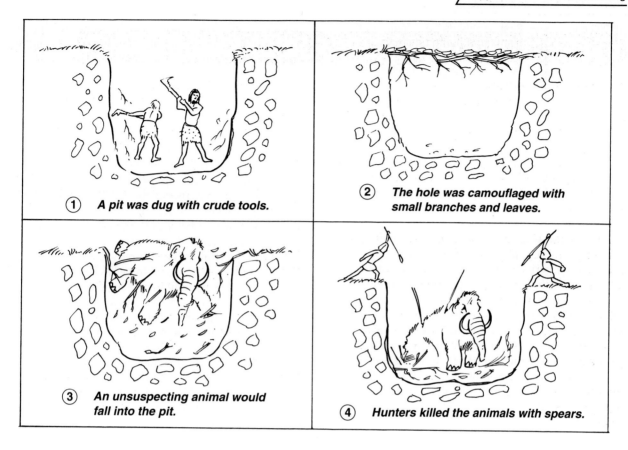

① **A pit was dug with crude tools.**

② **The hole was camouflaged with small branches and leaves.**

③ **An unsuspecting animal would fall into the pit.**

④ **Hunters killed the animals with spears.**

plants, and that they will grow more successfully if the hard ground is broken up first. Tribes gradually settled down to this farming way of life as their skills and knowledge developed.

Copymaster 77 is designed to reinforce children's understanding of the very earliest farming tools and methods, and also to illustrate the incredible changes that have taken place over the years. Pupils can either colour the four pictures at this stage, or colour and discuss each at the appropriate stage as the project progresses. Ask the children to give the drawings suitable labels – a Stone Age plough, a Saxon plough, a steam plough and a modern plough. The back of the sheet can be used for writing a sentence about each, and adding the appropriate dates when they were in use. Discuss the task that the plough is designed to do, and the ever-increasing efficiency of technology through time.

Activity 5: The beginnings of farming

A fundamental decision you will have to make is whether to introduce farming in other continents of the world in chronological sequence alongside British agriculture, or whether to do separate sub-topics on developments and methods in other lands. Whichever approach is adopted, it will be important at some stage to discuss the beginnings of farming, which took place in the Middle East.

Copymaster 78 provides an outline map of the area of the world where farming as a skilled activity began. Ask the children to colour in the already labelled Mediterranean, Arabian and Red Seas. They can consult

maps or a globe and write their own labels on the key rivers of the area – the Nile, Euphrates, Tigris and Indus. For less able children the names of rivers can be provided. Then they can colour in the areas where farming began and developed, along the courses of these rivers. (For more information and activities on farming in the area of the Nile, see the previous unit in this book, on Ancient Egypt.) Ask the children to complete the sentence beneath the map, and then discuss the various reasons – the climate was warm; the soil was rich, light and fertile; the rivers provided water and fertile mud.

Encourage the children to think and write about early discoveries that led to improvements in producing food: for example, weeding, preparing the soil, burning away old plants, fertilising the land with animal dung, giving soil a 'rest' from time to time, and selecting the best seeds to give the best crop results. Part of this writing can suggest how these important facts might have been discovered.

The above activities are very important in terms of background, as they introduce the key concept of transition from haphazard attempts at acquiring food to an organised system. This forms the basis for discovering and analysing how systems of agriculture have changed and developed through time, in parallel, of course, with changes in technology and scientific developments. Introduce these fundamental ideas to the class in preparation for study of key events through the ages, including the Agricultural Revolution.

This is a good point at which to start a farming timeline which can be added to and illustrated as the topic progresses. Here are some dates to start you off.

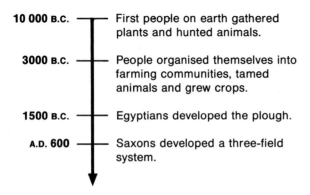

10 000 B.C.	First people on earth gathered plants and hunted animals.
3000 B.C.	People organised themselves into farming communities, tamed animals and grew crops.
1500 B.C.	Egyptians developed the plough.
A.D. 600	Saxons developed a three-field system.

Activity 6: The Anglo-Saxon three-field system

Learn about the three-field farming system of the Anglo-Saxon period. These settlers organised their farming into a three-year cycle of use for three different fields. Every third year, one of the fields was given a rest (allowed to lie 'fallow') to leave the soil to recover some of its nutrients. Use colour-coded cards to plan out the system (see below), or ask the children to draw their own plans and produce keys to indicate the use of the fields. This activity could be extended into drawing maps of the changing land-use of the three fields, an excellent integration with geography and the development of mapwork skills.

	YEAR 1	**YEAR 2**	**YEAR 3**
North field	FALLOW	Rye	Wheat
South field	Rye	Barley	FALLOW
West field	Wheat	FALLOW	Barley

Discuss and write about why this system was operated by the Anglo-Saxons. They did not understand the importance of manure and fertilisers. (For more information and activities concerning the three-field system, see the unit on the Anglo-Saxons in this book.)

Activity 7: Enclosures

Introduce and discuss the key concept of 'enclosures' – a system which developed during the Middle Ages. This was the enclosure of land with hedges, fences or walls, which had a dramatic impact on the countryside by the end of the fifteenth century. Read more about the implications of this new system, and write a list of the important changes that it caused.

Discuss why farmers enclosed their land. One fundamental reason was that many new enclosed fields were given over to sheep grazing because the woollen industry was growing rapidly in importance. Sheep were much easier to look after in enclosed fields rather than on open pasture. Furthermore, landowners needed fewer workers to tend sheep than to grow crops, so there were economic advantages.

Copymaster 85 allows much scope for pupils' imagination in demonstrating that they understand the principle of enclosures. Ask them to colour in the top half of the sheet to show land use before enclosures under the three-field system. They should show the three fields divided into strips, and one field lying fallow (for more information, see page 23 and **Copymaster 13**). A key can be devised and inserted by way of further explanation, if needed. The bottom half of the sheet shows the same three fields after rich farmers have enclosed them. Ask the children to use colour and a key to indicate the new use of the fields, drawing in the enclosing hedges/fences/walls. In both diagrams, indicate which land belongs to the villagers and which belongs to the wealthy landowners.

Discuss the ethics of enclosures – without doubt, the system enabled some people to get richer while others grew poorer. Ask the children to imagine that they are either a village farm-worker or a wealthy landowner and to write an account of the advantages (or otherwise) of enclosures from their personal point of view.

Activity 8: The woollen industry

Consider the nature and effects of the growth of the woollen industry in Tudor and Stuart times. England became the greatest wool manufacturing country in the world. Investigate the appearance and names of breeds of sheep that were reared. Draw pictures of them. Ask the children to find out and write about what is meant by the terms 'staple town', 'woolgatherers' and 'woolsack'.

Draw a series of diagrams to show the stages in production of wool from sheep to garment, *or* prepare a series of cards showing pictures of the stages of wool manufacture and ask the children to put them in order. (See below and overleaf.)

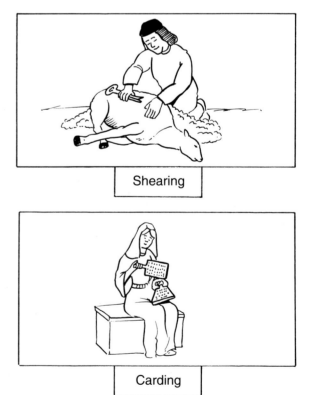

Shearing

Carding

124

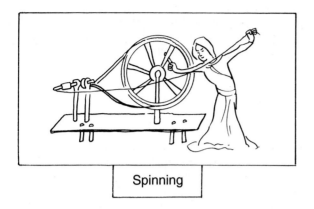

Spinning

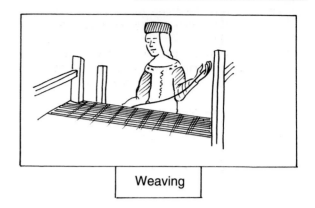

Weaving

Obtain samples of fleece and teach children how to clean the wool, and to card, spin and weave it. An entire sub-topic could be centred on the woollen industry, with excellent scope for integration of history with art, craft and technology.

Activity 9: The Agricultural Revolution
Introduce the term 'Agricultural Revolution', as applied to the great and rapid changes in farming which took place from the mid-eighteenth century onwards. A sub-topic on the Agricultural Revolution should highlight the reasons behind any changes, the nature of those changes and the notable people who helped to bring them about. Ask the children to find out about the lives and achievements of Jethro Tull, Lord Townshend, Robert Bakewell and Thomas Coke. The children could present their findings in diagrammatic form, as below, or perhaps in a series of wall-posters to show a progression of events. Time available will dictate to what extent the separate changes and discoveries are investigated, but to reinforce the main thrust of this period it would be useful to write about the life and work of one of the key men associated with the Agricultural Revolution, and to produce suitable illustrations connected with his contribution.

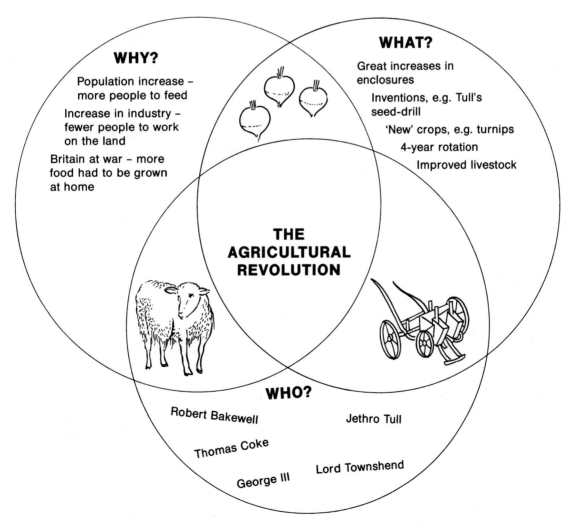

WHY?

Population increase – more people to feed

Increase in industry – fewer people to work on the land

Britain at war – more food had to be grown at home

WHAT?

Great increases in enclosures

Inventions, e.g. Tull's seed-drill

'New' crops, e.g. turnips

4-year rotation

Improved livestock

THE AGRICULTURAL REVOLUTION

WHO?

Robert Bakewell

Jethro Tull

Thomas Coke

Lord Townshend

George III

Write accounts, too, of the general situation in Britain at the time – the population was increasing rapidly; Britain was at war with France; and industry was expanding, leaving fewer labourers available to work in the fields.

Finally, the children could construct a mini-timeline of key dates in the Agricultural Revolution and/or add these to the farming timeline begun earlier.

The Agricultural Revolution – a timeline

1701	Jethro Tull's seed-drill
1730–38	'Turnip' Townshend transformed his Norfolk estate
1760	Beginning of great wave of Parliamentary enclosure (to 1850) Robert Bakewell began livestock breeding experiments at Dishley, Leicester
1776	Thomas Coke took over Holkham estate, Norfolk
1784	Andrew Meikle's threshing machine
1815	Corn Laws to protect farmers from threat of imported grain
1826	Patrick Bell's mechanical reaper
1830	'Swing' riots
1834	New Poor Law Tolpuddle Martyrs transported
1838	Royal Agricultural Society founded
1846	Repeal of the Corn Laws
1851	The Great Exhibition: British and American farm machines displayed
1850 (to 1875)	High Farming era: the Golden Age

Background information: *The Agricultural Revolution* Jethro Tull (1674–1741) invented a drill for sowing seeds. It could be pulled by horses, which was a major improvement – no longer did seeds have to be sown by hand.

Lord Townshend developed the four-crop rotation system (see Activity 10, following). He acquired the nickname 'Turnip Townshend'.

Robert Bakewell (1725–1795) experimented with the breeding of livestock. He maintained meticulous records of his work and, from the farmer's point of view, improved breeds of sheep, cattle, pigs and horses.

Thomas Coke (1754–1842) demonstrated new methods to his tenants, gave them long leases, and helped them financially to use modern techniques. He enriched his soil with marl and clover crops, grew swedes and potatoes, and kept herds of Devon cattle and flocks of Southdown sheep. He planted fifty acres of trees every year.

Activity 10: Four-year rotation
Copymaster 80 can be used with Activity 9 on the Agricultural Revolution, or as part of a progression in understanding the three-field system, enclosures, and then four-year rotation. The key to this progression is

the discovery and understanding of the importance of root crops such as turnips. Because they obtain their nutrients from much deeper in the soil than cereal crops, these root crops can eliminate the need for a fallow year. The four crops generally rotated in the system devised by Townshend are turnips, barley, wheat and clover.

Ask the children to devise a key and colour in on **Copymaster 80** the four fields in each of the four years, to show a sensible pattern of rotation. This activity is not as easy as it appears! Help can be given to younger or less able pupils by providing the key and colouring in a number of the rectangles as a starting point. The solution is:

YEAR 1		YEAR 2	
Turnips	Barley	Barley	Clover
Wheat	Clover	Turnips	Wheat

YEAR 3		YEAR 4	
Clover	Wheat	Wheat	Turnips
Barley	Turnips	Clover	Barley

Find out more about how root crops and cereal crops grow. Prove by evidence (visit a farm or grow them yourself) that the root systems of these two crops are very different.

Activity 11: Farming life in the eighteenth century
Write about life on a farm in the eighteenth century. Include references to milking cattle by hand, the stocking of turnips and the harvesting of corn with sickles. Draw pictures of the labourers tying the corn into sheaves in the fields.

Activity 12: Farmer George
Ask the children to guess or find out who 'Farmer George' was. Did the King have a role to play in the farming revolution?

The above activities highlight a critical turning point in British farming. Introduce the key idea that farming had become an industry. Years of serious depression in agriculture had been followed by a rapid and wide-ranging Agricultural Revolution, brought about by mechanisation and other discoveries. The new farming industry this created was here to stay.

Activity 13: The arrival of steam power
Study the invention of steam machines (ploughs, reapers and threshers). If possible, visit a farm museum to observe and sketch the actual evidence.

Make a list of improvements in agriculture that took place during the late nineteenth and early twentieth centuries, for example:

– the increased understanding and use of fertilisers;
– discovery of more adequate drainage materials;
– increased research, leading to improved yields from crops;
– development of livestock breeding;
– mechanisation.

Organise a class debate to consider whether such 'improvements' were always for the better. Aspects to consider could include:

– redundancies caused by mechanisation;
– damage caused to soil by certain farming practices;
– the trend towards 'factory farming' and intensive rearing of animals in small spaces.

Find out about the Tolpuddle Martyrs and the mysterious 'Captain Swing'. What was their attitude to these improvements?

TIME SPAN

Activity 1: The farming timeline
The activities suggested so far obviously cover a wide timespan, so it is important to make full use of your timeline to organise the key dimensions of the topic as a whole. This will help to reinforce the significance of change over long periods.

Activity 2: The times they are a-changing
Take a hypothetical farming village. Draw or make large collage pictures to show what the village would have looked like at different periods through time. For example, in the Middle Ages (A.D. 1000 to A.D. 1450), illustrate the house of the Lord of the Manor, the simple houses of the villagers, three large fields divided into strips which the Lord allowed the common people to farm, and common grazing land around the village.

For the same village in the eighteenth century (1700–1800), illustrate the squire's house, land in enclosed blocks rather than divided strips, storage barns for new crops such as clover and turnips, ditches for draining the land, villagers' cottages, a shop, the blacksmith and an inn.

The modern-day village would have farmhouses and outbuildings (including a dairy, grain store and machinery sheds), large fields with combine harvesters, tractors, fertiliser sprays etc., and people taking advantage of a modern transport system.

As an extension, make models of village buildings through the ages, to demonstrate an understanding of changing architecture and functions.

Activity 3: The breeding of livestock
A fascinating sub-topic which really highlights change through time is a study of animal breeds. Find pictures or photographs of some of the earliest breeds of sheep, cattle, pigs and poultry. Better still, visit a rare-breeds centre or a working farm museum. Paint pictures of the 'old and new', as shown below. Discuss how improvements in livestock and changes come about. This will involve reference to evolution and 'selective breeding' of animals, backed up by research and an understanding of what we want from farm animals.

Discuss some of the major changes that have occurred in farming and food production. Ask for a summary analysis of the key areas in which agriculture has altered radically – breeds and qualities of animals have changed, workers' jobs have changed, farming produce has changed. BUT point out that, despite all of this, farming is still basically about producing food for the people of the world to eat … just as it was in the Stone Age.

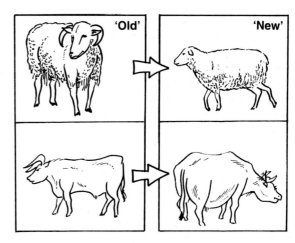

DEVELOPMENTS IN DIFFERENT PERIODS ▶

Activity 1: Key phases of development

Once again, a great deal of the material needed for this activity is incorporated in the preceding activities. A useful discussion might centre around key phases of development – were some periods of history (for example, the years of the Agricultural Revolution) more significant than others in terms of change? Debate the major inventions of farming – is it possible to single out two or three of these as being the most important?

Activity 2: Comparisons

Undertake a sub-topic on food and recipes through the ages, which will highlight developments in different periods. Here is an Elizabethan recipe you might like to try, even though the directions are not very precise.

To make Jumbolds

Take half a pound of almonds being beaten to a paste with a short cake being grated and two eggs, two ounces of caroway seeds being beaten and the juice of a lemon and being brought into paste. Roule it into round strings then cast it into knots and so bake it in an oven and when they are baked, yce them with rosewater and sugar and the white of an egg being beaten together, then put them againe into the oven a little while and then boxe them up and you may keep them all the yeare.

Research and write menus for typical meals of the following periods:

- prehistoric Britain
- Roman Britain
- medieval Britain
- sixteenth-century Britain
- seventeenth-century Britain
- eighteenth-century Britain
- nineteenth-century Britain
- twentieth-century Britain.

You could perhaps make a book for each of these historical periods, to include illustrated accounts of ingredients available at the time, cooking utensils and facilities, typical menus, and details of how and when a family would have dined. An excellent collection of recipes and background information for this purpose is provided in the books listed below (see *Resources*).

Along similar lines, make a series of class books on farming through the ages – perhaps a book for each century, or for each major historic period (as above). The class can be divided into groups, each to work on a different period. Allow scope for oral presentations of material, when there can be an emphasis on comparing and contrasting. Focus attention on comparisons by asking the children questions that tease out key factors, for example: 'What is one of the biggest differences between working life on a farm in the eighteenth century and today?' (A suitable answer is the number of people working there.) Prepare a series of such questions to be borne in mind as the work progresses.

Activity 3: Ingredients grid

As an alternative to producing period menus, organise the information about ingredients and, from research with books, ascertain in which periods of history these were available and commonly used in Britain. Record findings in a simple grid as shown below (tick boxes to show use).

Ingredients	Prehistoric	Medieval	Sixteenth century	Seventeenth century	Eighteenth century	Nineteenth century	Twentieth century
Vines							
Goose							
Milk							
Butter							
Crab							
Wheat							
Wild boar							
Turnips							
Mulberries							
Margarine							
Swedes							

and so on. . .

The list of ingredients is almost endless, and children will probably be very surprised at the early availability of certain items, such as crab (known in prehistoric times).

Continue the work into a discussion of the types of foods and menus commonly available (and indeed taken for granted) in Britain today that would not have been eaten a hundred years ago – pizza, curry, and a vast range of ready-prepared 'heat in the microwave' dishes. Talk about why we now have such a great range of ethnic and convenience food available to us. What, if any, are the implications of this for British agriculture?

Pay a visit to a local supermarket. Investigate the range of exotic fruits and vegetables that are on offer to us all around the year. Find out which countries they have come from, and how they were brought to Britain. If time allows, find out about the climate and farming practices in their countries of origin. Discuss why the availability of foreign produce all through the year is a fairly recent development. This introduces the all-important international dimension, which links into the next section of this unit.

Activity 4: War-time farming

It might be interesting for children to learn something about the importance of farming during war-time. Conduct a sub-topic on the role of the Women's Land Army during the early 1940s.

Ask the children to find out why so many women were encouraged to become 'temporary' farmers. Investigate why there were so many food shortages

---

10 000 Women Wanted For Farm Work

A FREE OUTFIT high boots, breeches, overall and hat.

MAINTENANCE during training.

TRAVELLING expenses in connection with the work.

WAGES 18/- per week, or the district rate, whichever is the higher.

MAINTENANCE during terms of unemployment up to four weeks.

HOUSING personally inspected and approved by the Women's War Agricultural Committee in each County.

WORK on carefully selected farms.

PROMOTION good work rewarded by promotion and higher pay.

AFTER THE WAR special facilities for settlement at home or overseas.

Don't Delay Enrol To-Day

Application Forms may be had at all Post Offices & Employment Exchanges

---

during the war, and how people tried to make their diets more nutritious and interesting. Explain how rationing was supposed to work. And what was the 'black market'?

LINKS ACROSS THE WORLD

As with the need to compare and contrast developments, this international dimension could well permeate the topic as a whole as it progresses, or it could be tackled as sub-topics.

Activity 1: An international timeline

Extend your existing timeline, or make a second, more complex one which allows for the recording of international developments. Shown here is part of such a timeline, which could be made on a large scale, with illustrations, maps, etc. Dates will, of course, be approximate and the scope for entries is limitless. However, even noting key events discovered through reading and research will help to put British happenings in perspective and enable the children to appreciate that many other nations were developing new aspects of agriculture too.

Activity 2: Farming abroad

Copymaster 81 draws attention to international developments in agriculture by asking pupils to link drawings of 'historic' farmers in various lands with maps of their countries. Ask the children to colour in

the drawings, draw a line to link each with its related map, and then use reference books to research an approximate date for each picture (dates are given below). The pictures could then form the basis of sub-topics, perhaps organised on a group basis. Each group could research and do a class presentation on one of the following:

Mountain farming in Peru Fifteenth-century peasants farmed in mountain villages in the days of the Incas.

Australian sheep farming Settlers arrived and started sheep farming on a large scale in the nineteenth century.

African tribal farming In the thirteenth century, tribes lived in tropic jungles, hunting animals and gathering seeds, berries and nuts for food.

Chinese farming of grain New crops such as maize were developed to feed an increasing population in the seventeenth century.

Cattle ranching in the United States of America Great herds of cattle were reared by cowboys in the nineteenth century.

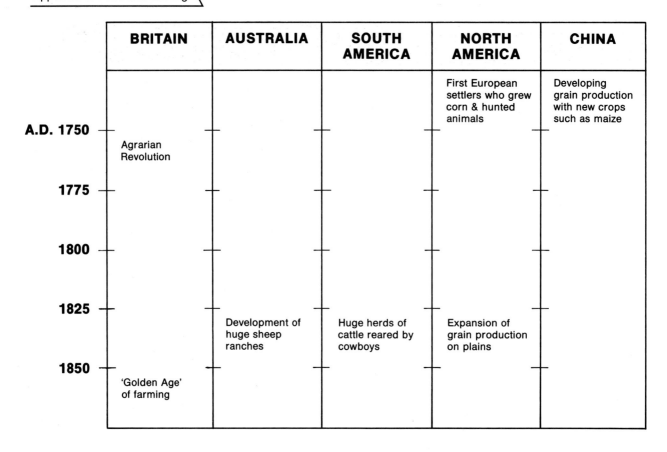

	BRITAIN	AUSTRALIA	SOUTH AMERICA	NORTH AMERICA	CHINA
				First European settlers who grew corn & hunted animals	Developing grain production with new crops such as maize
A.D. 1750	Agrarian Revolution				
1775					
1800					
1825		Development of huge sheep ranches	Huge herds of cattle reared by cowboys	Expansion of grain production on plains	
1850	'Golden Age' of farming				

Indian rice farming Twelfth-century villages watered fields to grow rice.

Extend this activity by asking the children to research and draw pictures of nations not represented on **Copymaster 81**, for example, Japan, the Middle East and other parts of Europe.

Activity 3: Farming today

Consider the main agricultural areas of Britain and/or the world today. Take an outline map of the British Isles and draw in the key farming areas. Discuss these locations with critical questions – for example, why are many sheep farms in upland areas? Why are large areas of the east given over the arable farms (cereals, potatoes, roots) and market gardens?

One very important conclusion to draw is that, despite the dramatic changes and improvements in agriculture that have occurred through time, farmers are still dependent on basic factors such as climate, height of land and soil types. Consider these fundamental questions: What has changed through the centuries? What has not changed? What factors can farmers control? What factors can they not control?

Activity 4: Food for thought

It is said that, in the reign of King Henry VIII, his cooks once baked a pie-crust and put it over a huge dish. Inside the dish were two dozen live songbirds, and when the pie was opened, a nursery-rhyme was born ... Ask

the children to imagine they were present when the pie was opened, and to produce illustrated creative writing about the event. Later, they might like to see how many songs and poems about farming and food they can find. Perhaps they could illustrate and learn to sing some of their favourites.

Tell the children some traditional harvest tales, such as the story of the feast of 'Harvest Home' and the legend of John Barleycorn. Ask them to find out in how many different ways barley was used in days gone by – baking barley bread, making barley water, making malt and brewing wine, feeding poultry with barley meal, and using barley straw as feed for cattle are just some of the uses.

Examine some of the old farming phrases we often use in a different context nowadays, such as:

all grist to the mill

make hay while the sun shines

the other man's grass is always greener

being *'pitchforked'* into something

having a *'furrowed brow'*.

Ask the pupils to explain what these expressions mean and where they might have come from. They may be able to 'glean' more ideas and information from other sayings. Do they know what the word 'pasteurised' means?

Read or tell stories involving farming and/or food – they could include *Oliver Twist* and *Farmer Giles of Ham*.

RESOURCES

Non-fiction

Lawrie, J. *Pot Luck: Cooking and Recipes from the Past,* A & C Black, 1991.

Food, 'Looking Back Series', Wayland, 1991.

Exploring Farming, 'Exploring the Past Series', Wayland.

Food Through the Ages, 'Through the Ages' Series, Simon & Schuster.

Fiction

Easy-reading and picture books

Avery, G. *Sixpence,* Collins, 1979. Farming with steam and harvest-fare in 19th-century Wales.*

Goodall, J. *Story of a Farm,* Deutsch, 1989. Early Middle Ages to the present day, in pictures.

Lasker, *A Medieval Feast,* Hamish Hamilton, 1976. Contrasting the wedding feasts of two couples, one poor and one rich, in the fifteenth century.*

Limb, S. *Meet the Greens,* Orchard, 1986. A young girl's crusade against factory-farming.

Willard, B. *Priscilla Pentecost,* Hamish Hamilton, 1970. Children's tasks on an eighteenth-century farm – bird-scaring, gleaning, stacking wood – and their daily fare.

Wills, J. *The Beechmount Barbecue,* Hamish Hamilton, 1991. A simple tale of children and a barbecue, which involves lots of sausages, chips and ice-cream.

Books for better readers

Allan, M.E. *A Strange Enchantment,* Abelard-Schumann, 1981. A story about a land-army girl. Older interest, but includes long descriptive passages about farming and rural conditions.*

Burton, H. *Kate Rider,* OUP, 1974. The first two chapters contain a good description of routines on a farm in the middle of the seventeenth century.*

Chard, B. *Ferret Summer,* R. Collings, 1975. Work on a small mid-10th century farm – mechanised, but not an agri-business.*

Garner, A. *The Aimer Gate,* Collins, 1978. Includes strong evocative description of a traditional corn harvest, ending with the rabbit kill in the last standing square.

Willard, B. *The Lark and the Laurel,* Longman, 1970. Set on a farm in early Tudor times. Seasonal routines, including a coney-catch.

Willard, B. *Farmer's Boy,* Julia MacRae, 1991. Traditional farming.

Willard, B. *The Miller's Boy,* Viking Kestrel, 1976. Rural life in fifteenth-century Sussex.*

Poetry

Harvey, A. *A picnic of poetry,* Blackie, 1988. Contains many poems dealing with customs and food in the past.

*These books are out of print but will be available from libraries and second-hand bookshops.

Blueprints links

You will find a valuable bank of related geographical material on food and farming in *Blueprints: Junior Geography Resource Bank.* The following other Stanley Thornes books will prove useful: *Investigating History: Food and Farming.*

TOPIC WEB

Voyages of exploration

- Early ideas on the shape of the world; mapwork
- The Spice Islands – journeys to the East
- Routes of exploration
- Voyages of Columbus
- Other explorers – Diaz, Vespucci, da Gama, Magellan, Cabot
- Navigation
- Life at sea
- Ships
- A Dictionary of exploration

Aztec civilisation

- Location of Mexico and Peru
- Evidence of the Aztecs
- Aztecs as warriors
- Daily life and homes
- Religious beliefs
- Priests and astrology
- Aztec calendars
- Food and cooking
- Clothing and hairstyles
- Writing and measuring
- King Montezuma
- Art and craft

EXPLORATION AND ENCOUNTERS 1450–1550

The Spanish Conquest

- Voyages of Cortes and Pizarro
- Cultural differences
- Reasons for the Conquest
- Atahualpa and the Incas
- Implications and legacy of the Conquest

VOYAGES OF EXPLORATION

Activity 1: Early views of the world

In this modern age we take the globe for granted, and a spherical portrayal of the world is no doubt a familiar sight in school classrooms. Children will probably be unfamiliar with the fact that people have not always believed that the world is round. Discuss these early views.

In the fifteenth century, people believed that if you sailed far enough away from home, you would reach the end of the world. Consider the logic of this position – after all, there was no evidence available to inform more accurate alternative views.

Many of the early peoples of history had strange ideas of how the world was constructed. The Vikings, for example, believed that the world was rather like a tray – flat, with sides and edges (see page 37). Sail too far, and you would plunge over the edge and be lost for ever. Ask the children to write imaginative accounts about 'falling off the edge of the world', and to produce some artwork. Spatial awareness of this nature is very difficult for children to grasp.

Background information: *Early views of the world*

By the fifteenth century, European merchants had been travelling across Asia to China and India in the east for many years, returning with gold, precious stones, cloth, spices and many other rarities. The extent of their world can be seen on **Copymaster 82**. The merchants knew much about the mountains, valleys and plains of distant lands, and about the many races and religions who populated them – but of the waters beyond the horizon they knew little. Sailors tended to stay within sight of the shore for fear of being swept away and lost: they told wild tales of seas that boiled or froze, of strange sea-monsters that could devour a ship whole, of fierce winds and whirlpools that could lure a ship to destruction, and of the very edge of the world where all the oceans cascaded downwards into endless green darkness.

Activity 2: Look at a globe

Study a globe and help the children to appreciate that it is indeed possible to travel all the way around it and arrive back in the same place. Discuss the limitations of two-dimensional maps in this respect. This aspect of the topic leads to excellent cross-links with the geographical skills of graphicacy and map projection.

Activity 3: The world is round!

Following on from the discussion in Activity 2, ask the children to suggest how people actually discovered more accurate ideas about the shape of our planet, leading to more accurate map-making. Hopefully, they will conclude that the only way to prove that it is possible to travel all the way around the globe is to do it … and you can then ask the question, 'Who did it, and when?' This will provide a useful lead into a study of voyages of discovery.

Activity 4: The first maps

It was not only the shape of the world that was in doubt. In the late fifteenth century, certain lands, notably America, had not yet been discovered by Europeans. People had totally inaccurate ideas about the location of global land and sea. Consider how people of this time thought the world looked, and how it actually looks. Draw maps to record this, as shown below. You may also find **Copymasters 83** and **84** useful here – together they provide an outline map of the world as we know it today.

A parchment effect can be created by soaking large sheets of cartridge paper in cold tea, and allowing them to dry before the children draw their 'antique' maps. A valuable source of colour illustrations of early maps is the book *The Explorers* by Richard Humble, published by Time-Life Books in the series 'The Seafarers' (1978).

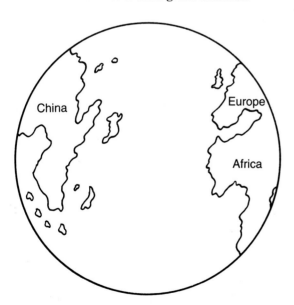

A view of the world in the 1450s

A view of the world in the 1990s

Activity 5: Early sea routes

Early travellers from Europe to China and the East went around the coast of Africa. Later, others thought it would be quicker to go westwards, but something got in their way – what was it? (America!)

Discuss the reasons for the early voyages to the East, notably to visit the Spice Islands. Investigate the use and importance of spices in Europe at that time.

Background information: *The use of spices*

Today we use spices such as pepper, cinnamon and cloves to add flavour to 'exotic dishes'. In the fifteenth century, spices were more of a necessity than a luxury because it was not possible to keep food fresh for any length of time (this was long before the days of tin cans, preservatives, refrigerators and freezers). Food was usually eaten fresh in the spring and summer, and taken from storage through the winter months. Many animals were slaughtered in autumn, so that their meat could be dried, preserved and eaten in winter. By this time, the fruits, vegetables and other foods that had been stored when fresh were beginning to decay, and spices did much to improve the flavour – though they did not help with preservation, as the habitually high number of deaths from dysentery, food poisoning and other stomach ailments testifies.

Activity 6: Where are the Spice Islands?

Use a modern atlas or globe to locate the position of the Spice Islands – to the south of Asia and halfway round the world from Europe. Early traders named them 'the Indies'; their modern name is the Moluccas. Find out about the spice trade, and draw simple diagrams showing what happened to the spices.

Plot on a map the original journey of the spices, silks, jewels and other goods traded from the East – up the Red Sea to Egypt, and by camel-train across land to Europe. There was no Suez Canal to aid their transit. Write imaginative stories about these journeys and paint pictures of camel-trains.

It was said that a merchant could buy 50 kilograms of cloves for a mere 4 ducats in the Spice Islands; and sell them in Europe for 400 ducats, thus making an enormous profit, even after paying for the cost of the expedition.

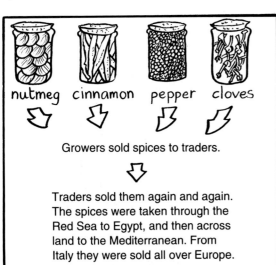

nutmeg cinnamon pepper cloves

Growers sold spices to traders.

Traders sold them again and again.
The spices were taken through the
Red Sea to Egypt, and then across
land to the Mediterranean. From
Italy they were sold all over Europe.

Activity 7: Sailing west to reach the East

Discuss the motivation for finding an easier route to the East. Who took up this challenge? Bartolomeo (or Bartholomew) Diaz and Vasco da Gama had explored routes by sailing eastwards around Africa, but it was Christopher Columbus who believed that he could reach the Spice Islands and perhaps even India or China by sailing due west. Discuss the significance and originality of his thinking.

Copymasters 83 and **84** together provide an outline map of the world that will be useful for several activities in this project. Use it to plot the routes of various explorers as the topic progresses. As each explorer is investigated, ask the children to draw a line (with arrows showing the direction of travel) to indicate the voyage. These can be colour-coded and identified in a key. Four key voyages are suggested here (see page 136), but there is space for recording others if you wish.

The four key voyages
Christopher Columbus: 1st voyage 1492–1493
John Cabot: 1st voyage 1497
Vasco da Gama: 1497–1499
Ferdinand Magellan: 1519–1522

Using cards or matching diagrams, help the children to match well-known explorers with their ships. Add small outline drawings of ships to the world map, labelled appropriately. Columbus's first voyage was made in the *Santa Maria*, and Cabot's in the *Matthew*. Vasco da Gama's ship was the *San Gabriel*, and Magellan sailed in 1519 in the *Victoria*.

Activity 8: Christopher Columbus

Make a study of the famous voyage of Christopher Columbus in 1492. This could perhaps be structured through a series of questions for the children to investigate, for example:

- Did Columbus actually reach the Spice Islands? (No)
- What nationality was Columbus? (Italian, from Genoa)
- Where did he set sail from? (Spain)
- What was the name of his flagship? (*Santa Maria*)
- Name some of the islands Columbus visited (San Salvador, Cuba, Hispaniola)
- Where had he actually landed? (the West Indies)

Paint pictures of the *Santa Maria* and her two accompanying ships, the *Pinta* and the *Nina*, approaching the coast of the Bahamas (San Salvador) with its sand and palm trees.

Write about and illustrate some of the fascinating things that Columbus and his crew might have brought back with them … perhaps plants and animals (and people!) that Europeans had never seen before. What fruit do the children think Columbus was describing when he wrote that it was:

'in the shape of a pine cone, twice as big, which fruit is excellent and can be cut with a knife like a turnip and seems very wholesome.'

Columbus's voyage would make an ideal subject for an historical newspaper – ask the children to imagine how our present newspapers might have reported his return.

In groups, they could prepare a front page 'exclusive', complete with banner headline, pictures, reports and maps of the journey. The same approach could be used with any of the other voyages of exploration contained in this study unit.

Investigate the three later voyages of Columbus, which resulted in his party reaching the mainland of America. Write illustrated reports about them.

Background information: *Christopher Columbus*

Columbus miscalculated when preparing for his voyage. He thought the distance he would have to travel before reaching China would be around 2500 miles: in actual fact, the distance was over four times as far. When Columbus landed on the West Indian island of Guanahani (which he renamed San Salvador), he thought he had reached offshore islands close to China. Even though he made three more voyages, eventually reaching mainland America, Columbus was unaware that he had discovered a whole new continent.

Species new to Columbus included the booby (a brown-feathered seabird), the man-of-war bird, the flamingo, land crabs, alligators, iguanas, flying fish and many other strange creatures. These are all illustrated in the Time-Life book *The Explorers*, published in 1978. (The fruit of which Columbus wrote was the pineapple.)

Activity 9: Who came after Columbus?

Find out which other explorers joined in these 'adventures to the west'. Include an account of the Italian, Amerigo Vespucci, who left Spain in 1499 heading across the Atlantic to South America. His second expedition took him even further south, discovering the country we now know as Argentina.

Whilst pursuing investigations into these exciting journeys to America, do not lose sight of the original aim of Columbus – to prove that the world was round. Set the children the challenge of finding out who eventually accomplished this. This activity will lead into the fascinating story of Ferdinand Magellan's voyage of 1519–22, with its successes and failures.

Plot the three-year voyage of Magellan on **Copymasters 83** and **84**. Write vivid accounts of life on board ship during this time – many of his crew contracted scurvy and other deadly diseases, or died of starvation. Tell of their bravery, the horrors of the world at sea, its dangers and excitements. The unfortunate Magellan was killed in the Philippine Islands but his ship, the *Victoria*, eventually returned home. This expedition proved beyond doubt that the world was round.

Activity 10: Life on board ship

Write a biography (or a series of extracts from the diary) of a sailor aboard the *Victoria*, entitled 'First Man Round The World'. Describe a typical day on board ship, the jobs to be done, the food available, the feelings and anxieties of enduring such a long and difficult adventure. Include in this story reference to how the ships of the time were navigated – by measuring the angle of the sun (see illustrations below and the background information following).

Use **Copymaster 85** to compare the technology and aids to navigation available to modern sea captains with those used in the early days of trans-oceanic voyages. Bear in mind also the problem of not having accurate maps to follow. Write about 'Hazards at Sea – predictable and unpredictable'.

Background information: *Aids to navigation*

In the fifteenth century the implements on board ship were not precise enough to allow really accurate navigation. These are some of the instruments used by seafarers.

The *compass* was the most important. Its needle always pointed north and so other points of direction could be calculated.

The *astrolabe* was held vertically with the pointer towards the sun. The navigator could then read off his latitude, or north–south position. Unfortunately the reading was usually incorrect, due to the fact that the boat was continually rocking.

The *cross-staff* was devised to try to improve on the astrolabe. The user lined up the short piece of wood with the sun and the horizon, and then calculated his latitude. Results were not precise. Timing was important.

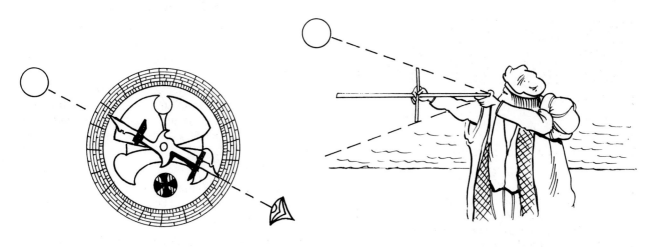

An astrolabe   **The cross-staff**

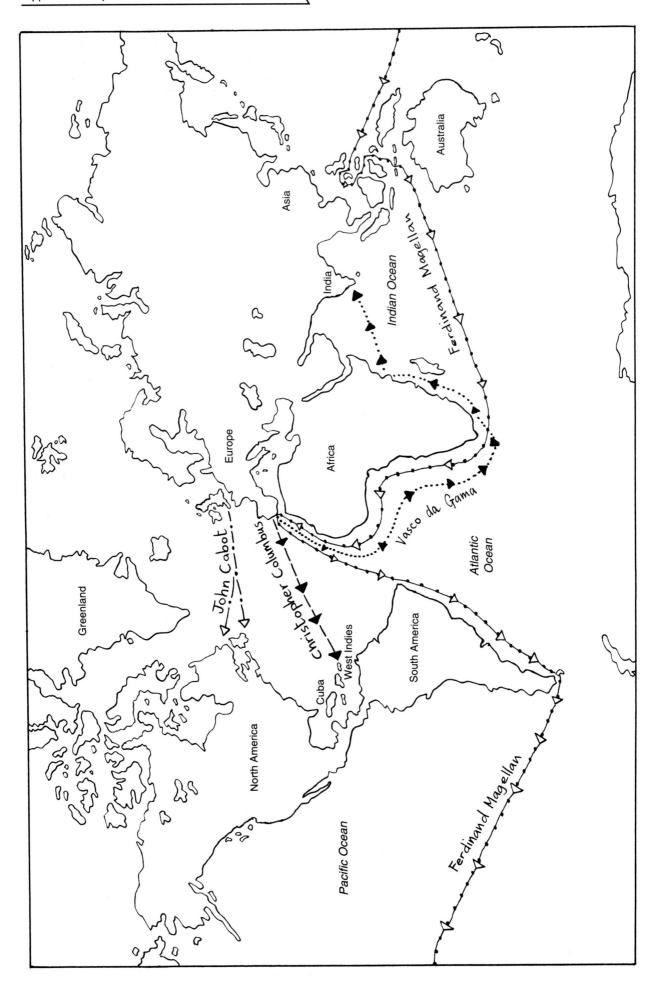

To keep track of time, sailors used an *hour-glass*. This was rather like a large egg-timer and had to be turned every thirty minutes. Accurate record-keeping was essential. Inevitably, human error made this an unreliable system.

Distance sailed was calculated by using a *log-line*. A log, tied to a rope, was thrown overboard. The rope was knotted at regular intervals, and as it was paid out the knots were counted. Over a given period of time, an average speed for the ship could be calculated in knots per hour.

Tacking was a sailing manoeuvre adopted in order to make headway against an opposing wind. No ship could sail directly into a wind blowing exactly opposite to the direction of the intended journey. Instead the ship would tack across the wind, sailing a zigzag course.

A *lead-line* – a line with a lead weight attached to it – was lowered overboard to discover the depth of water beneath the ship when sailors thought they might be approaching land. By taking 'soundings', the sailors could find out if the seabed was sloping upwards – towards land perhaps. Driftwood, such as branches, and land-birds were reliable indicators of a journey's end.

Lines of *latitude* and *longitude* form an imaginary grid over the surface of the Earth. They were devised and numbered to provide reference points even for featureless areas, such as oceans. Lines of longitude run north–south, and lines of latitude run east–west. The children will have encountered this concept when locating treasure by means of a squared grid over the map of a fictional island.

Activity 11: A sailing ship in detail

The outline drawing on **Copymasters 86** and **87** can be used in conjunction with descriptive writing about life at sea in the fifteenth century. The cross-section shows the interior of a ship, and can be coloured and labelled. Clearly, this can be used in a variety of different ways depending on the ability of the children. Either discuss the drawing in detail and provide labels to be inserted in the correct numbered places (see below), or ask the children to do their own research and investigate the key elements of the ship. They should try to fill in as many of the numbered items as possible and assemble some information about them. The labels for the copymasters are as follows:

①	mainmast	⑩	gun-deck
②	foremast	⑪	ballast
③	mizzen mast	⑫	brig (prison)
④	capstan	⑬	captain's cabin
⑤	keel	⑭	main cabin
⑥	helm	⑮	main hatch
⑦	poop-deck	⑯	galley stove
⑧	quarter-deck	⑰	swivel gun
⑨	forecastle	⑱	figurehead

A challenging task would be for the children (perhaps in groups) to try and build their own cross-section of a fifteenth-century sailing ship (complete with crew?). Alternatively, it may be possible to obtain model-making kits of some famous ships, such as the *Santa Maria*, for the children to assemble.

The subject of ships' figureheads can be a fascinating one. Ask the children to see how many different pictures of figureheads they can find, and then to sketch or paint as many as possible. A gallery of figure-heads designed by the children would make a striking display.

Activity 12: Other notable voyages

Find out in more detail about other notable voyages of the time, including those of Bartolomeo Diaz who battled through storms around the coast of Southern Africa (1487); Vasco da Gama who sailed from Portugal to India (1497); and John Cabot, who attempted to find a 'north-west passage' in the late fifteenth century.

Activity 13: A dictionary of exploration

Compile an illustrated 'Dictionary of Exploration'. As the children do their reading and research, ask them to note key names and ideas. Assemble these in alphabetical order to make up an illustrated dictionary. Sample entries are shown below.

Perhaps the easiest way to compile such a dictionary is to use a ring-binder and protect the children's work with polythene pockets. Make the dictionary a classroom resource – add to it on a regular basis, and allow the class access to it as part of their research material.

Children with access to information technology could record this information alongside notes on various journeys of exploration, in the form of a computer database.

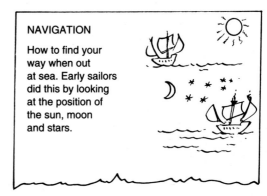

NAVIGATION

How to find your way when out at sea. Early sailors did this by looking at the position of the sun, moon and stars.

FLAGSHIP

The leading or most important ship in a sailing expedition. Columbus's flagship was the *Santa Maria*.

AZTEC CIVILISATION

C88–90

This section on the Aztec civilisation can be used as part of work on Study Unit 6, a past, non-European society.

Activity 1: Spanish exploration in South America

Link a sub-topic on the Aztec civilisation into the main theme of exploration by locating the homelands of the Aztecs and Incas on a map of Central and South America. When Spanish adventurers explored this territory they discovered two fascinating civilisations – the Incas in Peru and the Aztecs in Mexico.

Copymaster 88 will help the children to appreciate the location of these two civilisations – ask them to colour-code the key and to colour in on the map the empires of the Aztecs and the Incas. Label Mexico and Peru, and plot the lines of approach of the voyages which discovered them. Ask the children to colour the Aztec and Inca drawings, based on research, to raise awareness of the appearance of these striking people. Consultation of reference books at an early stage is important.

Activity 2: Who were the Aztecs?

Focus on a study of the Aztecs, as suggested by the National Curriculum documentation. The Aztec Empire possessed great power for about 100 years, until most of its civilisation was destroyed by the Spaniards in the early 1500s. Consider how we know about the history of the Aztecs – what firm evidence is available? Record sources of evidence on an illustrated pie-chart, first in general terms and then by adding specific items and examples as the sub-topic progresses (see below).

Discuss reasons for the success of the Aztecs and their dramatic rise to fame and fortune. Help the children to appreciate that the Aztecs gained their conquests and power largely by force of arms, as they were fierce warriors.

Background information: Who were the Aztecs?

The Aztecs were originally wandering, hunting and farming people who arrived on the shores of Lake Taxcoco in the valley of Mexico in about A.D. 1300. Two hundred years later, they ruled a vast empire stretching from the Pacific coast to the Gulf of Mexico. This area was inhabited by fifteen million people.

Activity 3: Aztec warriors

Copymaster 89 can be used as an introduction to studying the colourful life of an Aztec warrior. It could form the cover for a topic book on the Aztec civilisation, or be part of a wall-display 'line-up' of warriors. Ask the children to colour the pictures appropriately.

Write about the training of a young warrior. From the age of eight, boys went away to a school of their own clan (or 'telpochcalli') to train. They worked extremely hard and faced severe punishments for tasks not done well. They learned how to use weapons, and then accompanied adult warriors into battle.

Paint, make a collage picture or create a colourful wall-frieze entitled 'Battle of the Warriors', depicting two armies in combat, with vivid shields, clubs and sharp spears. The commanders on each side should have enormous feather head-dresses and fans on their shoulders. Give other warriors wooden helmets and animal-skin tunics (eagles or jaguars).

Make Aztec shields as an edging to the battle-scene display. Design these using Aztec patterns/mosaics, and decorate them with feathers (see opposite).

Activity 4: Aztec religion

Paint pictures of Blue Hummingbird, the god of war, whose temple stood in the middle of the city of Tenochtitlan, the capital of the empire. The name means 'Place of the Cactus'.

Find out more about daily life in Tenochtitlan. The city was built upon islands in the centre of a lake, and does not exist today (investigate what is there nowadays). The city scene was dominated by colossal temples, constructed from huge blocks of stone. Ask the children to suggest why the temples were so tall. Find out more about the building of the temples – new ones were regularly built on top of original ones, in the belief that a new temple should be built to demonstrate gratitude to the gods for the fact that the world had not come to an end.

The plan of Tenochtitlan below shows how the city was joined to the settlements on the shores of the lake by three causeways. Fresh water was brought in by aqueducts, and food and raw materials by canoes and human transport. Within the city there was an extensive canal system.

Background information: Aztec religion

The Aztecs thought that the sun had been created as a result of personal sacrifices by the gods, so it was their belief that blood should be sacrificed in return, to 'feed' the gods. Gruesome ceremonies of human sacrifice

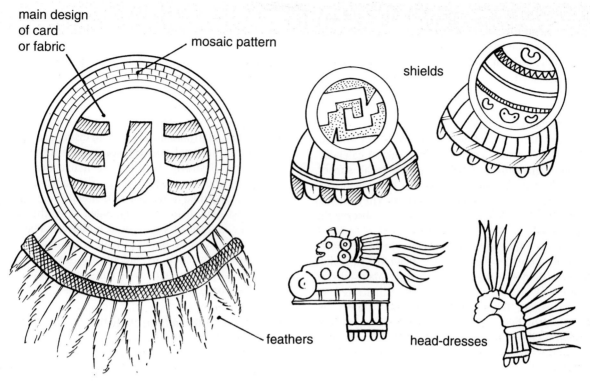

main design
of card
or fabric

mosaic pattern

shields

feathers

head-dresses

(usually prisoners captured in battle) were a regular part of Aztec religious life. The sacrificial knives were made of obsidian, flint or other hard stones. They sometimes had ornamental mosaic handles. As many as 20 000 men are said to have been sacrificed to the war god, Blue Hummingbird, at the command of Montezuma's elder brother Ahuitzotl (pronounced Ah-wit-zotl) when he was king. The name means 'water monster'. Montezuma did not approve of such large-scale bloodshed, arguing that other tribes would hate their Aztec masters for such cruelty and might rebel against them one day.

Activity 5: Aztec gods
Find out more about the Aztec gods, and write about them. Produce pictures of gods such as Coatlicue ('She of the Serpent Skirt'), who had two snake heads and a necklace of human hands and hearts.

Write about the New Fire Ceremony of the Aztecs, and discover the significance of the 52-year cycle by looking in reference books for details of the Aztec sacred calendar and the solar calendar. Aztec dates used a complex combination of these two calendars.

Background information: *Aztec gods*
The Aztecs believed that two gods, Ometecuhlti and his wife Omecihuatl, had created all life in the world. They had four sons – Xipe Totec (the Lord of the Spring Time), Huitzilopochtli (the Sun god), Quetzalcoatl (the Plumed Serpent), and Tezcatlipoca (the god of Night and Sorcery).

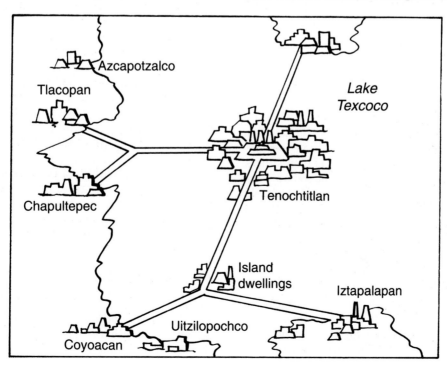

Once every 52 years, a man was sacrificed to the gods at a place called the Hill of New Fire. The 52-year cycle was very important to the Aztecs. They believed that on a certain day, once in every 52 years, the world might end. Rituals such as sacrifice and the casting aside of possessions were associated with this belief.

Activity 6: The astrologer priests

Many of the Aztec priests were astrologers too. Indeed, only astrologer priests could read the sacred calendar. The stars were observed by these priests at sunset, midnight and dawn. Boys destined to become priests went to a special school at the age of eight. They learned to read and write, to make medicines and to observe the stars.

Investigate the role of priests in the Aztec civilisation. Consider the obviously powerful influence that priests held over the common people. Make a list of the duties of an Aztec priest, suitably illustrated, to include perhaps, telling the fortune of a new baby, advising on the best time to go to war, healing people, and making sacrifices to the gods. Compare these duties with those of priests in our own society. What would people today think if priests began dispensing medicines and telling fortunes?

Activity 7: The naming of babies

Investigate the naming of Aztec babies. This will relate to work done on the sacred calendar. People derived their names from the name of the day on which they were born. There were twenty named days, including Monkey, Eagle, Lizard, Rain and Flower. Ask the children to do some research and complete the list. Make your own Aztec calendar, with appropriate illustrations in original style.

Which of the Aztec days would the children like to have been born on? Why? Which day appeals to them least? Why? Children who already know or can discover on which day of our week they were born might be able to create an Aztec name for themselves – what would it be? Perhaps the class could draw or paint themselves as Aztec children.

Ask the pupils to research, illustrate and write about the upbringing of Aztec children, and then to compare it with their own.

Background information: Aztec childhood

The lives of Aztec children were clearly laid down for them almost from birth. Boys were to become warriors, as well as continuing the everyday work of their fathers. They were presented with a tiny shield and some arrows, the symbols of the warrior, as well as small tools like those used by their craftsman fathers. Girls, on the other hand, were given tiny symbols of domesticity, such as a broom, a work-basket and a spindle.

Activity 8: Daily life

Find out more about the everyday life of an Aztec family. Peasant families dwelt in simple huts on the edge of the city. Draw pictures of the inside of such a home, with its bare rooms and floor-matting for sleeping on. This would be an ideal subject for a diorama or other model.

Domestic animals such as rabbits, turkeys and dogs were often kept in the garden of a home, and these were fattened up in readiness for special feasts. Everyday meals relied to a large extent on ingredients such as maize and beans. Maize was especially important as the basis for flour to make tortillas. Design a typical Aztec menu.

Make your own tortillas and find out how they are eaten today. Many books on Mexican dishes are available in the international cookery sections of libraries and bookshops. Basically, tortillas are maize flour mixed with water and moulded into large, flat pancakes, which can then be grilled or otherwise heated.

Discuss how dishes have changed since the days of the Aztec empire. If you visited a Mexican restaurant today, would you be likely to have roast dog, or other early delicacies such as tadpoles, frogs and newts? Consider why these items were consumed – was it from preference or perhaps through necessity?

Background information: Daily life

The Aztecs had three meals each day. They breakfasted on a bowl of maize gruel and ate a main meal in the middle of the day, with another bowl of gruel for supper. Favourite dishes included tomales (maize pasties filled with mushrooms, fruit, fish or sometimes savoury meat); and atole, a porridge mixed with honey or pimento. Beans with chilli peppers, onions, pumpkins, avocado pears, tomatoes, and lots of other fruits and vegetables were also part of the Aztec diet. Special treats included boiled grasshoppers, cactus worms, locusts and insect eggs!

Activity 9: Appearance and behaviour

Paint pictures to explain the everyday appearance of Aztec people. Research in appropriate reference books to make these as authentic as possible. Pay particular attention to hairstyles and jewellery, since clothes were an important way of showing rank. Strict rules dictated 'who could wear what'. Find out about the significance of feathers, jewellery and body paint.

Make a zig-zag book of hairstyles, with one style on each page and an explanation of the sort of person who might adopt each style. Dress up as Aztecs. Have an Aztec Day in the classroom and act out scenes from everyday and warrior life.

Find out about Aztec standards of behaviour. The Aztecs were very hard but fair in their attitudes and discipline, feeling that any misdemeanours reflected badly on the honour of the whole tribe. Merchants who dealt unfairly in the market-place could be punished by a beating or sometimes by being put to death. A law was even passed that any Aztec warrior found to be drunk in the streets would be killed unless he was a grandfather!

Activity 10: Aztec writing

Investigate Aztec writing and measuring. The Aztecs did not have an alphabet like we do, but wrote in pictures called 'glyphs'. **Copymaster 90** introduces the idea of colourful and elaborate glyphs. Two important glyphs are drawn in outline for the children to colour. They should then use reference books, find out more about the picture writing, and in the space on the sheet draw other symbols of their own choice.

Make an Aztec word or phrase book, a collection of tiny pictures with an explanation of what each picture means. Discuss the advantages and disadvantages of this form of written communication, and the importance of its legacy in terms of helping us to understand about Aztec life.

As well as lacking an alphabet, the Aztecs had no formal or regulated system for measurements or prices. Investigate their interesting alternative – trading goods of equal value. Goods were taken to market and exchanged for other necessities by bartering on items agreed to be equal in value. How could cloth, jewels, feathers and gold be exchanged fairly? Yet it appears that they were. Imagine an approach like this today!

Practice doing mathematics in the Aztec style, and record the results. Length was measured by parts of the human body – for example, in handspans, or by the distance from the tip of one outstretched hand to the other (reach). Discuss the reliability of such methods. Are your results consistent? Compare measurements within the class.

Activity 11: Montezuma, the Aztec king

Find out about the great king, Montezuma, who ruled the Aztec Empire at the time of the Spanish explorers in South America. Structure the investigation with suitable questions:

- When was he born? (1467)
- What did the name 'Montezuma' mean? (The Mighty Lord)
- How did he spend his childhood? (He trained as a boy priest, then as a warrior. He became very interested in astronomy, and predicting the future.)
- When did he become king? (1503)
- What were his duties? (E.g. to reward warriors, to collect taxes or tribute from conquered peoples.)
- How did he travel? (He was carried in a litter by nobles.)
- What was his main ambition? (To build an enormous and wealthy empire.)

Make a large collage picture of Montezuma being carried along on a golden litter, with fine clothing, elaborate head-dress and jewellery. Even when walking, Montezuma's feet were not permitted to touch the ground: servants moved ahead of him, spreading beautiful cloths for him to walk upon so that his gold and leopard-skin sandals would not become dirty. The Aztecs had to kneel and place their faces to the ground when their king passed by.

Background information: Montezuma

As a young man, Montezuma showed such fighting prowess that he was given the nickname of Xocoyotzin (pronounced Shoc-coy-ot-zin), meaning 'Prince Strongarm'. When he became king, Montezuma's lifestyle changed from the frugality of the warrior to the opulence expected of the ruler of a wealthy empire. He never ate from the same plate twice, or ever wore the same clothes for a second time. Only the finest and newest of everything was fit for the ruler of the Aztecs. What 'domestic' problems dc the children anticipate this caused? (Perhaps they could write a story from the point of view of a harassed steward or other official in the king's household.) What indication does this give about the economic position of the king?

Activity 12: Evidence of the Aztecs

Find out what remains of the life and possessions of Montezuma today, and where you would have to go to see them. Montezuma had a jade bust made of the god of the priests, Quetzalcoatl (pronounced Kwet-zal-coatull), which is now kept in the British Museum. A painted book telling the story of Quetzalcoatl, sent to Cortes by Montezuma, can now be found in a museum in Vienna.

Make replicas of art and craft work in the Aztec style, involving the skills of mosaic, featherworking, metalwork and carving. (In the case of the latter in particular, be aware of safety at all times.)

Set up your own 'Aztec Museum' in one corner of the classroom, with a range of items designed and made in appropriate media. Perhaps freestanding figures of an Aztec warrior and a Spanish conquistador could be made as part of this display.

THE SPANISH CONQUEST ▶

Activity 1: Setting the scene

Set the details of the conquest of the Aztec civilisation by Spain in the general context of voyages of exploration and discovery, and the great rivalry that developed between Spain and Portugal. What were they fighting over? What was the result of the intervention of the Pope? Draw a map of the 'New World', showing the Pope's division.

Read about the voyage of Hernando Cortes to Mexico in 1519, and plot this on a map (perhaps on **Copymasters 83** and **84**). Write about the aims of the Cortes expedition – to search for wealth and glory for

Spain, and to convert the heathen natives to Christianity. Cortes himself is said to have remarked, 'I come to get gold, not to till the soil like a peasant.'

Make a list of the fundamental differences between the Spanish (European) and Mexican cultures, religion being one. Ask pupils to imagine that they are Spanish adventurers (the word 'conquistador' means 'conquerors') arriving in Mexico in the early 1500s. They should describe what they find, and their sense of amazement at the richness, splendour and sophistication of the great cities.

Write about the battle to conquer the Aztecs. Enemies of the Aztecs, subjugated peoples such as the Tlaxcalans (pronounced Tlash-ca-lans), joined the Spanish side. The Spaniards launched a major attack on Tenochtitlan; many temples were destroyed and Montezuma himself was eventually killed. The Aztec Empire was at an end when the warriors surrendered in August, 1521. Cortes governed the country for the next seven years. Soon the Spaniards conquered the whole of Mexico and named it New Spain.

Discuss why so few invaders could destroy a mighty empire. What were the differences in the approach to warfare of the two opposing sides? What advantages did the Spaniards have?

Background information: Cortes and the Aztecs

Hernando Cortes was born in 1486. In 1519, at the age of 33, he landed in Mexico with a force of about 500 soldiers, 15 horses, 13 muskets and 7 small cannon. Once the force had disembarked, Cortes took the startling decision to burn all the ships so that there could be no turning back from the course he had set for the expedition – the conquest of the Aztecs.

The Aztecs had never seen guns or horses before. They were terrified of both, regarding the guns and gunpowder as magical weapons, and a man on horseback as forming one creature who must be worshipped as a god. Cortes was also greatly helped by a remarkable coincidence, in that his arrival came at a point in the sacred calendar when the Aztecs expected the god Quetzalcoatl to return. They believed that Quetzalcoatl had once been a king, who was driven out by the power of the war god, Blue Hummingbird, but who would return one day, bringing a new king to rule the Aztec people. Montezuma appears to have thought that Cortes was the long-awaited Quetzalcoatl, and welcomed him as an honoured guest – thus, ironically, hastening the end of his empire.

Activity 2: Pizarro and the Incas

Find out about Francisco Pizarro and his conquest of the Incas of Peru, under their emperor, Atahualpa (pronounced Atta-wal-pah). Why did Pizarro sail to Peru? Did he achieve his aim?

Background information: Pizarro and the Incas

Francisco Pizarro sailed from Panama to Peru in search of silver and gold. His expedition was financed by King Charles V of Spain, and consisted of 3 ships, 180 men and 27 horses. The Spaniards marched through the mountains of the Andes, and reached the Inca city of Cuxamalca in November 1532, to be confronted by an army of 40 000 Incas.

Pizarro sent messages of peace to Atahualpa, but then launched a surprise attack. The Incas were terrified by the horses and cannon of the Spaniards: a quarter of their army was slaughtered and Atahualpa was captured. Pizarro promised to release Atahualpa in

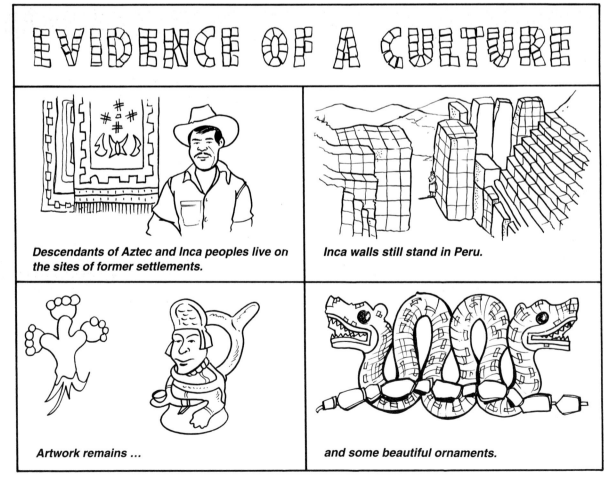

EVIDENCE OF A CULTURE

Descendants of Aztec and Inca peoples live on the sites of former settlements.

Inca walls still stand in Peru.

Artwork remains ...

and some beautiful ornaments.

exchange for a hoard of gold piled as high as the Emperor was tall. A room five metres wide and seven metres long was filled with gold to a height of almost three metres (perhaps it would be possible to find out how much this would be worth today?)

Sadly, Pizarro broke his promise by having Atahualpa put to death by strangulation. He soon captured the Inca capital of Cuzco, and by December of 1533 had installed a puppet emperor to rule the captive Incas. Pizarro established his headquarters in the city of Lima, where he exercised the real power behind the throne.

It is, perhaps, ironically satisfying that Pizarro's treacherous nature eventually brought about his downfall. He had a Spanish rival put to death, and friends of the victim took their revenge by killing Pizarro himself in June 1541.

Activity 3: The lives of the Incas

Using many of the suggestions given previously, help the children to find out more about the lifestyle and beliefs of the Inca people, and compare and contrast them with those of the Aztecs. Produce writing, painting, collage and craft work of all kinds.

Activity 4: The legacy of conquest

Analyse the implications of the Spanish conquest of Mexico. For example, discuss:

– the ending of Aztec and Inca religions;
– the cruel treatment of the remaining Indians by the conquerors;
– the removal of much gold and silver to Spain;
– the use of slaves;
– the spread of European diseases to the New World;
– the growth of trade between the Old and the New Worlds.

Make a large wall-display on the legacy of conquest, and decorate it with suitable Aztec/Inca-style art (see bottom of previous page).

Within fifty years of Columbus's discovery of the New World Spain was the world's richest nation, and her empire not only consisted of one third of the western hemisphere, but spanned the Pacific Ocean west to the Philippines. Ask the children to mark the approximate extent of the Spanish Empire of the 1550s on a suitable map (perhaps using **Copymasters 83** and **84**).

Portugal was also active in gaining wealth, through her colonies in India and the Moluccan Spice Islands. By 1542, Portuguese merchants had journeyed as far east as Japan in search of trade.

However, in 1540 the French king, Francis I, remarked somewhat sarcastically, 'I should like to see Adam's will, wherein he divided the earth between Spain and Portugal.' Other prominent maritime nations like the English and the Dutch agreed with these sentiments, and by the end of the fifteenth century they were all competing for empire across the known world.

RESOURCES ▶

Non-fiction

Wood, T. *The Aztecs*, See Through History Series, Heinemann.
Explorers 1450–1550, Collins Primary History Series.
Exploration and Encounters, Oxford Primary History Series.
The Aztecs, What Do We Know About Series, Wayland.
Columbus And The New World, Making History Series, Wayland.
Exploration and Encounters Pack, Heinemann.
The Usborne Book of Explorers, Usborne.
The Aztecs, Look Into The Past Series, Wayland.
Christopher Columbus, Life Stories Series, Wayland.

The British Museum has published an activity book on The Aztecs (British Museum General Enquiries – Tel: 0171-636-1555)

Fiction

Hodges, W. *Columbus Sails*, Bell, 1970. First published 1939; part biography, part story. (This book is now out of print but should be available through libraries.)

Poems

Columbus, from *The Emigrants*, by E.K. Brathwaite, in 'Every poem tells a story', comp. R. Wilson, Viking Kestrel, 1988.

Blueprints links

You will find a useful unit of work on ships and seafarers in *Blueprints: Topics Key Stage 2*. The following other Stanley Thornes books will prove useful: *Investigating History: Exploration and Encounters 1450–1550; History Timelines: Ships and Seafarers*.

SUMMARY SHEET

Name of child _____

| Date _____ | Date _____ |
| Study unit _____ | Study unit _____ |

Level and comments		Level and comments	
Level 2		Level 2	
Level 3		Level 3	
Level 4		Level 4	
Level 5		Level 5	

| Date _____ | Date _____ |
| Study unit _____ | Study unit _____ |

Level and comments		Level and comments	
Level 2		Level 2	
Level 3		Level 3	
Level 4		Level 4	
Level 5		Level 5	

SUMMARY SHEET

Name of child _____

Date _____	Date _____
Study unit _____	Study unit _____
Level and comments	*Level and comments*

Level 2		Level 2	
Level 3		Level 3	
Level 4		Level 4	
Level 5		Level 5	

Date _____	Date _____
Study unit _____	Study unit _____
Level and comments	*Level and comments*

Level 2		Level 2	
Level 3		Level 3	
Level 4		Level 4	
Level 5		Level 5	